W9-DBE-688

Landmarks in Modern American Business

Landmarks in Modern American Business

Volume 3

1974–2000

Edited by

The Editors of Salem Press

SALEM PRESS, INC.
Pasadena, California
Hackensack, New Jersey

Essays originally appeared in *Great Events from History II: Business and Commerce*, 1994; new material has been added.

∞ The paper used in these volumes conforms to the American National Standard for Permanence of Paper for Printed Library Materials, Z39.48-1992 (R1997).

Library of Congress Cataloging-in-Publication Data
Landmarks in modern American business / edited by the editors of Salem Press
     p.   cm. — (Magill's choice)
Includes bibliographical references and index.
ISBN 0-89356-135-5 (set : alk. paper). — ISBN 0-89356-139-8 (v. 1 : alk. paper). — ISBN 0-89356-143-6 (v. 2 : alk. paper). — ISBN 0-89356-149-5 (v. 3 : alk. paper)
    1. United States — Commerce — History — 20th century — Chronology. 2. Industries — United States — History — 20th century — Chronology. 3. Corporations — United States — History — 20th century — Chronology. 4. Commercial law — United States — History — 20th century — Chronology. I. Series.

HF3021 .L36 2000
338.0973—dc21

                  00-032962

First Printing

PRINTED IN THE UNITED STATES OF AMERICA

Contents
Volume 3

THE EMPLOYEE RETIREMENT INCOME SECURITY ACT OF 1974 IS PASSED

CATEGORY OF EVENT: Labor
TIME: September 2, 1974
LOCALE: Washington, D.C.

By establishing fiduciary, funding, vesting, and disclosure rules and plan termination insurance, ERISA attempted to protect employees' rights to retirement and other benefits

Principal personages:

JACOB JAVITS (1904-1986), a Republican senator from New York, cosponsor of pension reform legislation

RUSSELL B. LONG (1918-   ), a Democratic senator from Louisiana, chairman of the Senate Finance Committee

HARRISON WILLIAMS (1919-   ), a Democratic senator from New Jersey, cosponsor of pension reform legislation

RICHARD M. NIXON (1913-1994), the president of the United States, 1969-1974

JOHN H. DENT (1908-1988), a Democratic congressman from Pennsylvania, chairman of the General Subcommittee on Labor

GERALD FORD (1913-   ), the president of the United States, 1974-1977

RALPH NADER (1934-   ), a consumer advocate

Summary of Event

On September 2 (Labor Day), 1974, President Gerald Ford signed the Employee Retirement Income Security Act of 1974 (ERISA) into law.

ERISA established complex rules concerning employee benefit plan disclosure, fiduciary responsibility, funding, and vesting. Vesting refers to an employee's nonforfeitable right to a pension, a right earned, for example, after a fixed number of years of service. The law also established pension plan termination insurance and the Pension Benefit Guaranty Corporation.

ERISA was the culmination of eight years of investigations, hearings, and legislative proposals that responded to reports of abuse in the private pension and group insurance system, particularly with respect to the absence of vesting and funding standards in some plans. ERISA mandated practices that had become increasingly common among large corporate plans. The law's supporters thus included a wide range of interests, such as the American Bankers' Association and the United Auto Workers union. ERISA was moderate in scope and did not include certain reforms, such as the mandating of private employee benefit coverage for everyone in the work force, that were advocated at the time by Ralph Nader and other public interest advocates.

The American Express Company adopted the first pension plan in the United States in 1875. By 1940, more than four million American employees were covered by private pensions. The Revenue Act of 1942 allowed a company to receive a guarantee that pension contributions would be tax deductible, and this provision encouraged growth in coverage. The War Labor Board also encouraged growth during World War II by exempting employee benefit plans from wage freezes. A similar provision was made during the Korean War. Furthermore, in 1948 the Seventh Circuit Court of Appeals upheld a ruling in a case involving the Inland Steel Company that pensions are mandatory subjects of collective bargaining. This decision opened the door to collective bargaining by unions for employee benefits. Pension assets rose from $2.4 billion in 1940 to $52 billion in 1960. By 1970, more than twenty-six million American employees were covered by private pensions.

In 1958, the Welfare and Pension Plan Disclosure Act (WPPDA) established disclosure requirements for employee benefit plans. The WPPDA was amended in 1962 to establish criminal sanctions. The WPPDA's disclosure requirements, however, were limited in scope.

In 1963 and 1964, pension plans gained public attention when the Studebaker factory in South Bend, Indiana, closed. About forty-five hundred Studebaker employees under the age of sixty received only 15 percent of the retirement benefits they had earned, and many received no benefits at all. President John F. Kennedy had appointed a Committee on Corporate Pension Funds in 1962, and in 1965 the committee recommended stricter standards for plan funding and vesting of employees' pension benefits. This recommendation led to a 1968 House bill that would have established fiduciary standards for administrators of employee benefit plans, but the bill died.

In a message to Congress on December 8, 1971, President Richard M. Nixon proposed legislation to establish vesting and fiduciary standards and to permit individual retirement accounts (IRAs). A House Banking and Currency Committee task force investigated pension reform that year as well. In 1972, the National Broadcasting Company encouraged popular support for pension reform legislation by airing a television news documentary, *Pensions: The Broken Promise*, that depicted abuses in the pension system.

The House Ways and Means Committee, chaired by Wilbur Mills, held hearings in 1972 on H.R. 12272, the Nixon Administration's bill. H.R. 12272 included provisions on disclosure, fiduciary responsibility, and vesting, but not on funding and plan termination insurance. The most controversial part of the bill was its proposal for increasing the limits on the tax deductibility of pension benefits for self-employed individuals and their employees (Keogh or HR 10 plans) and IRAs. More than twenty national and local bar associations and the American Medical Association testified in favor of the Keogh plans and IRAs. The American Federation of Labor-Congress of Industrial Organizations (AFL-CIO) strongly opposed the Nixon bill because of these provisions. The bill died in the House.

In September, 1972, the Senate Labor and Public Welfare Committee, chaired by Harrison Williams, reported a bill that would have regulated pension plans, but the bill died when Senator Russell Long argued that it was primarily tax legislation and so was the province of his Senate Finance Committee. The Senate Finance Committee reported the bill out only after removing its provisions concerning vesting, funding, and termination insurance.

By early 1973, public support for pension reform was widespread, and jurisdictional disputes were to be swept aside. Congressman Carl Perkins, chairman of the Education and Labor Committee, testified that he had received several thousand letters in support of pension reform. Later that year, Ralph Nader and Kate Blackwell published *You and Your Pension*, a book that further encouraged popular support for pension reform by providing examples of insufficiently funded plans, the absence of vesting rules, and excessively complex plan provisions.

In September, 1973, the Senate Labor and Public Welfare Committee reported a bill cosponsored by Jacob Javits and chairman Harrison Williams. At the same time, the Senate Finance Committee sponsored a complementary bill. The two bills were merged into S. 4, which passed the Senate. The bill set minimum fiduciary, funding, portability, and vesting standards, established plan termination insurance, established IRAs, and extended limits on Keogh plans. (Portability refers to allowing employees to transfer pension assets to a new employer or to a centralized trust fund when they change jobs). Weeks later, in October, 1973, the House Education and Labor Committee reported H.R. 2, which omitted S. 4's provisions on portability, Keogh plans, and IRAs but was similar to it in other respects.

During 1972 and 1973, the House Ways and Means Committee held hearings concerning H.R. 12272; the Senate Labor and Public Welfare Committee held hearings concerning S. 4; and the General Subcommittee on Labor, chaired by John H. Dent, held hearings concerning H.R. 2. In the course of these hearings, organized labor gave only mixed support to pension reform legislation. For example, a representative of the Amalgamated Clothing Workers Union testified that jointly sponsored labor-management trusts should be exempt from retirement legislation. In fact, industry groups such as the national Chamber of Commerce and the American Bankers' Association, along with Towers, Perrin, Foster, and Crosby, a consulting firm, gave stronger support to the proposed vesting, disclosure, and fiduciary rules than did the AFL-CIO. The AFL-CIO did not testify during the S. 4 and H.R. 2 hearings. The United Steelworkers, the United Auto Workers, and other industrial unions, along with some craft unions, did not support the proposed legislation, especially its termination insurance provisions, probably because pension funds in the steel and auto industries were underfunded. In testimony concerning H.R. 2, Ralph Nader excoriated the labor movement for its weak support of pension legislation.

In February, 1974, the House Ways and Means Committee passed a revised H.R. 2 bill that included improvements to Keogh plans and established IRAs. The House-Senate conference committee reported a final compromise version of H.R. 2 and S. 4 in August, 1974. The conference committee's bill passed the Senate unanimously, 85-0. In the House, only two representatives voted against ERISA. President Ford signed the bill on September 2, 1974.

Impact of Event

ERISA established new rules on disclosure, vesting, eligibility, funding, and fiduciary responsibility. It established individual retirement accounts and increased the amount that self-employed individuals could contribute to their own pension plans. It established limits on contributions and benefits to highly paid individuals and restated the Internal Revenue Code's rules on integration of pensions with Social Security benefits. It also established the Pension Benefit Guaranty Corporation and a $1 per participant tax on single-employer plans to cover the newly created plan termination insurance.

With respect to disclosure, ERISA required that plan sponsors (both single employers and multiemployer trusts that sponsor benefit plans) provide participants with a summary of the formal, relatively technical, plan document that governs their pension plan. The summary, called a summary plan description, was required to be written in a manner calculated to be understood by the average plan participant. ERISA required that each plan administrator produce a detailed annual report that, in the case of pension and profit sharing plans, was required to be audited by a certified public accountant. It also required plan administrators to provide each plan participant with a summary of this annual report. Furthermore, the law required that the plan administrator provide an estimate of a participant's benefit upon request.

With respect to eligibility, ERISA required that plans could not require more stringent eligibility requirements than participants being twenty-five years of age or older, with at least one year of service, although with full immediate vesting, plans could require three years of service. Plans could no longer exclude employees because they were too old unless those employees began work within five years of the normal retirement age for the plan.

With respect to vesting, ERISA allowed plan participants to vest according to one of three rules: full vesting at ten years, the five to fifteen rule (25 percent vesting at five years of service increasing by 5 percent in the following five years and by 10 percent for five more years), and the rule of forty-five (50 percent vesting when the sum of age and years of service equals forty-five, increasing 10 percent per year thereafter). It also required that pension plans' normal form of benefit be a 50 percent joint and survivor benefit, that is, a pension amount at normal retirement age that has been actuarially reduced to provide a 50 percent benefit to the participant's spouse in the event of the participant's death.

With respect to funding, ERISA required that plans fully fund the cost accruing each year and that unfunded past service liabilities be funded over thirty years, with the exception of preexisting past service liabilities, which could be funded over forty years. With respect to fiduciary standards, ERISA required that plans name a fiduciary and that the named fiduciary and any cofiduciaries must act exclusively for the benefit of plan participants. The law required that fiduciaries act as would a prudent person in like capacity. The law also required that fiduciaries diversify assets and prohibited the exchange of property or lending of money between a plan and a party-in-interest, defined as a fiduciary or the relative of a fiduciary, a person providing services to a plan, an employer, or a related union.

With respect to Keogh plans and IRAs, ERISA raised the tax-deductible amounts that a self-employed person could contribute to $7,500, or 15 percent of earnings if less. It also allowed individuals not otherwise covered by a pension plan to establish an IRA.

With respect to limitations on contributions and benefits, it limited contributions to profit sharing plans to $25,000 or 25 percent of compensation, whichever was less, and limited benefits under pension plans to $75,000 or 100 percent of final average earnings, whichever was less. Both limits were indexed for inflation and were intended to prevent highly paid individuals from taking undue advantage of tax deductions for qualified pension plans.

Several writers, including Nader and Blackwell, raised important concerns about ERISA's efficacy. One characteristic of America's private system of pension and other benefits is that coverage is skewed toward higher-paid employees and employees of large firms. For example, in 1978, those whose preretirement income was more than 43 percent in excess of the median worker's had pensions worth 93 percent more than the median amount, as pointed out by Teresa Ghilarducci. Similarly, according to another study, in 1988, 65 percent of workers in firms with more than five hundred employees were covered by pension plans, while only about 12 percent of workers in firms with fewer than twenty-five employees were covered. By failing to mandate benefits and doing little to tighten restrictions on offsetting Social Security benefits from pension benefits (called integration), ERISA did little to alleviate the skew in coverage toward higher-paid workers.

The additional disclosures and plan termination insurance that ERISA required were costly, and administrative costs associated with compliance with ERISA may have had a depressing effect on plan adoption rates, especially among small firms. Although coverage rates of private pension plans grew from 15 percent of the work force in 1940 to 45 percent in 1970, the coverage rate remained constant at about 45 percent from 1970 to 1987. In particular, coverage among firms with fewer than twenty-five employees declined by about 15 percent from 1979 to 1988.

ERISA opened a floodgate for regulation of employee benefit plans. From 1974 through 1992, fifteen laws regulating employee benefit programs were passed. For example, the Tax Equity and Fiscal Responsibility Act of 1982 reduced the limitations on contributions and benefits, the Retirement Equity Act mandated further spousal benefits, and the Tax Reform Act of 1986 reduced the minimum years of service for vesting to five. The premium required for plan termination insurance increased dramatically, twentyfold for some plans. As of 1993, approximately half of the American work force lacked private pension coverage, and much of the remainder expected only modest benefits from the private pension system.

Bibliography

Beam, Burton T., Jr., and John J. McFadden. 5th ed. *Employee Benefits*. Chicago: Dearborn Financial Publications, 1998.

Ghilarducci, Teresa. *Labor's Capital: The Economics and Politics of Private Pensions*. Cambridge, Mass.: MIT Press, 1992. The best available analysis of the American pension system and its institutional context. The book is critical of the American employee benefit system and recommends several directions for reform.

Ippolito, Richard. *Pensions, Economics, and Public Policy*. Homewood, Ill.: Dow Jones-Irwin, 1986. A quantitative study of public policy on pensions by an official of the Pension Benefit Guaranty Corporation. Excessive emphasis on some unions' interest in plan termination insurance as a factor in ERISA's evolution.

Mamorsky, Jeffrey D. *Employee Benefit Law: ERISA and Beyond*. New York: Law Journal Seminars-Press, 1980-   . The 1992 version is by a prominent pension attorney. The best available legal analysis of ERISA and subsequent employee benefit plan regulation. Includes discussion of pension and profit sharing plans.

Nader, Ralph, and Kate Blackwell. *You and Your Pension*. New York: Grossman, 1973. Written by the country's leading consumer advocate and published one year before ERISA was passed. Includes illuminating anecdotes and recommendations for pension reform, many of which were adopted by Congress. The book was surprisingly well received by the pension community.

Rosenbloom, Jerry S. ed. *The Handbook of Employee Benefits*. Homewood, Ill.: Dow Jones-Irwin, 1984. Good introduction to practical administrative tasks associated with implementing ERISA and subsequent employee benefit regulation.

Turner, J. A., and D. J. Beller, eds. *Trends in Pensions 1992*. Washington, D.C.: U.S. Government Printing Office, 1992. Includes useful, up-to-date statistical data about pensions.

Mitchell Langbert

Cross-References

The Wagner Act Promotes Union Organization (1935); The Social Security Act Provides Benefits for Workers (1935); The Taft-Hartley Act Passes over Truman's Veto (1947); The Landrum-Griffin Act Targets Union Corruption (1959).

CONGRESS PROHIBITS DISCRIMINATION IN THE GRANTING OF CREDIT

CATEGORIES OF EVENT: Finance and consumer affairs
TIME: October 28, 1975
LOCALE: Washington, D.C.

The Equal Credit Opportunity Act passed in 1975 included policies to eliminate credit discrimination and eased the ability of women and minority group members to get loans

Principal personages:
WILLIAM BROCK (1930-   ), a senator from Tennessee
JOE BIDEN (1942-   ), a senator from Delaware
WILLIAM PROXMIRE (1915-   ), a senator from Wisconsin
JAKE GARN (1932-   ), a senator from Utah
PARREN J. MITCHELL (1922-   ), a congressman from Maryland
LINDY BOGGS (1916-   ), a congresswoman from Louisiana
PATRICIA SCHROEDER (1940-   ), a congresswoman from Colorado
FRANK ANNUNZIO (1915-   ), a congressman from Illinois
FERNAND J. ST. GERMAIN (1928-   ), a congressman from Rhode Island

Summary of Event
Portions of the Equal Credit Opportunity Act were enacted in 1974. The intent of this act was to protect individuals applying for credit from facing discrimination based upon gender and marital status. In 1975, the act was amended several times to prohibit credit discrimination based on race, color, national origin, religion, and age. The prohibition on age discrimination has one exception, in that an individual applying for credit must have

reached the age of majority in his or her home state and must be deemed competent to sign a legally binding contract.

On January 29, 1975, Senator William Brock proposed a bill in Congress to amend the Equal Credit Opportunity Act to ban age discrimination. Further amendments were proposed on June 9, 1975, when Senator Jake Garn suggested that the act encompass not only consumer loans but also all consumer lease agreements, since they were also forms of consumer credit. Later in the month, Senators William Proxmire and Joe Biden proposed further legislation related to consumer leasing requiring lenders to disclose all terms of leases to borrowers. On June 12, 1975, senators Biden and Proxmire proposed a bill encompassing criteria to prohibit consumer credit discrimination based upon the following personal characteristics: race, color, religion, national origin, political affiliation, sex, marital status, receipt of public assistance, or exercise of rights under this act. Both the original act and its amendments applied only to individuals applying for consumer credit, not business credit.

Credit is the process of obtaining funds from a lending institution in order to purchase goods and services. The ability of a consumer to obtain credit substantially raises his or her standard of living, as items can be obtained in the present and can be paid for with future income. The creditor (lender) has the ultimate authority as to whom will be granted credit and thus who will have this opportunity.

Traditionally in American society, those deemed by lenders as worthy credit applicants were white and male. There was some logic to this in the fact that prior to the 1960's a majority of the better-paid work force with greater likelihood of repaying loans fell into these two categories. The composition of America's work force began to change drastically in the 1960's as women and minority group members began to enter the work force in large numbers and take jobs with better pay, more responsibility, and greater longevity. This change increased the ability of women and minorities to derive incomes and to be able to repay their debts. Old paradigms die hard, however, and lenders were conditioned to believe that these groups were poor credit risks. Congress recognized the social changes taking place and the civil unrest erupting during this time period and enacted various legislation to guarantee equal opportunity. Equality in the process of receiving credit was a relatively low priority, so legislation regarding it was proposed relatively late.

The Federal Reserve Board was the primary regulator involved in monitoring banks' compliance with this act. Federal Reserve Regulation B was incorporated into the guidelines of banks and was monitored through bank examinations. This regulation codified the intent of the act.

Creditors are in the business of assessing and managing risk, or the chance of loss. Creditors need to assess five different things when evaluating a consumer credit request: character (will the borrower pay), capacity (can he or she pay), conditions (anything particular or unique to the loan request), capital (the borrower's accumulated wealth), and collateral (the security for the loan). A prudent lender would apply these "five C's" of credit to make a credit decision. These are the criteria that theoretically determine the creditworthiness of a borrower; factors such as age, sex, race, national origin, and religion are not accurate predictors of a borrower's willingness and ability to repay a debt and therefore should not be part of the lending decision. Passage of the amended Equal Credit Opportunity Act on October 28, 1975, thus reflected Congress' desire to exclude irrelevant factors from lending decisions.

Impact of Event

The passage of the Equal Credit Opportunity Act affected all parties involved in the granting and monitoring of consumer credit. This act was directly related to consumers and their attempts to obtain credit. It stipulated that creditors could not ask the sex, race, color, religion, or national origin of an applicant for credit. Loans using real estate as collateral or for home purchases were exempt because of dower rights of married applicants and government monitoring of other categories for fair housing. The law also established that no individual can be discouraged from applying for credit, each individual is entitled to have credit files maintained in his or her own name, a spouse is not required to sign a loan agreement unless he or she would be responsible for the credit (with the exceptions related to real estate mentioned above), and poor credit obtained with a former spouse could not be used against a borrower who had established good credit in his or her own name. Creditors may ask about obligations to pay child support or alimony and if applicants are receiving alimony, child support, or public assistance. This information did not have to be revealed and creditors were not allowed to use receipt of public assistance as a reason for denial of credit. In the case of female applicants, questions regarding types of birth control methods used and plans to have children were deemed illegal. Creditors had the right to determine whether applicants had reached the age of majority but could not deny a consumer credit because of his or her inability to obtain life insurance. Any other discrimination based on age was prohibited.

In the event that a consumer was denied credit, the Equal Credit Opportunity Act spelled out the procedures that must be followed. The lender had thirty days from the date of the application to inform the borrower of the decision on the loan. The creditor had to provide the borrower with the following information in writing: the action that had been taken (acceptance of the agreement, denial, or change in the terms), a statement of the consumer's rights, the name and address of the federal agency responsible for credit regulation, and whether information was obtained through a credit reporting agency.

Consumers were not the only parties affected by the passage of this legislation. Everyone in the business of granting credit to consumers was forced to comply with this legislation. The process of conforming began when a lender started to discuss the process of credit with an applicant. Lenders could not use sexist, racist, or other types of discriminatory language that might discourage or offend applicants applying for credit. Credit applications reflected the impact of this law. They included statements that the lender did not discriminate based on the disallowed factors. Individuals involved in the credit application process needed to have proper training to ensure that they were meeting the requirements of the law. Lenders needed not only proper training but also clerical staff to support the paperwork generated by the law, for example, written denial notices that had to be sent out on time. The act added direct costs to lenders through the paperwork, training, and compliance measures required. The paybacks for these added costs have been better customer relations, a more positive image of business, and the possibility of entering new and profitable markets as new groups were able to obtain credit.

The passage of any regulation requires monitoring by appropriate regulators. The Equal Credit Opportunity Act (ECOA) covers a vast spectrum of businesses, with different regulators each responsible for their own area. Commercial banks were regulated either by the Comptroller of the Currency or the Federal Reserve Board. Savings and loans were regulated by the Federal Home Loan Bank Board, and credit unions were regulated by the National Credit Union Association. Individual states also had responsibilities in ensuring compliance with the law.

Each regulator had various mechanisms to enforce the law. For example, a major portion of a commercial bank's examination dealt with consumer credit compliance. Bank examiners were often more concerned with loans that were denied then with loans that were made. Regulators have used compliance with ECOA and other consumer regulations in deciding whether to allow banks to merge with or acquire other banks.

Prior to 1986, small business owners were not protected under the Equal Credit Opportunity Act. Small businesses are viewed as high credit risks. Statistics show that more than half of new small businesses will fail within their first few years, with the most frequent cause of small business failure being inadequate financing brought about by inadequate cash flow. Applicants for small business loans commonly were bad at providing the following information to the lender: cash flow forecast, a clearly stated purpose for the loan, the amount of the loan, and the time frame and source of repayment. Lenders often required a loan proposal including the above information and a detailed business plan. Most small businesses and their owners are one and the same. Even though loan requests are for business purposes, loans are made to individuals. Congress decided to extend equal credit opportunity to business owners as well as consumers.

On March 19,1985, Parren J. Mitchell and Lindy Boggs proposed a bill to the House of Representatives to amend the Equal Credit Opportunity Act to include owners of small businesses. The bill particularly focused on small business loans to women and minority group members. Congresswoman Patricia Schroeder, Cochair of the Congressional Caucus on Women's Issues, presented details regarding the discrimination women experienced in obtaining credit to finance small businesses. Her arguments included the fact that women were rapidly entering the work force as the owners of their own companies and that women were playing a critical role in the creation of jobs. Congressmen Frank Annunzio and Fernand J. St. Germain also played critical roles in the passage of this amendment through their work as members of the Subcommittee on Consumer Affairs and Coinage of the Committee on Banking, Finance, and Urban Affairs. St. Germain remarked that this bill was special to him because he had floor managed the original act in 1974. The amendment exempted large businesses from protection. All banks, savings and loans, credit unions, department stores, credit card issuers, and car and appliance dealers had to comply with this regulation and act without discrimination in their credit decisions regarding loans to small businesses.

The Equal Credit Opportunity Act had major effects on those involved in granting, receiving, and regulating consumer credit. The 1986 amendments extended those effects to those involved with loans to small businesses and to the businesses themselves. The economic environment of the late 1980's and early 1990's favored small businesses, and women and minority group members were the fastest-growing segments of small-business owners. This was brought about in large part by the Equal Credit Opportunity Act amendments prohibiting credit discrimination and increasing opportunities for all borrowers.

Bibliography
Beares, Paul. "Regulation of Consumer Credit." In *Consumer Lending*. Washington, D.C.: American Bankers Association, 1987. An excellent

book dealing with all phases of consumer credit. Written from a banker's perspective, but easy reading for the layperson. Discusses in detail the process of consumer credit, the five C's of credit, and consumer credit management. A must for all consumer lenders.

Board of Governors of the Federal Reserve. *A Guide to Business Credit and the Equal Credit Opportunity Act*. Washington, D.C.: Author, 1986. A twelve-page brochure explaining the requirements to obtain a small business loan. Lists federal enforcement agencies and alternative sources of capital.

Burda, Joan M. *An Overview of Federal Consumer Law*. Chicago: American Bar Association, 1998. Practical guide prepared by the American Bar Association.

Cole, Richard H. "Regulation of Consumer Credit." In *Consumer and Commercial Credit Management*. 8th ed. Homewood, Ill.: Irwin, 1988. Chapter 6, "Regulation of Consumer Credit," goes into consumer lending regulation in detail. The book is an excellent reference on both consumer and business credit.

Federal Reserve Bank of Philadelphia. *How the Equal Credit Opportunity Act Affects You*. Philadelphia: Author, 1986. Puts the ECOA into perspective for the average individual. Describes who ECOA applies to, lenders' responsibilities, what to do in the case of errors, and consumer remedies. A straightforward publication that is easy to understand.

Sirota, David. "Other Government Activities in Real Estate Finance." In *Essentials of Real Estate Finance*. Chicago: Real Estate Education Company, 1992. This chapter lists all federal government regulations pertaining to residential real estate financing. The book in general covers all aspects of consumer real estate finance. An excellent reference for all mortgage lenders.

U.S. Congress. House. Committee on Banking, Finance and Urban Affairs, Subcommittee on Consumer Affairs and Coinage. *To Amend the Equal Credit Opportunity Act*. 99th Congress, 2d session, 1986. House Document 1575. Government hearings and testimonies amending the ECOA to include small businesses. Includes arguments pertaining to the amendment from both opponents and proponents.

U.S. Congress. Senate. Committee on Banking, Housing, and Urban Affairs, Subcommittee on Consumer Affairs. *Equal Credit Opportunity Act Amendments and Consumer Leasing Act—1975*. 94th Congress, 1st session, 1975. Summary of the legislation and discussions prior to enacting the ECOA. Includes the bills proposed in Congress and testimony regarding them.

William C. Ward III

Cross-References

The Federal Reserve Act Creates a U.S. Central Bank (1913); Congress Passes the Equal Pay Act (1963); The Civil Rights Act Prohibits Discrimination in Employment (1964); Congress Passes the Consumer Credit Protection Act (1968); Congress Passes the Fair Credit Reporting Act (1970); Congress Deregulates Banks and Savings and Loans (1980-1982); Bush Responds to the Savings and Loan Crisis (1989).

JOBS AND WOZNIAK FOUND APPLE COMPUTER

CATEGORY OF EVENT: Foundings and dissolutions
TIME: April 1, 1976
LOCALE: Santa Clara Valley, California

In 1976, Steven Jobs and Stephen Wozniak founded Apple Computer, Inc., which became the world's second-largest manufacturer of personal computers

Principal personages:
STEVEN JOBS (1955-   ), a cofounder of Apple Computer
STEPHEN WOZNIAK (1950-   ), a cofounder of Apple Computer
MIKE MARKKULA (1942-   ), a former Intel marketing manager appointed as Apple's first chairman in May, 1977
MICHAEL SCOTT (1943-   ), the first president of Apple Computer
JOHN SCULLEY (1939-   ), a business executive who joined Apple Computer in 1983 and later became chief executive officer

Summary of Event

Apple Computer was officially founded on April 1, 1976, by twenty-one-year-old Steven Jobs and twenty-six-year-old Stephen Wozniak. Their initial idea was to assemble computers for their friends. They did not realize the potential that their ideas had to revolutionize the personal computer industry. Ultimately, their goal became making computer technology widely accessible to the mass population. These entrepreneurs recognized that most consumers at that time saw computers as too expensive and too complex to use. Jobs envisioned the firm offering products that contributed to human efficiency as much as had the electric typewriter, the calculator, and the photocopy machine.

Jobs and Wozniak were graduates of Santa Clara's Homestead High

School and began collaborating in 1976 at the Home Brew Computer Club, a group of young computer enthusiasts located in Palo Alto, California. Wozniak was a superior product engineer and designer, while Jobs had a grasp of the demands of the marketplace. They designed their first machine in Jobs's bedroom and used $1,300 from the sale of Jobs's Volkswagen and Wozniak's scientific calculator to assemble their first working model in Jobs's parents' garage. They chose Apple as the name for their venture as conveying a nonthreatening yet high-technology image. The name also recalled Jobs's fond memories of time he spent on an Oregon farm. Jobs and Wozniak's original plan was to limit production to circuit boards. After Jobs's first sales call yielded an order for fifty units, they rethought their strategy and decided to offer fully assembled microcomputers.

The first model, the Apple I, was introduced and sold without a monitor, keyboard, or casing, at a price of $666. It was the first single-board computer with on-board read-only memory (ROM), which told the machine how to load other programs from an external source, and with a built-in video interface. Orders for their "personal computer," mainly from hobbyists, soon reached six hundred units. Jobs and Wozniak now faced the problem of improving the original model without sacrificing its key selling features, its simplicity and compactness. Their efforts resulted in the introduction of the Apple II, the first fully assembled, programmable microcomputer that did not require that users know how to solder, wire, or program. The Apple II featured considerable versatility and inspired numerous independent firms to develop third-party add-on devices and software programs. The resulting software library soon included more than ten thousand programs ranging from games to sophisticated business applications.

Demand soon outstripped the founders' ability to produce the machine. They turned to Mike Markkula, who had been a marketing manager at Intel, a fast-growing manufacturer of integrated circuits. Markkula contributed at least $91,000 to the company (by some estimates, as much as $250,000), secured a line of credit with the Bank of America, raised over one-half million dollars from venture capitalists, and was named chairman of the company in May, 1977. One month later, Michael Scott was brought in as president of the firm.

Markkula wrote Apple's first business plan. Its objectives included capturing a market share at least twice that of the nearest competitor, realizing at least 20 percent pretax profits, and growing to $500 million in annual sales within ten years by continuing to make significant contributions to the home computer industry. In addition, the plan called for the establishment and maintenance of a corporate culture that was conducive to personal growth and development for the firm's employees. The plan also called for an "easy exit" for its founders within five years, should they wish to disassociate themselves from the enterprise.

The firm's strategy called for continual marketing of peripheral products for the basic computer so as to generate sales equal to or greater than the initial computer purchase, the allocation of funds for research and development to guarantee technological leadership, and the ability to attract and retain outstanding personnel. The plan called for initially targeting the hobbyist market, as a stepping-stone to wider distribution. The company also sought to refine manufacturing processes to reduce costs. Apple computers were to be designed and marketed as more economical than a dedicated system in specific applications, even though a particular user might not use all the features of the computer.

By the end of 1977, Wozniak had improved substantially upon the original model by adding a keyboard, a color monitor, and expansion capabilities for peripheral devices. These features gave the new model, the Apple II, considerable flexibility and enticed a number of companies to develop software programs for the company, as well as a plethora of add-on devices.

By 1980, with the help of Regis McKenna, a well-respected public relations expert in Silicon Valley, the California center for computer technology, Apple had sold more than 130,000 units. Revenues grew from less than $8 million in 1978 to $117 million. The company went public in 1980 with one of the largest stock offerings in history, underwritten in cooperation with Morgan Stanley, Inc. The first day of trading took Apple stock from the underwriters' price of $22 per share to $29, bringing the market value of Apple to $1.2 billion.

The Apple II Plus model did not fare as well as its predecessors. The Apple III, aimed at the professional market, was hampered by production problems that resulted in a recall of some units. These problems and the attention required to solve them offered International Business Machines (IBM) an opportunity to introduce its long-awaited entry in the personal computer market.

The problems with the Apple II Plus and Apple III models were at least partially responsible for the firm's first major managerial shake-up. Apple president Michael Scott fired forty employees. Scott was then dismissed by Markkula, who became president. Jobs assumed Markkula's former position as chairman. Meanwhile, Wozniak was injured in 1981 and took a leave of absence from the firm. After his recovery, Wozniak founded an organization dedicated to fostering a spirit of cooperation among people. He expressed an interest in returning to Apple in a trouble-shooting capacity, with a mission to restore the spirit that led Apple to its early successes.

In January, 1983, Jobs announced the introduction of the Apple IIe, a successor to the Apple II Plus. He simultaneously announced the introduction of Lisa, the first of a generation of computers aimed at the business market. Lisa incorporated many of the technological advances to date and added several unique features, including the first hand-held "mouse" input device. This mechanism allowed the user to execute commands by invoking a series of user-friendly "menus" by moving the mouse and clicking buttons rather than by typing commands. This innovation also allowed the user to more easily produce high-quality graphics that previously would have required a complex series of keystrokes. Computer novices could now master use of the computer in a matter of minutes, rather than the weeks mastery had taken in the past.

As the company evolved, its approach to management changed dramatically. Realizing that selling computers had become a more complex marketing problem, Jobs sought help. Computers no longer would sell themselves on the basis of their technological innovations. In April, 1983, perceiving that marketing expertise was lacking within the firm, Jobs recruited John Sculley from PepsiCo. The move was controversial given that Sculley had developed his reputation selling soft drinks in a mature market, an environment very unlike the growth industry of personal computers. Some foresaw a conflict of corporate cultures between the freewheeling style of Silicon Valley and the more traditional style that Sculley embodied. Although an outsider, Sculley brought marketing skills to Apple that had been missing.

Impact of Event

In 1984, Apple introduced the Macintosh. This model, dubbed the computer "for the rest of us," incorporated a graphical user interface inspired by Xerox's Alto Computer. Macintosh was developed for the business (focusing on productivity and desktop publishing) and education markets. Its compact design and ease of use caught the attention of the market, though the original models were criticized for lacking the computing power required for some business applications. After a series of modifications and upgrades, the computer gained widespread acceptance.

In 1985, after a series of tumultuous conflicts with Sculley and Apple's board of directors, Jobs resigned his position, closing the chapter on Apple's origin and founders. Jobs later formed his own firm, Next, Inc., dedicated to providing sophisticated workstations for the education markets.

By 1986, with the introduction of the Mac Plus and the Laserwriter printer, Apple had begun to make significant inroads into the business market. The company also embarked on a cost- and price-reduction program, allowing it to sell aggressively to large businesses, a historically weak market for Apple. Combining traditional computer applications such as word processing and spreadsheets with pioneering concepts such as desktop publishing, three-dimensional computer-assisted design, and interactive multimedia tools (with text, animation, and sound) carried the Apple tradition for innovation forward.

Apple's unique approach to personal computing altered the manner in which computer manufacturers compete. Apple pioneered the concept of integrating hardware and software to offer new possibilities. For example, integration of high-resolution displays with scalable fonts (alphanumeric characters that could be printed in a variety of sizes) and graphics capabilities allows people to create sophisticated documents on their personal computers. Through the integration of a microphone and a CD-ROM drive with specialized software, people could now work with sound, video, and animation. Most other computer manufacturers could not integrate hardware and software as expediently because they did not manage the software development for their systems. Most, instead, licensed the same system software (MS-DOS) from the same company (Microsoft). As a result, many of their products were indistinguishable and companies often competed solely on the basis of price. Manufacturers of "clones" of IBM computers set off price wars in the hardware arena. Although Apple lowered prices to remain competitive, much of its sales growth has come through product innovation.

In a surprising change in direction, given the maverick style of the firm's beginnings, strategic partnerships became increasingly important for Apple. The company collaborated with Sony in introducing the Macintosh Powerbook notebook computer, and in 1990 Apple announced that it was working with Sharp on a pen-based group of products to include electronic books and communication devices. In 1991, in a move that shocked the computer industry, Apple and rival IBM announced a joint venture to develop new software, operating systems, and hardware that would allow easier integration of the products of the two firms.

Apple Computer rose from origins in a garage to become the second-largest manufacturer of personal computers, behind IBM. The company's Macintosh line became known for its user friendliness and superior graphics capabilities. Although some significant product features have been mimicked by competing firms, Apple has successfully redefined how general users view personal computing. As a result of planning and the vision of Jobs and Wozniak in Apple's early years, personal computing has become accessible to the general population. Through a continual series of product innovations, the firm has continued to redefine how people process and transmit information.

Bibliography

Levering, Robert, Michael Katz, and Milton Moskowitz. *The Computer Entrepreneurs: Who's Making It Big and How in America's Upstart Industry.* New York: New American Library, 1984. A series of brief biographical sketches of the pioneers of the computer industry, including Apple's founders and their contemporaries.

Linzmayer, Owen W. *Apple Confidential: The Real Story of Apple Computer, Inc.* San Francisco: No Starch Press, 1999.

Moritz, Michael. *The Little Kingdom: The Private Story of Apple Computer.* New York: William Morrow, 1984. Covers the early history of the firm and provides behind-the-scenes insight into the founders and the unique corporate culture they fostered.

Price, Rob, Jill Savini, and Thom Marchionna. *So Far: The First Ten Years of a Vision.* Cupertino, Calif.: Apple Computer, 1987. Although published as a public relations vehicle for the firm, this richly-illustrated volume provides an interesting and entertaining historical overview of the firm's early years.

Rose, Frank. *West of Eden: The End of Innocence at Apple Computer.* New York: Viking Press, 1989. A behind-the-scenes account of the managerial upheaval at Apple Computer that led Steve Jobs to leave the company as it sought to penetrate the business market.

Sculley, John. *Odyssey, Pepsi to Apple: A Journey of Adventure, Ideas, and the Future.* New York: Harper & Row, 1987. A readable personal account of the firm from the standpoint of Apple's chief executive officer and successor to Steve Jobs. Focuses on the struggle between Sculley and Jobs and its implications for the direction of the firm.

Andrew M. Forman
Elaine Sherman

Cross-References

IBM Changes Its Name and Product Line (1924); CAD/CAM Revolutionizes Engineering and Manufacturing (1980's); Electronic Technology Creates the Possibility of Telecommuting (1980's); IBM Introduces Its Personal Computer (1981); *Time* magazine Makes an E-commerce Pioneer Its Person of the Year (1999); Dow Jones Adds Microsoft and Intel (1999); The Y2K Crisis Finally Arrives (2000).

MURDOCH EXTENDS HIS MEDIA EMPIRE TO THE UNITED STATES

CATEGORY OF EVENT: Foundings and dissolutions
TIME: December, 1976
LOCALE: New York, New York

By purchasing the New York Post, *Rupert Murdoch extended his successful tabloid style of newspaper publishing from London and Australia to the United States*

Principal personages:
RUPERT MURDOCH (1931-   ), a newspaper magnate
DOROTHY SCHIFF (1903-1989), the owner and publisher of the *New York Post* who sold it to Murdoch
OTIS CHANDLER (1927-   ), the longtime head of newspaper operations for the Times Mirror Company
GEORGE E. MCDONALD, (1920?-   ) the president of the Allied Printing Trades Council
WILLIAM KENNEDY, the president of the Pressmen's Union

Summary of Event

In December, 1976, newspaper magnate Rupert Murdoch purchased the *New York Post* for $30 million from Dorothy Schiff. Murdoch's premise in purchasing an American newspaper was founded on his previous success in publishing mass circulation newspapers. If his tabloid approach to journalism was successful in London and Australia, he believed, it should also be successful in the United States. Murdoch's purchase created an international and transatlantic newspaper connection, one that rankled the established newspaper world of New York City and created contention in other

615

parts of the United States. The U.S. publishing community generally opposed Murdoch's incursion, partly because of his aggressive dealings in purchasing newspapers and expanding his paper kingdom and partly because of his tabloid format, which sensationalized the news and relied heavily on pictures. His formats were far removed from those of such major newspapers as *The New York Times* and *The Christian Science Monitor*, along with most other New York newspapers.

British journalist Anthony Smith, writing in *The Nation*, describe Murdoch's approach as an unceasing flow of titillation, sensationalism, and voyeuristic excitement, devoid of information. Edwin Diamond later suggested in the same publication that Murdoch seemed unconcerned with the conventional standards of taste imposed by advertisers aiming at an educated middle-class audience. A journalistic variant of Gresham's Law appeared to be at work, in which newspaper publishers believed that bad journalism drives out good journalism. Murdoch believed that newspapers do not create taste, they merely reflect it.

Murdoch's American advertising agency comprised a team that often repeated, "You've got to hit 'em hard, mates, hard," referring to the readers. Soon, Murdoch realized why his formula was not working in New York City as well as it did in London: The United States did not have the same sharply divided class structure. In 1977, Murdoch was asked in an interview whether his "cheeky working-class formula" was applicable to New York. Murdoch replied that New York City was middle-class and did not have a working class.

Lines of battle between Murdoch and the rest of the New York newspaper establishment were drawn even more sharply when the pressmen struck in 1978. George E. McDonald was president of the Allied Printing Trades Council, the coordinating group to which nine of the ten newspaper unions belonged. He was also the president of the Mailers' Union. William Kennedy was the president of the Pressmen's Union.

Murdoch was serving as the president of the Publishers Association of New York City. Following a breakdown in negotiations, McDonald suggested bringing in Theodore Kheel as a mediator. Most of the principals in the strike opposed bringing in Kheel. Kennedy, the president of the Pressmen's Union, feared that Kheel would be the middleman in a cabal of publishers and unions other than his. The publishers were wary because the peace Kheel had brought in past strikes had come at a high price. Joseph Barletta of the *Daily News* had vetoed Kheel as a mediator in a Newspaper Guild strike at his paper the previous June. Distrust among the principals caused an early deterioration.

Meanwhile, McDonald planned a strike by his mailers' union against the already struck newspapers as a means of giving himself sufficient direct involvement to call for Kheel's designation as mediator. Once Kheel was called in as mediator for the mailers' union, McDonald thought it would be natural for him to mediate the pressmen's strike. Instead, Kheel suggested that he enter negotiations as an adviser rather than as a mediator. Kenneth Moffett, deputy director of the Federal Mediation Conciliation Service in Washington, D.C., thought that Kheel could be a positive influence. A controversy occurred when Murdoch learned of a private meeting between Kheel and Walter E. Mattson, executive vice president and general manager of *The New York Times*. Murdoch was enraged because this meeting was contrary to the understanding he had when he became president of the Publisher's Association. The original understanding was that none of the principals would discuss the terms of a settlement with anyone outside the group except by mutual agreement, and that Murdoch would be the central figure in all such moves. After a series of meetings and misunderstandings, Murdoch made a separate pact with the union and abandoned the bargaining table. He launched a Sunday edition of the *New York Post*, complete with a television supplement similar to one that the *Daily News* had been quietly planning. Murdoch thus expanded his subscriber base while other papers suffered from strikes. After the strike was settled, the *Daily News* went on a campaign to bury Murdoch by going after his subscribers and advertisers in an effort to win them away from Murdoch and thus bring down his expanding newspaper kingdom. Joseph Barletta stated in a 1979 interview that newspaper publishing in New York is not an "old boys' club," but that if Murdoch was going to be a street fighter, the establishment could play his game.

By 1979, Murdoch still had only a small share of total U.S. newspaper revenues as well as a small portion of U.S. newspaper holdings. His sprawling international media empire annually grossed close to $600 million, netted more than $45 million after taxes, and sold two and a half billion copies of ninety-two publications, mainly in Australia and Great Britain. His American properties included the *New York Post*, the weekly *Star*, two papers in San Antonio, Texas, and *The Village Voice*. The Gannett Company during the same period published seventy-seven newspapers in thirty states, dwarfing Murdoch's American holdings. The Times Mirror Company, publisher of the *Los Angeles Times*, made three times as much money as Murdoch's entire empire. Otis Chandler, head of newspaper operations for that company, stated that he was waiting to see how long it would take for Murdoch to fail in the United States.

Rather than fail, Murdoch continually analyzed his losses and adjusted the formats of his papers. Although tabloids such as *The National Enquirer* existed prior to Murdoch's arrival on the scene, those papers had gradually changed to adjust to the market. Murdoch also adjusted. After his use of lurid headlines pertaining to the Son of Sam murders in the *New York Post*, the Murdoch formula declined in the United States. Murdoch knew he had to adapt. By 1979, the *New York Post* began to display upgraded quality, even though it still featured crime, scandals, gossip, and occasional bouts of hysteria. The paper now carried a solid financial section and reported more international and metropolitan news. American newspaper publishers also learned from Murdoch. He was becoming part of the American newspaper establishment.

Impact of Event
When Murdoch bought the *New York Post* from Schiff in 1976, the initial reaction from the newspaper establishment was fear that the Murdoch format of sensationalism would squeeze out the more conservative papers that appealed to the middle and upper classes. Publishers also objected to his agressive style of acquisitions. His style and format precipitated a "bury Murdoch" campaign. The Gannett Company, a complex of publications, organized an effort to identify and reclaim every subscriber who had switched to the *Post*.

Murdoch drew criticism and animosity while generating fear among the established newspaper publishers. His aggressive manner in acquiring newspapers was abhorred, and his tabloid format caused fear among more established publishers that the quality of the newspaper world was going downhill. Some observers believed, however, that American newspapers were becoming more elitist. Murdoch offered choices by offering another style of journalism. His presence in the American market worked in two ways. Murdoch continued to adapt his style in order to make his newspapers sell, and the established media had to scramble to maintain their subscription lists. At the same time that Murdoch was becoming Americanized, he prompted action in response to his style. Other publishers had to react, going after potential subscribers in a shifting demographic environment and making other changes in their publishing operations. Many of the changes should have been made twenty years earlier. Murdoch's entry into U.S. publishing made his new competitors move faster.

Murdoch's News International Company encompassed holdings in England, Australia, and the United States, resulting in an international press network different from any in the past. Murdoch kept a tight rein on every phase of his publishing empire, compared with the American style of departmental authority. Murdoch passed judgment on his publications in every department rather than assigning authority in the various phases of publishing. He even brought in American editors to replace some of his overseas editors.

Murdoch's ownership of the *New York Post* from 1976 to 1988 was marked by flamboyance. Abe Hirschfeld acquired the *Post* in 1988. By 1993, *The Wall Street Journal* and *The New York Times* were carrying news of its bankruptcy and a subsequent bid by Murdoch to take over the newspaper once again.

A 1990 article in *The Economist* featured Murdoch's News Corporation, describing how nobody had exploited the booming media industry of the late 1980's better than Murdoch. In addition, few had borrowed more money to do it. Murdoch's willingness and ability to borrow money gave him opportunities unavailable to most others. Newspaper articles on his bids and holdings show years of being deeply in debt, but he always managed eventually to show a profit. Murdoch continued, into the 1990's, to make bids to purchase media holdings including newspapers, magazines, and radio and television stations throughout the world.

Bibliography

Diamond, Edward. "Low Road to Oblivion: Murdoch and the *Post*." *The Nation* 230 (May 24, 1980): 615-617. Explains what was often cited as Murdoch's "S" formula: scare headlines, sex, scandal, and sensation, with a fifth "S" for New York—Studio 54 people. Explains the ups and downs in readership of the *Post*. Also explains how the newspaper shutdown of 1978 helped create a *Post* monopoly until the strike was over.

Gottlieb, Martin. "Cuomo Backs Murdoch's Bid for Post." *The New York Times*, March 25, 1993.

Kennedy, Carol. "Tough Guy in the Gentlemen's Club." *Maclean's* 94 (March 2, 1981): 10. Theorizes about why Rupert Murdoch became so aggressive, suggesting that he tried to live up to his father's reputation as a respected newspaperman. Also contains viewpoints of Murdoch's executives.

Raskin, A. H. "A Reporter at Large, II: Intrigue at the Summit." *The New Yorker* 54 (January 29, 1979): 56-85. Penetrating report about the personalities involved in the pressmen's strike of 1978.

Reilly, Patrick M. "Murdoch to Offer Interim Proposal to Acquire *Post*." *The Wall Street Journal* (March 26, 1993): B7. Describes Murdoch's submission of a plan to a federal bankruptcy judge for the purchase of the *New York Post*.

Shawcross, William. *Murdoch: The Making of a Media Empire*. Rev. & updated. New York: Simon & Schuster, 1997.

Tuccille, Jerome. *Rupert Murdoch.* New York: D. I. Fine, 1990. Describes Murdoch as standing at the center of a communications revolution that is reshaping ways of receiving information. Describes his media empire and the deals that created it.

Welles, Chris. "The Americanization of Rupert Murdoch." *Esquire* 91 (May 22, 1979): 51-59. Explains how Murdoch created intense animosity in a short time. He brought his own "game rules" with him, but his rules and those of the newspaper establishment changed and to some extent meshed.

Corinne Elliott

Cross-References

Station KDKA Introduces Commercial Radio Broadcasting (1920); Congress Establishes the Federal Communications Commission (1934); The 1939 World's Fair Introduces Regular U.S. Television Service (1939); The Cable News Network Debuts (1980); Cable Television Rises to Challenge Network Television (mid-1990's).

AT&T AND GTE INSTALL FIBER-OPTIC TELEPHONE SYSTEMS

CATEGORY OF EVENT: New products
TIME: April, 1977
LOCALE: Chicago, Illinois, and Long Beach, California

With the installation of the AT&T and GTE fiber-optic telephone systems, the potential for high-quality, expanded telephone service was in place, as was the impetus to find other uses for the new technology

Principal personages:

JOSEPH H. MULLINS, the man responsible for the transmission equipment of the AT&T installation

MORTON I. SCHWARTZ (1934-   ), the man responsible for the optical cable splicing techniques used in the AT&T installation

BERT E. BASCH (1942-   ), the project leader responsible for GTE system design and installation

ROBERT B. LAUER (1942-   ), the project leader of the GTE optoelectronics group

WILL A. REENSTRA (1923-   ), the man responsible for installation of the AT&T equipment

HOWARD CARNES (1943-   ), a designer of the GTE system

RICHARD A. BEAUDETTE, a designer of the GTE system

WILLIAM POWAZINIK, the man responsible for the fabrication of the GTE light-emitting diodes

JOSEPH ZUCKER (1928-   ), the man responsible for the GTE optoelectronics devices

STEWART D. PERSONICK (1947-   ), the man in charge of measuring the quality of transmission and splice losses in the AT&T installation

Summary of Event

In April of 1977, General Telephone and Electronics (GTE) installed fiber-optic telephone service over a 5.6-mile path between a Long Beach, California, switching office and a local exchange in Artesia, California. Shortly thereafter, American Telephone and Telegraph (AT&T) switched on its own fiber-optic communications system under the streets of Chicago. The first fiber-optic public telephone systems were in place and operating, and their success or failure in providing reliable and economical expanded services would determine the fate of the infant technology of fiber optics and the divergent uses that might develop for it.

Developments in optical communication were minimal until the introduction of the laser. Charles Townes and Arthur Schawlow of Bell Laboratories proposed the concept of the laser as an intense light source in 1958, and by 1960 Theodore Maiman of Hughes Research Laboratory had succeeded in creating a functional laser. The most significant event leading to the establishment of optical fiber as a viable transmission medium was the publication of a paper in 1966 by K. C. Kao and G. A. Hockham of Standard Telecommunication Laboratory in England, in which they proposed that optical fiber could be used as a transmission medium provided that the loss in the fiber could be reduced to 20 decibels per kilometer. At the time, signal losses in optical fiber were typically about 1,000 decibels per kilometer, making the fiber almost useless as a transmission medium.

In 1970, scientists at Corning Glass Works achieved the manufacture of optical fibers with losses measuring less than 20 decibels per kilometer. With the advent of the laser as an intense light source and the development of high-quality optical fibers, the stage was set for researching the possibility of establishing a fiber-optic communications network.

Fiber optics refers to a technique for transmitting information that has been modulated with a light source from a laser or light-emitting diode (LED) along optical fibers. Light has a higher frequency on the electromagnetic spectrum than other forms of electromagnetic radiation commonly used to transmit information, such as radio waves and microwaves. Because of the higher frequency of light, a fiber-optic channel can carry much more information than can other means of data transmission. Optoelectronics is a discipline of electronics having to do with electronic devices that generate, detect, transmit, and modulate electromagnetic radiation in the infrared, visible, and ultraviolet parts of the electromagnetic spectrum. One of the basic functions of optoelectronics is to transform electrical pulses to light, then back again.

For the telephone companies, the pursuit of fiber-optic communication, over the short term, had a logistical basis. The appeal of fiber optics, in the light of increasing demand for telephone service, was that fiber-optic cable could go anywhere copper-wire pairs could go, so service could be expanded over established paths and over the same real estate. Some of the foreseeable economic and technical advantages of fiber-optic systems included longer distances between repeaters or terminals resulting from decreased signal loss, higher rates of data transmission because of greater available bandwidth, and freedom from the electromagnetic interference typical of a copper-wire environment.

GTE's Long Beach, California, fiber-optics system was designed and developed by GTE Laboratories Inc. of Waltham, Massachusetts. The pulse code modulation (PCM) equipment that provided the 1.544 megabits per second digital signals to the optical communications link was manufactured by GTE Lenkurt Incorporated of San Carlos, California. General Cable Corporation of Greenwich, Connecticut, developed the optical-fiber cable using fibers manufactured by Corning Glass Works.

The GTE system carried twenty-four simultaneous telephone conversations on two of six optical fibers. Although the total distance between switching offices was 5.6 miles, the fiber-optic cable was looped back on itself so that the total distance for the system spanned 21.6 miles, connected through eight repeaters. According to Lee L. Davenport, then president of GTE Laboratories, the success of the Long Beach, California, installation proved that fiber-optic circuits are significantly quieter than copper-wire circuits and that it is feasible to use optical transmission systems on a permanent basis.

The installation of the Chicago fiber-optic system was a cooperative effort among American Telephone & Telegraph Company, Bell Laboratories, Western Electric Company, and Illinois Bell Telephone Company. The optical-fiber cable in the Chicago experiment contained two ribbons of twelve optical fibers each. The optical fibers were made by the Modified Chemical Vapor Deposition Process (MCVD), which was invented at AT&T Laboratories. Video encoders and other terminal equipment had been installed to enable the system to provide customer voice and data transmission, Picturephone Meeting Service (PMS), and interoffice trunk service. Most of the system's traffic was digitized and transmitted at the 44.7 megabits per second rate necessary to convey Picturephone video signals.

The half-inch-diameter Chicago cable contained two twelve-fiber ribbons. According to Joe Mullins, then head of the Bell Laboratories Fiberguide Trunk Development Department, a single pair of fibers could carry 576 conversations. One of the fiber-optic ribbons was used for commercial traffic, such as the transmission of voice, data, and video information. The rest of the fiber-optic lines were used for tests and measurements. The total distance of the Chicago optical link was about 1.6 miles.

The successful installation and operation of the Chicago system gave AT&T the necessary field experience that it would soon need for other fiber-optic installations. The success in Chicago convinced management that such systems were economically effective and led to lightwave trunk development that began in 1978 and resulted in the first standard commercial service in September, 1980. The Chicago project was also a precursor to a later AT&T commitment to lay the first transatlantic and transpacific fiber-optic cable systems, completed in 1988 and 1989, respectively.

The installation of the early fiber-optic telephone systems was the first step taken by two telecommunications giants toward the deployment of a new technology that had heretofore only been tested in the laboratory. This step signaled the beginning of a new era that would see changes in the way the world perceived the technology of telecommunications. Voice, data, and video transmissions were now riding a beam of light to their destination, instead of a copper wire. The success of the fiber-optic telephone systems was a major technological and historical event that opened the floodgate from which would be unleashed a torrent of entrepreneurial efforts taking advantage of the new technology.

Impact of Event

From its beginning with the experimental telecommunications systems in Chicago and Long Beach that demonstrated that it was technologically and economically feasible to combine electronic, laser, and fiber-optic technologies to create high-quality telecommunication systems, the science of fiber optics has grown and flourished. New telephone systems almost exclusively use optical fiber instead of copper cable, and old systems were upgraded. As of the early 1990's, only the final link between the American home and the telephone branch exchange remained predominately copper-wire pairs. That also began to change, not because the telephone companies wanted to provide subscribers with better-quality voice service, for twisted-wire pairs offer excellent voice transmission to the home, but because other services such as high-definition TV (HDTV) and data require high-bandwidth optical technology or coaxial cable to carry the broadband signals. Therein lies a conflict between the telephone companies and the cable television industry.

Most U.S. households have telephones and television sets. About one-fourth have personal computers, and about half subscribe to cable television. Telephone companies have access to these homes by means of the twisted-wire pairs that connect to the family telephone. Cable television companies gain entry by coaxial cable.

The Cable Act of 1984 prevents telephone companies from owning or operating cable television businesses within their designated service areas. Free of any real competition, the cable television industry experienced tremendous growth, and its companies, for the most part, operated as unregulated monopolies. Seeing that the cable television industry was no longer a small, struggling business in need of protection from competition, the Federal Communications Commission (FCC) began investigating the possibility of recommending the repeal of the Cable Act of 1984, thereby allowing telephone companies to transmit television signals and enter into competition with the cable television industry.

If the repeal of the Cable Act takes place, a race to provide optical fiber to the home will begin. Huge profits can result from using high-bandwidth optical technology to provide telephone service as well as high-definition television, data, and other services. Because coaxial cable is not an efficient conductor of electronic pulses over long distances, signals traveling over it need to be amplified about every quarter mile. Coaxial cable is efficient over stretches of less that three hundred feet when carrying conventional video, but an HDTV signal would start to distort after only about one hundred feet. Signals traveling over fiber-optic cable need reamplification only about every thirty miles.

Telephone companies have the advantage of already having a fiber-optic backbone installed for their communications networks but would have to bear the expense of supplying fiber optics to the home if they are to reap the profits resulting from customer demand for expanded services. Manufacturers of optical fiber and optoelectronics devices see tremendous potential profits in supplying the material necessary to provide fiber optics for the local telephone loop.

The monumental quantities of information already traveling over fiber-optic telecommunications networks on beams of flashing light are blurring the distinction between telephone voice information, entertainment systems, and computer data. It is all simply digital data, ones and zeros. Those who would control this surging sea of information are playing for high stakes. Losses could be staggering, but the rewards could be in the hundreds of billions of dollars. To this end, alliances began forming in the early 1990's among telephone, cable television, electronics, computer, entertainment, video game, and publishing companies that were destined to change the face of television from a simple cyclopic box allowing the viewing only of programs that happen to be on the air to an interactive control center from which can be ordered selections from a huge library of movies, arcade-type video games, retail-store merchandise from video catalogs, and any program from five hundred television channels. Music, text, and instructional programs will also be available on demand. Many more innovative services were in various stages of development. Their implementation depended in large part on public demand and legislation.

Bibliography

Carey, John, and Neil Gross. "The Light Fantastic: Optoelectronics May Revolutionize Computers—and a Lot More." *Business Week*, May 10, 1993, 44-49. Looks at the fiber-optics revolution that essentially began with the deployment of fiber-optic telephone systems in 1977. Modern uses for fiber optics from medicine to aircraft wings are discussed.

Free, John. "Fiber Optics Head for Home." *Popular Science* 238 (March, 1991): 64-95. Discusses the many services that will be available in the home via fiber-optic lines.

Kuecken, John A. *Fiberoptics*. Blue Ridge Summit, Pa.: Tab, 1980. A well-written book that covers the history, basics, applications, and theory of fiber optics.

Leon, Jose C. de, ed. *Selected Articles from the GTE Lenkurt Demodulator*. San Carlos, Calif.: GTE Lenkurt, 1976. Several chapters cover events leading to the development of the concept of fiber optics. Light sources such as light-emitting diodes and lasers are discussed, as is the future role of optical communication in the telephone industry.

Noll, A. M. "The Broadbandwagon!: A Personal View of Optical Fibre to the Home." In *Telephone Company and Cable Television Competition*, edited by Stuart N. Brotman. Boston: Artech House, 1990. Noll discusses the impending conflict between telephone companies and the cable television industry over service to the home. Technical and economic issues concerning fiber-optic cable installation are viewed, and historical parallels of services are drawn.

Schwartz, M. I., W. A. Reenstra, J. H. Mullins, and J. S. Cook. "The Chicago Lightwave Communications Project." *The Bell System Technical Journal* (July/August, 1978): 1881-1888. A clear, readable description of the Bell System Chicago fiber-optic telephone system installation in 1977.

Schwartz, Morton I. "Optical Fiber Transmission—From Conception to Prominence in Twenty Years: Emerging from Infancy into the Limelight." *IEEE Communications Magazine* 22 (May, 1984): 38-48. Includes a brief historical description of the evolution of optical fiber communications, a technical discussion of fiber-optic cable, and an overview of AT&T Bell Laboratories' fiber-optic field trials. Although some parts of this paper are slightly technical, the language is clear and very readable.

Waller, Larry. "Fiber's New Battleground: Closing the Local Loop." *Electronics* 61 (February, 1989): 94-96. An excellent article describing the conflicts between cable television and the telephone companies. Suggests solutions to some of the problems and discusses the costs and profits of providing fiber optics to the home.

Weinstein, Stephen B., and Paul W. Shumate. "Beyond the Telephone." *The Futurist* 23 (November/December, 1989): 8-12. Looks at innovative communications concepts that may drastically change the way people live.

Jose C. de Leon

Cross-References

Congress Establishes the Federal Communications Commission (1934); Electronic Technology Creates the Possibility of Telecommuting (1980's); Cable Television Rises to Challenge Network Television (mid-1990's).

THE ALASKAN OIL
PIPELINE OPENS

CATEGORY OF EVENT: Transportation
TIME: July 28, 1977
LOCALE: Prudhoe Bay to Valdez, Alaska

The trans-Alaskan pipeline between Prudhoe Bay and the port of Valdez, long delayed by environmental considerations, opened nearly ten years after discovery of a major oil field at Prudhoe Bay

Principal personages:
ROBERT O. ANDERSON (1917-   ), the head of Atlantic Richfield Company, the principal actor in both the discovery of oil in Alaska and the construction of the pipeline
THEODORE "TED" STEVENS (1923-   ), the primary spokesman for Alaska in the Senate
MORRIS UDALL (1922-1998), a congressman who was the most vocal critic of the pipeline in the House of Representatives

Summary of Event

The opening of the trans-Alaskan pipeline on July 28, 1977, represented a victory of energy considerations over environmental concerns and of technology over a bewildering array of problems. Tremendous problems had to be overcome in order to produce oil in the frozen wilderness of Alaska's North Slope and then transport it across nearly a thousand miles to an open port without disturbing, to any significant extent, the area's fragile physical and biological landscape.

The story of Alaska's oil begins with the creation of the Naval Petroleum Reserve on the territory's North Slope in 1923. The history unfolds essentially in three stages from that moment to the opening of the pipeline more than a half century later. During the first of these stages, which lasted until

628

the 1960's, exploratory drilling in Alaska occurred intermittently, usually at times of projected oil shortages in the continental United States and usually more as a hedge against future shortages than as the first step in a massive commercial development of Alaska's oil wealth. Even if the technological difficulties in producing and transporting Alaskan oil could be solved, the costs involved would have made the product prohibitively expensive. The discovery of cheap oil in Kuwait and exploration of other rich oil fields in the Middle East during the late 1940's and early 1950's further dampened interest in Alaska. Exploratory drilling there slowed.

Changes in the world oil market during the late 1950's and early 1960's inaugurated the second period, one of growing interest in Alaskan oil that lasted until the "eleventh hour" discovery of oil in Prudhoe Bay in 1967. As the oil companies of the Western world began to lose the control they had exercised over the world petroleum market for half a century, particularly after the birth of the Organization of Petroleum Exporting Countries (OPEC) in 1960, interest was rekindled in finding closer-to-home sources of oil. Meanwhile, steady increases in the posted price of oil during the 1960's closed the gap between the cost of producing Alaska's oil and the price that it could fetch on the world market.

During the mid-1960's, world oil prices increased. At the same time, world politics and the economic power of OPEC made the supply of cheap oil from abroad less secure. These conditions combined to lure an expanding number of American firms into exploratory ventures abroad and at home, chiefly along the Outer Continental Shelf. Among these adventurers was the Atlantic Richfield Company, later known as ARCO. Under the direction of Robert O. Anderson, one of America's last great oil wildcatters, Atlantic Richfield obtained the majority of the governmental leases then being granted for exploratory and developmental activity in Alaska. The company then began its search. Even after its initial well on Alaska's North Slope proved to be dry in 1966, Anderson pressed on with exploratory efforts. On December 26, 1967, in temperatures thirty degrees below zero, Atlantic Richfield struck a pool of oil that would eventually be estimated to contain ten billion barrels. This was the largest oil field ever discovered in North America.

Then came the third period, the most frenzied of all, in which Atlantic Richfield struggled for permission to build the pipeline necessary to ship oil from the often-frozen tundra of the North Slope to southern markets. While Atlantic Richfield was confirming the size of its find and evaluating its potential, environmental groups began to mobilize in opposition to the construction of any pipeline running south across Alaska's frozen landscape. Their hand was strengthened enormously by the Santa Barbara oil spill in 1969 and the National Environmental Protection Act (NEPA) passed in its wake, at approximately the same time that oil companies were requesting a federal right-of-way to build a trans-Alaskan pipeline. The NEPA required the United States Department of the Interior to prepare a justifying environmental impact statement before granting permission to begin any project likely to have substantial effects on the environment.

On March 20, 1970, the Department of the Interior sought to comply with the letter of the law by issuing an eight-page impact assessment that substantially downplayed the risk of environmental damage being caused by a Prudhoe Bay-to-Valdez pipeline. Within a week, a group of respected environmental organizations jointly sued the Department of the Interior for violating the National Environmental Protection Act. Three weeks later, a court injunction halted construction on the pipeline until such time as a definitive court ruling on compliance with the NEPA could be obtained.

The trucks and the half million tons of pipeline previously rushed to Alaska so that work could begin on the pipeline ultimately remained in storage for nearly four years. Two of those years were spent in judicial wrangling. On March 20, 1972, the Department of the Interior produced a nine-volume environmental impact statement to justify its approval of the pipeline's construction, but the injunction remained in effect until August 15 of that year, when the case was appealed to the Supreme Court. Then came the October, 1973, Arab-Israeli war and resultant Arab oil embargo on Western countries that assisted Israel in that war. OPEC emerged as a cartel that was effective in controlling the price and production of oil. Almost overnight, the price of oil from OPEC countries quadrupled to nearly $12 per barrel. Opposition in Congress to the construction of the trans-Alaskan pipeline collapsed. A measure to approve the Interior Department's last environmental impact statement, relieve the Department of the Interior from further obligations under the NEPA, and approve the construction of the trans-Alaskan pipeline from Prudhoe Bay to Valdez was passed on November 16, 1973, less than a month following the announcement of the Arab oil embargo on shipment of petroleum to the United States. By April, 1974, the monumental task of constructing an environmentally friendly pipeline was at last under way.

Impact of Event

Almost every aspect of the production and transportation of oil in Alaska represented a technological and environmental challenge to the petroleum industry. Environmentalist groups that sought to block the development of Alaska's oil reserves were not entirely wrong when they claimed that the industry, when oil was first discovered at Prudhoe Bay, had lacked the technology to exploit the field without significant damage to the environment.

The environment of icebound Prudhoe Bay was unique in the oil industry's experience. Temperatures could drop to and remain at sixty-five degrees below zero for long periods in winter. The tundra would freeze solid. The layer of permafrost below the tundra could be as thick as a thousand feet. Steel pilings then in use for rig construction were useless.

Laying an eight-hundred-mile pipeline across the terrain posed equally taxing problems. Once thawed, the tundra took on a spongelike property and was thus unable to provide the stability needed for a pipeline. Except in winter, the ground could be extremely delicate, so delicate that even light trucks could easily disfigure it. On the other hand, laying the pipeline below the tundra posed serious threats to the permafrost itself. Unless precautions were taken, oil being pumped from wells would enter the pipeline at temperatures above 150 degrees. Oil rushing through the pipeline at that temperature could melt the permafrost.

Meanwhile, all along the stretch from Prudhoe Bay to Valdez, construction of the pipeline and the pipeline itself posed threats to the landscape as well as to the migratory paths of caribou and other animals. Environmentalists feared the damage that would be caused by construction crews as they worked and also questioned how animals would respond to the pipeline once it was in place. Subsequent shipment of Alaskan oil to California by means of tankers traveling from Valdez through Prince William Sound carried yet another set of environmental risks, as the 1989 wreck of the *Exxon Valdez* would underscore.

So formidable were the technological and environmental challenges confronting ARCO that its executives considered another pipeline route—one running across Alaska and then Canada to consumers in the American Midwest—as well as other options including shipment of oil from Prudhoe Bay by icebreaker-tankers. The Valdez route was the shorter and generally less expensive option. In addition, because it did not cross national borders, it was also the option most in keeping with security-of-oil-supply concerns. Furthermore, it did not require negotiating tricky right-of-passage agreements with a foreign country that the trans-Canada route would have required. Nor was the Canadian route without environmental risks of its own.

At a cost of $7.7 billion, the pipeline was completed in 1977. Within a year, it was carrying a million barrels of oil per day from the North Slope to the port facilities in Valdez. Within another year, as a result of another international oil crisis and another doubling of the price of OPEC oil to more than $36 per barrel, investors in the pipeline were earning handsome profits. The principal remaining problems associated with the trans-Alaskan pipeline revolved around the problems of abundance.

By the early 1980's, the amount of oil being transported had doubled, stemming America's appetite for imported oil but also overwhelming California's ability to absorb the oil available for shipment from Alaska. Finding other outlets for Alaskan oil thus became an unforeseen inconvenience of the pipeline's success, but it was only an inconvenience. The brake placed on the growing flow of imported oil into the United States more than offset such unforeseen consequences of the shipment of Alaskan oil. Moreover, although the flow of oil from Alaska came too late to prevent a second oil crisis from occurring in 1979, it played an important part in contributing to the general decline in Western demand for OPEC oil. That decline in demand exerted such pressure on the cohesiveness of the OPEC organization that OPEC substantially lost control over the production rates of its member states and was powerless to prevent the virtual collapse in the posted price for a barrel of OPEC oil in the mid-1980's.

Bibliography

Anderson, Robert O. *Fundamentals of the Petroleum Industry.* Norman: University of Oklahoma Press, 1984. Slick, illustrated, readable, and informative, this work offers just what the title suggests: a guide to and history of U.S. and foreign oil industries, their on- and offshore operations, and the relationship between the worlds of oil and government. For beginners and general audiences.

Berry, Mary Clay. *The Alaska Pipeline: The Politics of Oil and Native Land Claims.* Bloomington: Indiana University Press, 1975. An insightful account of the impact of the Alaska pipeline on the development of the "two Alaskas," one of natives and one of oil.

Bradley, Robert L. *Oil, Gas, and Government: The U.S. Experience.* Lanham, Md.: Rowman & Littlefield, 1996.

Chasan, Daniel Jack. *Klondike '70: The Alaska Oil Boom.* New York: Praeger, 1971. Another good account of the impact of oil on Alaska, this time in the form of a very readable narrative covering the first days of the oil rush that followed Atlantic Richfield's discovery of oil.

Coates, Peter A. *The Trans-Alaska Pipeline Controversy: Technology, Conservation, and the Frontier.* Bethlehem, Pa.: Lehigh University Press, 1991. A good study of the confrontation between environmentalists and energy developers seeking to build the trans-Alaskan pipeline, examined in the context of a century of confrontations between environmentalists and developers over Alaskan resources.

Davidson, Art. *In the Wake of the Exxon Valdez.* San Francisco, Calif.:

Sierra Club Books, 1990. An in-depth, often technical analysis of the spill of approximately ten million gallons of petroleum in Prince William Sound in 1989.

Dixon, Mim. *What Happened to Fairbanks?: The Effects of the Trans-Alaska Oil Pipeline on the Community of Fairbanks, Alaska.* Boulder, Colo.: Westview Press, 1978. Two years of field work produced a volume of considerable insight and a few surprises pertaining to the unintended effects of the pipeline's construction on life in Fairbanks.

Jorgensen, Joseph G. *Oil Age Eskimos.* Berkeley: University of California Press, 1990. A solid interpretation of the effect of energy development on one of the poorest groups of native Americans. Compensation for the oil on their Alaskan homelands later relieved poverty.

Tussing, Arlon R., and Linda Leask. *The Changing Oil Industry: Will It Affect Oil Prices?* Anchorage, Alaska: Institute of Social and Economic Research, University of Alaska, 1999.

Yergin, Daniel. *The Prize: The Epic Quest for Oil, Money, and Power.* New York: Simon & Schuster, 1991. A massive study of the development of the international oil industry, with as much attention to the personalities and politics involved as to the historical events that marked the evolution of the petroleum industry in the modern world.

Joseph R. Rudolph, Jr.

Cross-References

Discovery of Oil at Spindletop Transforms the Oil Industry (1901); The Supreme Court Decides to Break Up Standard Oil (1911); The Teapot Dome Scandal Prompts Reforms in the Oil Industry (1924); Atlantic Richfield Discovers Oil at Prudhoe Bay, Alaska (1967); Arab Oil Producers Curtail Oil Shipments to Industrial States (1973); The United States Plans to Cut Dependence on Foreign Oil (1974).

CARTER SIGNS
THE AIRLINE
DEREGULATION ACT

CATEGORY OF EVENT: Transportation
TIME: October 24, 1978
LOCALE: Washington, D.C.

Although deregulation gave managers more flexibility to develop their business strategies, the subsequent shakeout in the airline industry underscored the need to avoid poorly planned rapid expansion

Principal personages:
JIMMY CARTER (1924-   ), the president of the United States who signed the Airline Deregulation Act
DAVID C. GARRETT (1922-   ), the president and chief executive officer of Delta Air Lines at the time of deregulation
ALFRED KAHN (1917-   ), the chairman of the Civil Aeronautics Board in the late 1970's, a chief advocate of deregulation
HARDING L. LAWRENCE (1920-   ), the chief executive officer and chairman of the board of Braniff Airways at the time of deregulation

Summary of Event

The Airline Deregulation Act of 1978 gave the airline trunk carriers more freedom to develop their business strategies by relaxing the constraints imposed by the Civil Aeronautics Board (CAB) under previous legislation. The term "trunk carriers" refers to major airlines that primarily serve large cities and high-density routes. In contrast, local-service carriers link small cities with large traffic centers. In 1978, the United States trunk airline industry consisted of eleven major carriers: American Airlines, Braniff Airways, Continental Air Lines, Delta Air Lines, Eastern Airlines, National

Airlines, Northwest Airlines, Pan American World Airways, Trans World Airlines, United Air Lines, and Western Air Lines.

Prior to the Airline Deregulation Act, signed by Jimmy Carter on October 24, 1978, the CAB strictly regulated airline routes, fares, and mergers. For example, before a trunk carrier could provide service on a new route, it had to petition the CAB for approval. Approval was contingent upon the CAB's judgment regarding three issues: need for additional service on the route, which airline should be awarded the route, and whether the route tied into an airline's existing network. Incumbent airlines usually contended that the petitioned route could not support any additional service, so proceedings often dragged on for years.

The CAB regulated air fares by establishing maximums, minimums, or both maximums and minimums. Each carrier was required to obtain permission before introducing a new fare. The CAB ruled on these fare changes to determine whether they were reasonable. Although the CAB designed the fare limits to provide a rate of return on investment equal to 12 percent, this target was rarely reached.

Mergers were a third area in which the CAB exercised control. The airlines used mergers to acquire the route networks and aircraft capacity of other carriers. This strategy was often more expedient than petitioning the CAB for individual routes because the acquiring carrier could receive many new routes simultaneously. The CAB generally approved a merger, however, only if it prevented a carrier from going bankrupt, with the result that a particular geographic area would lose air service.

The CAB regulations effectively prevented trunk carriers from competing on the basis of fares and routes. Although the airlines could offer different in-flight amenities, each aircraft had approximately the same level of comfort. Because their product was undifferentiated, airline managers realized that customers were more concerned with scheduling the most convenient flight than with maintaining brand loyalty. As a result, frequency of service became the most important determinant of market share. The CAB did not regulate flight frequency except to prevent de facto abandonment of routes.

Proponents of deregulation argued that the CAB regulations were responsible for increasing the cost of air transportation. Their argument was based on the premise that as the airlines scheduled more flights to increase market exposure, each flight carried fewer passengers. Costs, and thus fares, rose because the fixed cost of each flight was spread among fewer passengers. They argued that deregulation would permit the airlines to differentiate their product and provide a wider range of fares and services. One anticipated outcome was lower prices.

Jimmy Carter's administration began the work of deregulating transportation industries that was continued by Ronald Reagan. (White House Historical Society)

Advocates of deregulation also argued that the legislation would result in greater efficiency and flexibility. First, by increasing a carrier's flexibility to improve route structures and flight schedules, deregulation would permit better aircraft utilization. Second, assets would not be wasted simply to seek future route awards. Under regulations, some carriers had used artificially low fares to strengthen their bargaining position when seeking future routes. Third, carriers would have more leverage when dealing with labor unions because the U.S. government would not be obligated to aid an ailing airline.

With the exception of United Air Lines, the trunk carriers either vehemently or tacitly opposed deregulation. They argued that the absence of entry restrictions on the more profitable routes would result in duplication and overcapacity. Because more planes would fly these routes, higher rather than lower fares would result. If increased competition resulted in excess capacity, then profitability would decline because each flight would carry more empty seats. In addition, they argued that deregulation would diminish stable and reliable air service. In a deregulated environment, an airline could enter a market on weekends or holidays and carry full flights by offering reduced fares. During periods of reduced traffic demand, however, the carrier could suspend its service. Finally, critics feared that rate wars would develop as airlines offered cut-rate fares to establish themselves in new markets. As incumbent airlines lowered their fares to remain competitive, profits would be reduced. As a result, carriers would have difficulty replacing their fleets.

Opponents of deregulation also argued that smaller cities would suffer reduced or suspended service because the trunk carriers would concentrate their equipment capacity on the lucrative long-haul routes between high-density population centers. This argument was similar to a cross-subsidy issue: The trunk airlines claimed that they used profits from their long-haul routes to negate losses on their shorter, less profitable routes. If deregulation eliminated these profits, then carriers would not be able to offset the losses from their shorter routes and might have to abandon them.

Flights over shorter distances are relatively more expensive in terms of cost per mile because fixed costs, such as passenger and luggage processing, are spread over fewer miles. In addition, slower average aircraft speeds cause higher labor costs per seat mile. Finally, fuel costs per seat mile are proportionately higher because the rate of fuel consumption is greater during takeoff and landing than it is during flight. Because other forms of transportation, such as the automobile, are relatively attractive at shorter distances, demand is highly elastic; that is, customers are very likely to choose a substitute form of transportation if prices go up. As a result, the higher costs of shorter flights cannot be offset by fares that reflect those costs and allow as much profit as earned on longer flights.

These arguments were never substantiated. Several studies were conducted to determine the extent of cross-subsidization, with results indicating that the trunk carriers did not rely heavily on this practice. The Airline Deregulation Act protected small communities by stating that an airline providing the only service on a route had to continue that service until a replacement carrier was found, thus defusing one criticism of deregulation.

Impact of Event

The aftermath of airline deregulation underscored the need for managers to accurately evaluate corporate strategy. For many years, the airlines preferred to pay the costs of CAB regulation rather than face the uncertain environment that would exist without controls. Once the industry was deregulated, however, many carriers were lured by the freedom to expand and increase market share. The result was that many airlines overexpanded, faced overcapacity, sold their product at low prices, and suffered declining profits.

Although airlines earned record profits in 1978, the trunk airline industry exhibited declining performance and reported a net loss in 1980. The loss was incurred because managers did not accurately assess the effects of their strategies on competitors' behavior and profitability. Instead, they engaged in debilitating price wars and provided excess capacity on the more popular routes. Low fares in conjunction with rising fuel and operating costs caused declining profits in the first years of deregulation.

Prior to deregulation, managers were enamored of the concept of flight frequency. Because CAB regulations severely limited the trunk carriers' ability to compete on the basis of fares and routes, flight frequency became the most important determinant of market share. This led to the widespread practice of using long-term debt to finance large aircraft fleets that could provide frequent service. As a result, trunk carriers were highly leveraged, faced large interest charges, and were adversely affected by the 1980-1981 recession that reduced air traffic demand.

A brief description of the corporate strategies implemented by Delta Air Lines and Braniff Airways following deregulation illustrates these points. Delta and Braniff implemented strategies that resulted in good and poor performance, respectively. Both companies used a hub-and-spoke route network prior to deregulation, and both carriers flew the less popular routes to small and medium-sized cities. These flights were then aggregated at a hub city and efficiently scheduled to connect with the carrier's more profitable long-distance flights. This system minimized passenger inconvenience resulting from layovers and made the airlines less dependent on other carriers for their feeder traffic.

A major advantage of this type of network was that each airline was generally a monopoly carrier on its short-haul routes. Consequently, older planes could be used without worrying about flight frequency, competition, or price wars. As a result, these carriers entered the deregulated era in better financial shape than did the larger carriers. Delta had one of the industry's lowest debt ratios, whereas Braniff's leverage was commensurate with the industry average. These two carriers also tended to be more profitable than the larger carriers.

Following deregulation, Braniff changed its strategy and placed more emphasis on adding long-haul routes. In 1979, for example, Braniff added new routes to Europe and the Far East, even though it lacked marketing exposure in these areas. Braniff hoped that the new domestic and international routes would feed each other and increase traffic flow through its domestic hub cities. It also expected that new traffic patterns would help smooth demand over the entire system. This rapid expansion strategy was not compatible with the environment. Braniff tried to expand its operations during a period of rising interest, fuel, and operating costs, but it had to lower prices to remain competitive on existing routes and offer promotional fares to increase its market exposure on the new routes. Braniff ignored the importance of flight frequency and its relationship to market share. In many cases, Braniff initiated only one flight on its new routes, sometimes with an inconvenient arrival or departure time. As a result, Braniff was not able to schedule its system as efficiently as it initially hoped. Braniff also shifted capacity from markets in which it previously held a prominent position, with the result that competitors entered these cities and stole market share.

In contrast to Braniff, Delta maintained its position as one of the trunk industry's most profitable carriers. It did not deplete its resources in price wars on the more popular routes, adding routes only when it perceived a need for additional service. Delta also added routes that could be profitable in the short term. As a result, it initiated service to fast-growing regions in the Pacific Northwest, California, and Texas. Delta did not sacrifice flight frequency in its traditional markets to provide service on these new routes. When Eastern Airlines increased flight frequency to Atlanta, Delta's major hub, Delta countered by simultaneously adding more flights. To combat the tendency toward providing excess capacity, Delta introduced flight complexes at its Atlanta hub. Thirty or forty planes would converge on Atlanta at two-hour intervals, exchange passengers, and fly to different spoke cities. The strategy kept a greater percentage of passengers within the feeder and connector system. Passenger layover was minimized through efficient scheduling which, in turn, reduced the chance that passengers would defect to another airline. Delta became one of the dominant U.S. carriers, and Braniff filed for bankruptcy in 1982.

The Carter Administration made initial progress toward deregulating the truck, railroad, airline, and banking industries. Ronald Reagan also supported deregulation during his two terms in office. As illustrated in the airline industry, success in a deregulated environment would require careful attention to corporate strategy and avoidance of short-term tactics with long-term pitfalls.

Bibliography

Dempsey, Paul Stephen, and Andrew R. Goetz. *Airline Deregulation and Laissez-Faire Mythology.* Westport, Conn.: Quorum Books, 1992. Good retrospective critique of the outcome of deregulation. The authors contend that several key assumptions made by free-market economists were erroneous. The authors advocate some regulatory reform.

Fruhan, William E., Jr. *The Fight for Competitive Advantage: A Study of the United States Trunk Air Carriers.* Boston: Division of Research, Graduate School of Business Administration, Harvard University, 1972. Good resource that analyzes the competitive environment in the trunk airline industry under the auspices of the Civil Aeronautics Board.

Lewis, W. Davis, and Wesley P. Newton. *Delta: The History of an Airline.* Athens: University of Georgia Press, 1979. Comprehensive review of the history of Delta Air Lines from 1929 to 1979. The authors take an easy-to-read historical point of view rather than conducting a rigorous economic or business analysis.

MacAvoy, Paul W., and John W. Snow, eds. *Regulation of Passenger Fares and Competition Among the Airlines.* Washington, D.C.: American Enterprise Institute for Public Policy Research, 1977. Collection of studies conducted by the United States Department of Transportation and other public and private agencies regarding the likely impact of deregulation on airline costs and service.

Saunders, Martha D. *Eastern's Armageddon: Labor Conflict and the Destruction of Eastern Airlines*. Westport, Conn.: Greenwood Press, 1992. An interesting case study that examines the demise of Eastern Airlines from both historical and organizational behavior perspectives. Eastern Airlines was acquired by Texas Air in 1986 and ceased operations in January, 1991. The author analyzes the conflict between Eastern's unions and Texas Air's management, especially Frank Lorenzo. Several airlines failed following deregulation, but Eastern's bankruptcy often is viewed as one of the more tragic.

M. Mark Walker

Cross-References

The DC-3 Opens a New Era of Commercial Air Travel (1936); Amtrak Takes Over Most U.S. Intercity Train Traffic (1970); Congress Deregulates Banks and Savings and Loans (1980-1982); Air Traffic Controllers of PATCO Declare a Strike (1981).

THE PREGNANCY DISCRIMINATION ACT EXTENDS EMPLOYMENT RIGHTS

CATEGORY OF EVENT: Labor
TIME: October 31, 1978
LOCALE: Washington, D.C.

The Pregnancy Discrimination Act expanded employee benefit provisions, clarified the need for nondiscriminatory fetal protection policies, and led to state and federal laws mandating parental leave

Principal personages:
SUSAN C. ROSS (1945-   ), the codirector of the Campaign to End Discrimination Against Women Workers
JIMMY CARTER (1924-   ), the president of the United States, 1977-1981
WENDY WILLIAMS, a coauthor of the Pregnancy Discrimination Act

Summary of Event

The passage of the Pregnancy Discrimination Act in 1978 was the first federal attempt to expand rights and protection for pregnant workers. The Pregnancy Discrimination Act (PDA) is an amendment to Title VII of the Civil Rights Act of 1964 and prohibits discrimination in employment based on pregnancy, childbirth, or related medical conditions. Although women are protected by the act against such practices as being fired or being refused a job or promotion because of pregnancy, the major impact of the PDA relates to employment benefit policies.

The PDA requires employers with fifteen or more employees to provide the same benefits for pregnancy-related conditions as they provide for other medical conditions. For example, a woman unable to work for pregnancy-related reasons is entitled to disability benefits or sick leave on the same basis as an employee unable to work because of physical injuries from an accident. If a firm allows salary continuation for victims of heart attacks, it must do so for pregnant workers as well. It would be illegal, on one hand, to allow eight weeks of unpaid leave for cancer treatment but, on the other hand, to limit maternity leave to four weeks. If employees are entitled to get their jobs back after a leave for surgery or illness, so are women who have been unable to work because of pregnancy. In addition, any health insurance coverage provided must cover expenses of pregnancy-related conditions on the same basis as expenses for other medical conditions. In essence, employers may not differentiate between pregnancy and illness.

Changes in the legal treatment of pregnancy discrimination in the work force have their roots in action begun in the 1960's concerning sex discrimination. The most comprehensive federal law dealing with sex discrimination is Title VII of the Civil Rights Act of 1964. Title VII prohibits discrimination in employment decisions based on race, religion, color, national origin, and sex. Although discrimination in all aspects of employment on the basis of sex was banned, Title VII did not address whether discrimination based on pregnancy was a form of sex discrimination.

Congress established an enforcement agency, the Equal Employment Opportunity Commission (EEOC), to administer and interpret Title VII's provisions. Immediately after the passage of Title VII, the EEOC took the position that denying benefits to pregnant employees would not be discriminatory. Continued congressional debate concerning protection against sex discrimination brought about a reversal of that opinion. In 1972, the EEOC issued its guidelines on discrimination because of sex, which state that work disabilities resulting from pregnancy or pregnancy-related illness are temporary disabilities, and that leave, medical, disability, seniority, and reinstatement rights comparable to those provided to nonpregnant employees must be provided to pregnant employees or those with pregnancy-related disabilities.

Following the issuance of the EEOC guidelines, many states passed legislation requiring employers to offer coverage for pregnancy-related disabilities comparable to that offered for other disabilities. Lower courts consistently ruled that denying benefits to pregnant women that were available to nonpregnant employees violated Title VII. Despite the EEOC guidelines and lower court rulings, many employers tended to treat pregnancy differently from other medical conditions. Frequently, pregnant workers were not allowed to use disability plans, and other benefits such as seniority rights and medical insurance were often discontinued during unpaid maternity leaves. Female employees challenged such policies and charged that they constituted a form of sex discrimination in employment under Title VII of the Civil Rights Act.

Two cases that reached the United States Supreme Court were the catalysts for congressional debate and passage of the PDA. In 1976, the Supreme Court held in *Gilbert v. General Electric Corporation* that employers could exclude pregnancy-related disabilities without creating sex discrimination. The plaintiff in the case had applied for benefits, under the company's temporary disability plan, for pregnancy-related complications while she was on maternity leave. The firm refused her claim because she was on maternity leave. She sued under Title VII, and the lower courts ruled in her favor. The Supreme Court, however, held that the denial of disability benefits for a pregnancy-related condition did not constitute discrimination. The Court concluded that men and women were covered for the same risks except for pregnancy, and the exclusion of a risk affecting only women did not constitute discrimination based on sex. One year later, in *Nashville Gas v. Satty*, the Supreme Court ruled that the denial of sick-leave pay to pregnant employees was not a violation of Title VII.

The reaction to these two cases was immediate and intense. A coalition of women's organizations, civil rights organizations, and labor unions formed in support of legislative reform. Wendy Williams, coauthor of the Pregnancy Discrimination Act, commented at congressional hearings that the Gilbert decision reflected an attitude that women are marginal, temporary workers. To eliminate employers' use of women's role as childbearers as a justification for inequitable treatment, Sue Ross, codirector of the Campaign to End Discrimination Against Pregnant Workers, called for an explicit federal law eradicating discrimination based on pregnancy and childbirth. Congress responded by passing the Pregnancy Discrimination Act.

Impact of Event

The passage of the Pregnancy Discrimination Act was the first attempt at a national policy on maternity that would influence personnel policies related to job security, hiring and promotion, safety standards, and employee benefit plans. Although compliance with the PDA was far from universal, many companies expanded employee benefit plans and initiated innovative programs to help pregnant women in the workplace. The PDA provided employers with the initiative to examine fetal protection policies and laid the foundation for state and federal regulations and laws concerning parental leave.

The primary impact of the PDA related to employee benefits plans.

Although some companies provided equal benefits for pregnant and non-pregnant employees prior to the PDA, compliance with the PDA has been far from universal. Subsequent to the passage of the PDA, many companies evaluated their policies and adjusted them in order to comply with the law, while others were unsure as to what was required. Compliance with the PDA is highly correlated with organizational size. Immediately following enactment of the PDA, most large firms had adjusted benefits in order to comply with the law, but noncompliance was common among small organizations. Only about half of the firms with fewer than one hundred employees complied with the PDA by 1981. Small firms that ignored the law claimed that they did not know what was required to comply. A survey of small firms indicated that they were confused as to whether employers were required to provide health insurance, disability insurance, and sick-pay benefits for pregnancy-related conditions or merely to adjust existing benefits to cover pregnancy-related conditions equitably.

Prodded by the PDA, some companies expanded employee benefits and incorporated innovative features into their personnel policies. One new feature was to permit new fathers to take up to six months of unpaid leave to care for a newborn. Another benefit extending beyond the PDA requirements related to unpaid leave. American Telephone and Telegraph (AT&T) provided disability payments to pregnant employees before they gave birth and before they were certified as disabled. In drawing up new plans affecting pregnant employees, AT&T adjusted treatment of other employees as well. Employees who were not pregnant also became eligible for time off in advance of an anticipated disability.

As a result of the Pregnancy Discrimination Act, some companies instituted programs for pregnant workers aimed at holding down the costs of expanding benefits and maintaining employee productivity. Cash incentives or alternative care arrangements, such as in-home nursing care following the birth, were offered to employees who leave the hospital earlier than expected. Such efforts lowered the cost to employers of health insurance and disability insurance premiums.

Numerous companies ran workplace seminars aimed at helping pregnant employees develop good health habits. According to occupational health nurses, these seminars on prenatal health care help reduce absenteeism during pregnancy and reduce the average length of maternity leave.

The issue of pregnancy-related discrimination has been examined by employers in the context of fetal protection policies. Companies concerned about reproductive hazards have instituted policies intended to protect fetal health. Some of these policies excluded women from jobs and occupations involving exposure to risks to the fetus. Johnson Controls, for example, refused to employ women in departments where lead was used because of concern about potential fetal injury.

The courts have ruled that policies that exclude women from jobs that may pose hazards to their reproductive health or the health of a fetus are direct violations of the Civil Rights Act of 1964 as amended by the Pregnancy Discrimination Act of 1978 unless the threat cannot be abated by means of control of the risk or other protection from it. In three separate court cases, stringent tests for fetal protection policies were established. The courts ruled that a fetal protection policy may discriminate against women if persuasive evidence exists that the risk to the fetus is real and likely to occur and that the risk is confined to women or fetuses.

Employers responded to the prohibition of discriminatory fetal protection policies in several ways. Several large companies initiated research studies aimed at identifying potential connections between occupational exposures and adverse reproductive effects. Larger corporations offered protection from reproductive hazards through temporary job transfers of pregnant workers to jobs of comparable work at equal pay and began taking steps to try to minimize reproductive hazards for both female and male employees.

In response to the passage of the PDA, states addressed issues concerning pregnant workers through laws and regulations. Although only a few states had enacted laws pertaining to reproductive hazards by the early 1990's, a majority of states had addressed some aspect of work as it pertained to pregnant women. A number of states enacted laws or promulgated regulations covering pregnancy under disability laws and prohibiting discrimination in hiring and promotion decisions based on pregnancy.

One trend concerns laws governing maternity leave not related to disability. Under the PDA, employers must grant disability leave to pregnant employees to the same extent as offered to other employees for different types of disabilities. The PDA does not require employers to grant leave for child care. Several states passed laws mandating unpaid parental leave or maternity leave. Because the PDA provides for equal treatment, employers must offer the same parental leave to fathers as to mothers.

American companies typically did not offer maternity leaves that extended beyond the period of disability. The Family and Medical Leave Act passed by the Bill Clinton Administration addressed that issue. The primary provisions of the FMLA centered on requiring a fixed number of weeks of unpaid parental leave, continued health benefits, and job security.

Employers are faced with difficulties in setting parameters with respect to pregnancy leave. Under the PDA, employers are prohibited from placing limits on the length of pregnancy leaves unless they also place identical limits on other disability leaves. This restriction has led to substantial state legislation regarding family and medical leaves as well as to the proposal of the federal Family and Medical Leave Act.

Bibliography

Bureau of National Affairs. *Pregnancy and Employment: The Complete Handbook on Discrimination, Maternity Leave, and Health and Safety.* Washington, D.C.: Author, 1987. Provides an overview of legal developments covering pregnancy discrimination and maternity-leave issues. Reviews issues involving reproductive hazards to pregnant workers. Details programs initiated by employers.

Dabrow, Allan, and Gina Ameci. "What You Should Know About Pregnancy and the Law." *Management Review* 80 (August, 1991): 38-40. Examines several lawsuits subsequent to the PDA relating to discrimination in employment. Discusses trends relating to parental leave at the state and federal levels.

Fried, Mindy. *Taking Time: Parental Leave Policy and Corporate Culture.* Philadelphia: Temple University Press, 1998. Part of Temple University Press's Women in the Political Economy series.

Kamerman, Sheila B., Alfred J. Kahn, and Paul Kingston. *Maternity Policies and Working Women.* New York: Columbia University Press, 1983. Discusses why maternity benefits are important and presents the evolution of federal maternity policies for working women. Also discusses the benefits mandated at the state level. Includes examples of maternity benefits from specific companies.

Kohl, John P., and Paul S. Greenlaw. "The Pregnancy Discrimination Act: Compliance Problems." *Personnel* 60 (November/December, 1983): 65-71. Summarizes the origins of the Pregnancy Discrimination Act and reports the results of a study investigating compliance with the PDA.

Zigler, Edward F., and Meryl Frank, eds. *The Parental Leave Crisis.* New Haven, Conn.: Yale University Press, 1988. Provides a history of maternity-leave policies. Discusses why parental leave is important and examines the need for a national parental-leave policy. Useful for understanding the impact of women in the work force on laws and employer policies.

Iris A. Pirozzoli

Cross-References

Congress Passes the Equal Pay Act (1963); The Civil Rights Act Prohibits Discrimination in Employment (1964); Nixon Signs the Occupational Safety and Health Act (1970); The Supreme Court Orders the End of Discrimination in Hiring (1971); The Supreme Court Upholds Quotas as a Remedy for Discrimination (1986).

THE THREE MILE ISLAND ACCIDENT PROMPTS REFORMS IN NUCLEAR POWER

CATEGORY OF EVENT: Consumer affairs
TIME: March 28, 1979
LOCALE: Harrisburg, Pennsylvania

The nuclear power plant accident at Three Mile Island exposed weaknesses and led to new safety measures designed to avoid a repetition elsewhere

Principal personages:
DICK THORNBURGH (1932-   ), the governor of Pennsylvania, 1979-1987
WILLIAM W. SCRANTON III (1947-   ), the lieutenant governor of Pennsylvania, 1979-1987
JOSEPH M. HENDRIE (1925-   ), the chairman of the U.S. Nuclear Regulatory Commission, 1977-1979
JIMMY CARTER (1924-   ), the president of the United States, 1977-1981

Summary of Event

On March 28, 1979, the Three Mile Island (TMI) nuclear power plant on the Susquehanna River near Harrisburg, Pennsylvania, nearly suffered a catastrophe as its Unit Two malfunctioned, setting into play events that resulted in the most serious accident to that time in the history of the commercial nuclear power industry. Had it not finally been contained, the malfunction would have resulted in devastation similar to that caused by the plant in Chernobyl, Ukraine, in 1986.

The TMI accident exposed many weaknesses in nuclear power plant design, management, and operation. The ineffectiveness of the Nuclear Regulatory Commission (NRC) and inadequacy of emergency preparedness were also exposed, leading to proposal of many changes by the many investigators deployed to study the event, including a presidential commission and congressional committees, the Nuclear Regulatory Commission, Pennsylvania governmental groups, and industrial organizations. In 1980, the comptroller general published a report to Congress that reviewed eight of the other reports and gave its own independent observations.

The Three Mile Island Unit Two, as well as its sister, Unit One, was a pressurized water reactor. It generated electric power by boiling water into steam, which then spun the blades of a turbine generator. The heat to convert the water to steam was produced by chain reaction fission of uranium in the reactor's core. This core was covered with water as its primary coolant and encapsulated in a structure forty feet high with walls of steel eight inches thick. The coolant was radioactive and under pressure, which allowed it to be superheated to 575 degrees Fahrenheit without boiling. It then was pumped to a steam generator, where the coolant heated cooler water in a secondary system. Under less pressure, the water turned to steam and spun turbine blades, propelling a generator. The steam passed through a condenser, changing it back to water. It then began its circuit through to the boiler and back again through this secondary system, also called the "feedwater" circuit.

At 4 A.M. on Wednesday, March 29, 1979, two pumps in this system shut down; the steam turbine followed a few seconds later. Its steam was released. What little coolant was left in the secondary system boiled. The primary coolant could not transfer its heat load and it too began to boil, increasing pressure in the reactor and in the primary system. A relief valve opened, allowing radioactive water and steam to drain into a tank to prevent a primary coolant explosion. This valve should have shut off after thirteen seconds, but it remained open for more than two hours.

Less than a minute later, emergency backup pumps automatically engaged to add water to the secondary system. No water was added, however, because valves controlling the flow had been closed for maintenance two weeks earlier. According to Nuclear Regulatory Commission rules, the plant was to be shut down if these valves were closed for more than seventy-two hours.

Two minutes into the crisis, the emergency core coolant system kicked in to add water to the reactor core. Technicians, however, believed that the reactor was already full of water. They also assumed that the pressurizer relief valve was closed when it was not.

Four minutes later, with pressure in the primary cooling loop high, it was thought that the system was filling with water. Since additional increases in pressure could cause the system to blow, one emergency pump was stopped. Twelve and one-half minutes into the incident, the other was reduced to one-half speed. This was proper procedure, since the attendants believed the system was filling with water. This condition is known as "going solid" and must be avoided to lessen the possibility of the primary system's breakdown. The reactor core in fact was not covered by water, and temperatures began rising toward the meltdown point of 5,000 degrees Fahrenheit. There were no meters that could measure the depth of water in the reactor core, so the operators could only guess about this critical information.

At eight and one-half minutes into the crisis, the closed valves on the feedwater system were opened, filling the secondary system with water, which helped to draw heat from the primary system. The relief valve allowed primary cooling water to drain into a tank that spilled its radioactive water onto the containment building's floor. The water then was pumped into a tank in the nearby auxiliary building. Radioactivity was released in this final procedure at 4:38 A.M.

Pockets of steam collected in two sets of pumps for reactor cooling, resulting in vibrations that caused them to be turned off. With no cooling system in operation, the reactor suffered severe damage. The twelve-foot-tall fuel rods were only half covered with water. The shields around the rods themselves were destroyed by the intense, rising heat, releasing radioactive debris into the primary coolant, which itself was spilling onto the floor. Hydrogen and radioactive gases from the coolant collected in the containment building. Radiation levels rose within the buildings and was released into the atmosphere. At 6:50 A.M., a general emergency was declared.

Early Wednesday afternoon, hydrogen that had accumulated in the containment building exploded. Hydrogen continued to be created by the uncovered core, fueling fears of a catastrophic explosion.

Another scenario envisioned was the so-called "China Syndrome." In the scenario, the core would become so hot (about 5,200 degrees Fahrenheit) that it would melt. This superheated material would bore its way through the bottom of the plant and down through the ground until it hit water. The water would become high-pressure steam and would erupt from the earth, spewing radioactivity into the air all around the plant. A typical nuclear reactor could release about the same radiation as would a thousand bombs of the size used at Hiroshima.

A 1975 study estimated that a plant slightly larger than Three Mile Island could cause thirty-three hundred deaths and forty-five thousand radiation injuries immediately. Forty-five thousand cancer and forty thousand thyroid tumor fatalities would result in the longer term. Fourteen billion dollars of damage to property would also occur.

Controlled and uncontrolled radiation leaks from the plant continued through Wednesday, March 28, and Thursday, March 29. On Friday, Governor Richard Thornburgh ordered an evacuation of pregnant women and small children within five miles of the facility. A hydrogen bubble began to grow in the reactor vessel. It was thought that it could self-ignite in five to eight days, resulting in a possible meltdown. A general evacuation was considered by Thornburgh and Lieutenant Governor William W. Scranton III but was not ordered. It was thought that it might set off an evacuation panic and result in more injuries than it might prevent.

On Saturday morning, John Herbein, the Metropolitan Edison vice president for generation, said that the bubble had decreased in size by two-thirds and that the danger was over. Harold Denton of the NRC disagreed and said that the bubble actually had increased in size. Lack of information, poor communication among the numerous people from the varied agencies involved, incorrect wire service reports, and alarmist news reports fueled the mounting alarm on the part of the public, both locally and nationally. More than half of the families within a twelve-mile radius of the plant evacuated at least one member.

Later on Saturday, Harold Denton told Thornburgh that the size of the hydrogen bubble had been reduced. Joseph M. Hendrie, a commissioner of the NRC, had a group working on the same problem. They reported that the bubble could be explosive in six or seven days.

On the afternoon of Sunday, April 1, President Jimmy Carter visited the facility. At about the same time, the hydrogen bubble shrank, eliminating the possibility of explosion, and the crisis wound down.

Impact of Event

Numerous changes were made in the operation of nuclear power plants as a result of the Three Mile Island incident. This was a contingency for which there had been no plan, since it was thought to have a negligible probability of happening.

Until TMI, nuclear plants were constructed with three levels of safety built in, known as "defense in depth." The first level involved using quality construction standards and emergency practices to prevent accidents. It is inevitable that mistakes will be made, accidents will happen, and equipment will break down. These factors required another level to prevent or control their effects. These were built into the original design. The last level of safety assumed that special design features would fail. The containment building could mitigate or slow the release of radioactive particles from the plant should that happen.

In a complete meltdown, the core would eat through the floor of the plant, contaminating the groundwater supply. Radiation might also quickly breach the containment building and result in many deaths and injuries. Because it might be impossible to contain a meltdown, design features to delay the release of radioactivity were suggested. They provided more time to evacuate the area. They included core "catchers" to slow the core melting through the floor, a filtering system to provide for filtering and release of gases in the containment building to prevent overpressurization, and hydrogen control systems to prevent or minimize the formation of a hydrogen bubble, which was so potentially dangerous at TMI. Control room design changes were adopted that made controls more recognizable and accessible to operators in emergency situations.

Prior to 1979, nuclear plants were located close to major population areas. It was thought that the probability of radiation exposure to the public was quite small. After the accident, it became apparent that anything made by man was subject to failure. A return to the policy of constructing plants far from populated areas was thought to be prudent.

The inadequate qualifications and training of operators contributed to the severity of the accident. Training programs had been geared toward running the plant under normal conditions rather than under stressful emergencies. Supervisory and management personnel knew little about actual operations and were not able to help the operators mitigate problems.

The Nuclear Regulatory Commission now requires more operators, who are better qualified and have passed a more stringent licensing examination. Supervisors need engineering expertise, training is more rigorous, and simulators are used to prepare operators to deal with emergency situations, sometimes even duplicating the TMI conditions.

Studies found that initial situations similar to that at TMI had occurred at other plants, but operators were able to react before a major emergency developed. There was no system in place at the NRC or within the nuclear power industry to collect or distribute information to other operators about the problems encountered. A system to review and analyze information was implemented to collect data on American and foreign nuclear reactors. The Office for Analysis and Evaluation of Operating Data was created to be the focal point of this effort.

At the time of the TMI accident, the quality assurance programs of both Metropolitan Edison and the NRC were deficient. Standards used in the construction and operation of power plants were to be monitored by an independent department within each utility to ensure compliance. The NRC reviewed the utilities' efforts. These standards did not apply to equipment unrelated to safety or to radiation survey monitors. Equipment not related to safety had a significant involvement in the accident, and many of the radiation monitoring instruments at TMI did not work. An acknowledgment from the NRC that rigid quality assurance standards and their strict implementation were essential was expected to lessen the likelihood of a future similar event.

Emergency procedures on the part of the NRC and state and local governments were found to have been lax or nonexistent. The accident demonstrated that an emergency was possible, prompting emergency and evacuation plans to be implemented or upgraded for existing nuclear power plants. In addition, operating licenses would be granted to new nuclear generating plants only if state and local governments had federally approved emergency plans. The Federal Emergency Management Agency, rather than the NRC, became responsible for evaluating emergency plans.

During the emergency, numerous TMI employees were assigned various emergency response duties. Many had received no training and did not understand what needed to be done. Additionally, half of the radiation dose rate monitors were not operable. The NRC became more rigorous in requiring emergency training and equipment maintenance. Each of the five members of the Nuclear Regulatory Commission had equal responsibility and authority in all decisions in 1979. The chair had vaguely defined administrative and executive functions, but decision-making power lay with joint action of the commissioners and not with the chair. With no one ultimately in command, slow, inefficient management resulted. After reorganization of the NRC in 1980, the chair had more power, although the commission as a whole still set the framework within which the chair could operate. The chair was allowed to act in the name of the commission in an emergency, determining policies, giving orders, and directing all actions concerning the emergency. The chair gained the ultimate responsibility for emergency decision making. This was expected to provide more timely responses instead of the delays involved with management by committee.

Overall, the TMI accident prompted reconsideration of nuclear power as a source of energy. Although relatively inexpensive, nuclear power posed the risk of disasters and the problem of nuclear waste disposal. Regulators had to decide how many costly safety requirements to impose, and the federal government faced choices of which energy sources to promote and even whether to allow construction of new nuclear power plants. The 1986 nuclear disaster at Chernobyl renewed these concerns worldwide.

Bibliography

Cantelon, Philip L., and Robert C. Williams. *Crisis Contained: The Department of Energy at Three Mile Island.* Carbondale: Southern Illinois

University Press, 1982. Evaluation of the Department of Energy's performance during the emergency.

Del Tredici, Robert. *The People of Three Mile Island*. San Francisco: Sierra Club Books, 1980. Interviews with local people and others connected with the event.

Gray, Mike, and Ira Rosen. *The Warning: Accident at Three Mile Island*. New York: W. W. Norton, 1982. A very readable investigative report that dramatically pulls the reader through the complex events of the Three Mile Island disaster itself after reviewing prior problems experienced at other nuclear plants. Less technical than some of the other publications; fast and informative reading.

Ramsey, Charles B. *Commercial Nuclear Power: Assuring Safety for the Future*. New York: J. Wiley, 1998.

Sorensen, John H., Jon Soderstrom, Emily Copenhaven, Sam Carnes, and Robert Bolin. *Impacts of Hazardous Technology: The Psycho-Social Effects of Restarting TMI-1*. Albany: State University of New York Press, 1987. Reviews the background of TMI and projects the effects of starting the undamaged sister reactor, TMI-1.

Starr, Philip, and William Pearman. *Three Mile Island Sourcebook: Annotations of a Disaster*. New York: Garland, 1983. This book is divided into three sections. The first provides a chronology of media coverage from TMI's announcement of opening in 1966 until 1981. Three local newspapers, *The New York Times*, and *Newsweek* are surveyed. The next section is annotations of state and federal documents. The last covers books, articles, and other publications written about TMI.

Stephens, Mark. *Three Mile Island*. New York: Random House, 1980. Written by a staff member of the presidential commission. Recounts the immediate events of the incident and offers suggestions to avoid future problems.

U.S. General Accounting Office. *Three Mile Island: The Most Studied Nuclear Accident in History*. Washington, D.C.: Author, 1980. This inquiry was made to determine whether the investigations done up to that time were thorough and accurate in their presentation of the facts and their conclusions as to the causes of the accident. Eight investigative reports, as well as other materials, were reviewed. The General Accounting Office found that although reports varied as to depth and detail, the facts and conclusions were consistent. Equipment breakdowns, insufficient training of operators, poor design, and inadequate emergency and operating procedures were the chief culprits. Blame was also placed on the Nuclear Regulatory Commission with its poor structure, practices, and attitudes.

John R. Tate

Cross-References

The U.S. Government Creates the Tennessee Valley Authority (1933); GPU Announces Plans for a Commercial Nuclear Reactor (1963); The Environmental Protection Agency Is Created (1970); The United States Plans to Cut Dependence on Foreign Oil (1974); The Alaskan Oil Pipeline Opens (1977).

THE SUPREME COURT RULES ON AFFIRMATIVE ACTION PROGRAMS

CATEGORY OF EVENT: Labor
TIME: June 27, 1979
LOCALE: Washington, D.C.

In United Steelworkers of America v. Weber, *the Supreme Court upheld the legality of preferential treatment in the Weber case, making it possible for affirmative action programs to continue*

Principal personages:
BRIAN WEBER (1946-   ), a production worker at Kaiser Aluminum, Inc.
WILLIAM J. BRENNAN, JR. (1906-1997), the Supreme Court justice who wrote the majority opinion
WILLIAM H. REHNQUIST (1924-   ), the Supreme Court justice who wrote the dissenting opinion

Summary of Event

The passage of Title VII of the Civil Rights Act in 1964 made it illegal for employers to discriminate against anyone on the basis of race, sex, color, religion, or national origin. Title VII was supposed to create an atmosphere of equal opportunity, in which all candidates theoretically had the same chance to secure a job and other employment benefits. It was soon recognized, however, that prohibiting present and future discrimination would not fully remedy the consequences of past discrimination. Members of groups disadvantaged by prior discrimination did not have the experience, credentials, status, or contacts to compete on an equal footing with those who had never been the target of discrimination.

The government therefore imposed on federal contractors the duty to undertake "affirmative action," that is, to engage in special efforts to hire and promote members of groups that were underrepresented in their work forces. The overall goal was to bring groups that had been discriminated against into statistical parity in the work force at a faster than natural rate. Affirmative action required employers to compare the relevant labor market to their present labor force and to identify discrepancies and situations in which minorities and women were underrepresented. They then had to file written affirmative action plans that included goals, timetables, and strategies to correct the deficiencies.

Opponents soon chose to test the validity of affirmative action by questioning the legality of the results the legislation created. Affirmative action has been interpreted in several ways. It was commonly understood that an employer undertaking affirmative action would actively recruit underrepresented groups, eliminate managerial prejudices toward underrepresented groups, and remove employment practices that put victims of previous discrimination at a disadvantage. There has never been a question about the legality of these types of practices. To most employers, however, the safest way to comply with affirmative action involved extending preferential treatment to qualified members of underrepresented groups through the use of hiring quotas. This meant, for example, that if women were underrepresented in a particular company, and a woman and a white man applied for a job and had the same qualifications, the woman would be given preference. At the extreme, quotas might also result in less-qualified women and people of color being preferred over white men. Such practices resulted in what was called reverse discrimination against members of groups that were adequately represented, in particular, white men.

Such a result appeared to be in conflict with Title VII (section 703), which specifically prohibits employment discrimination based on race, gender, color, religion, or national origin. The basic issue was therefore whether an affirmative action plan that classifies people according to their race, gender, and national origin and then makes employment decisions at least partially based on those classifications violated Title VII. Opponents of affirmative action argued that its practical effect mandated preferential treatment for certain groups of people, while Title VII specifically stated that it did not require the granting of preferential treatment. A series of court cases, most of which reached the Supreme Court and culminated in the ruling in *United Steelworkers of America v. Weber*, eventually decided the fate of affirmative action.

The Supreme Court initially seemed to take a position against preferential treatment, in *Griggs v. Duke Power Co.* (1971). This case concerned a company that had unintentionally produced a discriminatory effect against

African Americans by requiring tests and educational credentials that were not job related. The decision made it clear that the court considered these practices to be violations of Title VII and that artificial and unnecessary barriers to employment had to be removed. The court also specifically stated, however, that no person or group had a right to preferential treatment simply because of membership in a particular group or because of being the target of prior discrimination.

The arguments against preferential treatment seemed to grow stronger in 1976 with *McDonald v. Santa Fe Trail Transportation Company*. Three men, two white and one black, were charged with the same indiscretion. The company fired the two white men but gave the black man a warning. The two white men charged the company with discrimination, but the company responded that Title VII was meant to protect the disadvantaged and that the two white men therefore had no protection. The Supreme Court disagreed, eventually ruling that the term "race" was all-inclusive and Title VII therefore also prohibited discrimination against whites.

Another 1976 ruling, this time by a lower court, ordered American Telephone and Telegraph (AT&T) to pay damages to a white man who had lost a promotion to a woman with less experience and seniority. The promotion decision had been made in the context of a federal consent decree, in which AT&T had agreed to hire and promote women and people of color into jobs previously dominated by white men. The male employee believed that he was nevertheless the victim of sex discrimination, and the court agreed, contending that "innocent employees" should not be made to pay for a company's past discriminatory practices.

A more direct blow was dealt to affirmative action in *Regents of the University of California v. Bakke* (1978). The university reserved a percentage of its medical school openings for minority students. A white applicant was denied admission to the University of California at Davis Medical School because the white allotment had been filled and the only slots open were those saved for minority candidates. In a narrow and indecisive ruling, the Supreme Court affirmed a lower court order to admit Allan Bakke to the medical school, claiming that the university's admission system violated both the Constitution's equal protection amendment and Title VII. The Court made it clear that quotas based exclusively on race were illegal in a situation in which no previous discrimination had been shown. The justices did not, however, outlaw the use of quotas in situations where previous discrimination had occurred. The Supreme Court further muddied the waters when it also ruled that although race could not be the sole deciding factor, the university could continue to take race into consideration in its selection system.

The net effect of these decisions placed employers in a difficult position and affirmative action in potential jeopardy. In the light of the various rulings, employers believed that they had to find ways to increase the presence and position of underrepresented groups without causing any discrimination against the white majority. Such a balancing act was extremely difficult, if not impossible. The controversy was finally decided in 1979 with *United Steelworkers of America v. Weber.*

In 1974, the United Steelworkers of America and Kaiser Aluminum voluntarily entered into a fifteen-plant collective bargaining agreement that included an affirmative action plan designed to remedy racial imbalances in Kaiser's skilled craft work force. The plan reserved half of the openings to in-house craft training programs for African Americans until the percentage of black craft workers at Kaiser mirrored the local labor force. The litigation arose from a charge at the Gramercy plant in Louisiana, where 1.83 percent of the skilled craft workers were black, while 39 percent of the local work force was black. After the plan was put into operation, seven black and six white workers were selected from the production work force to enter the training program. Brian Weber, a white production worker, bid for admission into the program and was rejected; he had more seniority than all the black workers who were selected. Weber subsequently filed a class action suit, alleging that the plan discriminated against whites and was therefore in violation of Title VII.

The basic issue was whether a private sector employer could voluntarily implement an affirmative action plan that involved preferential treatment when there was no proof of prior discrimination but the work force did demonstrate racial or sexual imbalance. The majority opinion, authored by Justice William J. Brennan, Jr., ruled that any employer or union that was trying to eliminate imbalances in its work force could voluntarily use a plan that involved preferential treatment, even if that plan benefited individuals who had not themselves been the victims of discrimination. In reaching this decision, the justices emphasized that Kaiser's affirmative action plan was the result of negotiation and agreement between the company and the union. The Supreme Court further stipulated that although Title VII does not require preferential treatment, neither does it prohibit it.

The *Weber* decision did not legitimize all quota systems. It stated that in order for a quota system to be lawful, it must be part of a permissible affirmative action plan. The court offered the following guidelines as to what constitutes a permissible affirmative action plan: It is designed to break down old patterns of discrimination; it does not needlessly trammel the interests of white employees; it does not create an absolute bar to whites; it is a temporary corrective measure; and it has the goal of eliminating racial imbalance.

There was a strong dissent in the *Weber* case, authored by Justice William H. Rehnquist. The minority quoted convincing evidence from the *Congressional Record* that indicated that some members of Congress, including strong proponents of the bill, did indeed intend that Title VII prohibit all preferential treatment.

Impact of Event

Review of the findings of *Weber* and the previous cases results in a four-faceted scenario. If an employer has been found guilty of employment discrimination, affirmative action involving preferential treatment appears to be sanctioned by Title VII, which allows the courts to impose any relief or affirmative action deemed appropriate. In these cases, the affirmative action is viewed as a remedy for illegal behavior, that is, a way to redress an imbalance created by deliberate discrimination. On the other hand, if an employer has an imbalanced work force but has not been found guilty of discrimination, the courts have no power to order any plan involving preferential treatment. A firm is free, however, to voluntarily adopt measures that result in preferential treatment, provided they are part of a permissible affirmative action plan. Although "permissible" has never been specifically defined, the five criteria laid out in *Weber* are regarded as useful guidelines. Finally, a firm cannot voluntarily adopt preferential treatment tactics that are not part of a permissible affirmative action plan.

The *Weber* ruling is especially noteworthy because it is one of the few in judicial history in which a court has rejected the actual wording of a statute in favor of what it interprets as the legislative intent. The Court acknowledged that Title VII does indeed prohibit all racial discrimination but contended that the law had to be interpreted in the context of the history and purpose of Title VII. The Court held that the primary concern of Title VII was the plight and position of African Americans, and it was therefore illogical to assume that the act would therefore ban all voluntary and race-conscious efforts to correct the effects of past discrimination. In effect, the Court said that despite the inevitable result of reverse discrimination, preferential treatment is permissible when its goal is the correction of longstanding social problems. Based on this reasoning, and despite subsequent challenges, most major firms in the United States implemented affirmative action, and most plans involved some degree of preferential treatment.

The battle, as of the early 1990's, was probably far from over. From its inception, affirmative action has had its detractors and its defenders. Both proponents and opponents of affirmative action continued to make valid and legitimate points about the evils and the benefits of preferential treatment. Some voiced moral and societal objections; opponents protested that it is unfair to require present generations to pay for the sins of predecessors, that affirmative action causes discrimination against white men, and that all employment decisions should be based solely upon merit. Detractors further argue that any legislation that allows preferential treatment is bound to increase hostility toward the groups it is meant to help. Others point out, however, that to rely on the natural progression of time to correct the effects of past discrimination would take far too long and would perpetuate an untenable situation.

Although the *Weber* ruling may have settled prominent legal questions about preferential treatment and affirmative action, it by no means ended the controversy. The continuing debate again took center stage in the late 1980's, when a more conservative Supreme Court handed down a series of decisions unfavorable to affirmative action and equal employment opportunity legislation. Congress quickly responded with the Civil Rights Act of 1991, which basically undid all the conservative Court decisions.

Legislative and judicial activity continued to generate uncertainty for businesses, as they did their best to hire and promote women and people of color while still trying to treat individual white men fairly. This balancing act appeared to be producing mixed results. Because of affirmative action, women and people of color gained entry into organizations, but they were not being promoted into higher and more influential positions. Whether affirmative action can be declared a success, therefore, had yet to be determined.

Bibliography

Buchholz, Rogene A. "Equal Employment Opportunity." In *Business Environment and Public Policy*. 4th ed. Englewood Cliffs, N.J.: Prentice-Hall, 1992. Chapter 12 provides a concise and understandable synopsis of affirmative action. Gives insight to both sides of the issue. Excellent summary of major cases dealing with affirmative action.

Dudley, William, ed. "Does Affirmative Action Alleviate Discrimination?" In *Racism in America: Opposing Viewpoints*. San Diego, Calif.: Greenhaven Press, 1991. Presents a series of articles arguing both for and against affirmative action. Provides moral and societal context. Lively style, interesting points.

Eisenberg, Theodore. *Civil Rights Legislation*. 3d ed. Charlottesville, Va.: Michie, 1991. Provides a lengthy reprint of the *Weber* ruling and other significant affirmative action cases. Written in lawbook fashion. Somewhat difficult to understand for those not versed in the law.

Hall, Kermit L., ed. *The Oxford Guide to United States Supreme Court*

Decisions. New York: Oxford University Press, 1999. Multiauthored collection of essays on more than four hundred significant Court decisions, with supporting glossary and other aids.

Ledvinka, James, and Vida Scarpello. *Federal Regulation of Personnel and Human Resource Management.* 2d ed. Boston: PWS-Kent, 1991. Provides an excellent history of the controversy surrounding preferential treatment. Easy to read.

Player, Mack. *Federal Law of Employment Discrimination in a Nutshell.* 3d ed. St. Paul, Minn.: West, 1992. A "nutshell" reference guide to employment discrimination law. Lays out highlights in a brief, orderly fashion.

Weiss, Robert J. *"We Want Jobs": A History of Affirmative Action.* New York: Garland, 1997.

Marie McKendall

Cross-References

Congress Passes the Equal Pay Act (1963); The Civil Rights Act Prohibits Discrimination in Employment (1964); The Supreme Court Orders the End of Discrimination in Hiring (1971); The Pregnancy Discrimination Act Extends Employment Rights (1978); *Firefighters v. Stotts* Upholds Seniority Systems (1984); The Supreme Court Upholds Quotas as a Remedy for Discrimination (1986); Bush Signs the Americans with Disabilities Act of 1990 (1990).

AMERICAN FIRMS ADOPT JAPANESE MANUFACTURING TECHNIQUES

CATEGORY OF EVENT: Manufacturing
TIME: The 1980's
LOCALE: The United States

American firms, in response to gaps in productivity and quality, adopted various techniques developed in Japan

Principal personages:
TAIICHI OHNO (1912-1990), a vice president of Toyota Motor, inventor of just-in-time concepts
SHIGEO SHINGO (1909-1990), an engineer and consultant who invented just-in-time inventory practices in collaboration with Ohno
KIICHIRŌ TOYODA (1925-   ), the president of Toyota Motor

Summary of Event

The adoption of just-in-time inventory practices by American firms in the early 1980's helped American industry to respond to the Japanese challenge. Firms were making vigorous efforts to close gaps in their productivity and quality, which had both fallen behind the performance of Japanese firms. The United States had been directly confronted by the productivity and quality levels achieved by Japanese industry, which seriously threatened the competitiveness of American firms.

The typical Japanese business orientation maintained that a company that allows exploitation, including that of consumers, cannot achieve long-term success. The astonishing results obtained in Japan through focusing on quality, long-range strategic planning, partnership with suppliers, and adoption of the principle that the employees are the company necessitated a rethinking of priorities and a change of outlook on the part of American industry. Many Western managers believed that Japanese techniques could not be applied in Western companies and that matching Japan's successes would be impossible. Evidence refuted notions that these accomplishments resulted from cultural differences, and managers became willing to experiment with the techniques.

Japan's fundamental economic goal since 1945 had been to achieve full employment through industrialization. As a means of attaining this goal, the Japanese employed a strategy to gain dominance in selected product areas. They imported technology, concentrated on achieving high productivity, and embarked on a drive to improve quality and reliability. Two basic concepts behind the drive toward dominance were elimination of waste and respect for people. Elimination of waste involved such tactics as keeping plants small and specialized, using workers in groups to take advantage of teamwork and cooperation, producing with just-in-time methods, and minimizing setup times for jobs. Respect for people involved lifetime employment, unions sponsored by companies, use of automation and robotics to eliminate tedious and dangerous tasks for humans, management by consensus or committee, and quality circles. The Japanese recognized that every worker could make a contribution, often beyond his or her immediate tasks, and that suppliers often could assist in improving a company's productivity or in reducing its costs.

Some of the new Japanese techniques were difficult to translate into the American industrial environment because of cultural factors or resistance on the part of workers. Many, however, were appropriate and practical, such as the just-in-time philosophy, minimized setup time, and concentration on quality. The just-in-time philosophy acted as a framework and organizing principle for other innovations.

Most accounts agree that the just-in-time philosophy was developed in Japan at Toyota Motor Corporation. Until the late 1970's, the technique was limited in use to Toyota and its family of key suppliers. In 1949, Toyota had found itself on the brink of bankruptcy. At that time, the United States was far more productive than Japan in automobile production. Kiichirō Toyoda, president of Toyota Motor Corporation, issued a challenge to his company to catch up with the United States within three years. Responding to the challenge, Taiichi Ohno, a company vice president, pointed out that the lack of success was a result of wastefulness in the production process. Ohno proceeded to organize a production system dedicated to elimination of waste. In collaboration with Shigeo Shingo, an engineer, he invented the just-in-time system. Under that system, parts arrive at the company or at individual workstations just in time for their use, rather than being stockpiled. The company thus saves the costs of carrying large inventories of parts or components. The system also encourages greater coordination of plans both within the company and with outside suppliers.

Toyota's subsequent success has been attributed to implementation of an integrated production system based on the elements described previously. The system, however, was not a quick solution to management problems. Experts estimated that such a system might take as long as ten years to develop and integrate because it involved such a radical overhaul of management philosophy and worker orientation to jobs.

Ohno realized that managers needed to change their concept of how business was done, at all levels of the company. The secret of success was a never-ending search for improvements in productivity and quality. Ohno was inspired by his observation of an American supermarket, in which items selected from shelves by customers were replaced just in time for the next round of customers. He saw that as a model of efficiency.

The production system developed at Toyota did not receive much attention until the 1970's, when other Japanese firms began to recognize the potential suggested by the system. During the late 1960's, managers in the United States began to realize that systems for production management and

In order to compete with Japanese imports, American automobile manufacturers have had to adopt elements of Japanese manufacturing techniques. (PhotoDisc)

scheduling were imposing costs that were larger than necessary. Managers therefore began to concentrate on efficiency in production. At the same time, however, firms were also concerned with diversifying into new fields and improving the quality of their products. Within this context, the emphasis on efficiency was lost.

The financial burden associated with large inventories produced a revolution in production scheduling and resulted in a shift in priority to focusing on reducing inventory costs through such just-in-time systems as materials requirement planning (MRP). The conviction that MRP was the answer to the just-in-time challenge survived until the mid-1970's, when American managers noticed that Japanese firms operating without MRP still obtained better results. As they studied the Japanese approach, American managers noticed that it was considerably simpler. To attain the best results, however, it was necessary to introduce radically new approaches and modes of thinking.

Impact of Event

A survey in 1984 found that American firms that had applied just-in-time methods had obtained extraordinary results. Not uncommon were 90 percent reductions in throughput time, 90 percent reductions of work in process, 10 to 30 percent reductions in manufacturing costs, 75 percent reductions in setup times, and 50 percent reductions in the floor space required for production. Similarly, a study of eighty European plants revealed typical benefits of 50 to 70 percent reductions in throughput time, 50 percent reductions in average inventories, 20 to 50 percent increases in productivity, 50 percent reductions in setup times, and an average payback for investments in just-in-time methods of less than nine months.

In 1976, a Quasar plant in Chicago that manufactured Motorola television sets was purchased by Matsushita. Within two years, with the same full-time work force, Matsushita doubled output, increased product quality twentyfold, and reduced the costs of servicing warranties by more than 90 percent. General Motors began using Japanese techniques in 1980 and soon cut inventory costs by about 75 percent, increasing the turnover of inventories almost fivefold. Other American automobile manufacturers obtained similar results.

General Electric, Westinghouse, and RCA also reported impressive results. The computer system division of Hewlett-Packard increased productivity by 55 percent, decreased welding defects by more than 90 percent and rejected items by 95 percent, and reduced the lead time for production by 90 percent. Other American companies that profitably adopted Japanese production techniques, including just-in-time inventory practices, included

Black & Decker (power tools), Deere & Company (heavy machinery and farm equipment), and American Telephone and Telegraph. In Europe, gains were equally impressive. Firms benefiting from the techniques were as diverse as Olivetti (typewriters), Michelin (steel cord), Fiat (aircraft engine parts), Famitalia Carlo Erba (pharmaceuticals), Lever Industriale (detergents), and Europa Metalli (metals).

Just-in-time practices were applied to processing industries such as production of chemicals, pharmaceuticals, and metals as well as to production to order and to more traditional manufacturing. Just-in-time practices proved applicable in service industries as well as in the factory. The successes, however, did not mean that implementation of Japanese production techniques was free of problems or provided the solution to every difficulty. Many problems refused to go away quickly. Resistance to change by both managers and workers, underestimation of education and training needs, shortages of parts or components as production scheduling changed, and lack of commitment were commonly reported.

The 1980's will be remembered as a period of dramatic change in Western manufacturing. Changes for the most part had their source in the overwhelming success of Japanese industry in lowering costs and improving quality, as demonstrated by Toyota, Suzuki, and many manufacturers of electronic components, among other firms. Once they realized that they had fallen behind in the productivity race with Japan, many Western managers thought that they were beaten. Until the end of the 1970's, many of them believed that catching up would be impossible. They had preconceived notions about the sources of Japanese success, including a belief that Japan had unbeatable advantages in labor costs, the number of labor hours per worker, worker attitudes, and punctual suppliers. Western managers did not believe that these conditions could be matched in their environments. Facts soon demolished all of these alibis for poor performance, and Western managers had no choice but to try to understand the Japanese lesson and make serious efforts to close the productivity and quality gaps.

The Japanese successes particularly affected American industry, as the two countries competed in many product lines, but other countries also found themselves challenged. American managers launched their own revolutions in strategy, organization, management, and workplace culture, sometimes modeling efforts on Japanese successes and other times creating new techniques to fit the American environment.

Management philosophy came to accept that quality rather than efficiency was the top priority and that operating horizons had to be expanded beyond the short term to achieve long-term success. Clients were to be satisfied as well as possible, even if that meant spending money in the short term. Suppliers were partners in the production process, and employees were not merely suppliers of labor but instead could make valuable contributions through their ideas and simply through becoming more motivated and more concerned about the welfare of the company. Further developments set in motion by the advent of just-in-time techniques included focusing on rapid development and introduction of new product lines and achieving competitive advantage through flexibility in manufacturing.

Bibliography
Cutcher-Gershenfeld, Joel. *Knowledge-Driven Work: Unexpected Lessons from Japanese and United States Work Practices.* New York: Oxford University Press, 1998.
Hay, Edward J. *The Just-in-Time Breakthrough.* New York: Wiley, 1988. A dynamic, comprehensive, practical, and clearly written explanation of just-in-time concepts and their relationship to quality, vendors, management, systems, and technology. Written from the perspective of an experienced practitioner. Outlines the process of getting started and cautions against the pitfalls.
Hernandez, Arnaldo. *Just-in-Time Manufacturing: A Practical Approach.* Englewood Cliffs, N.J.: Prentice-Hall, 1989. Explains the fundamental concepts from a theoretical angle, covers critical operational rules, and provides specific instructions for starting a just-in-time system from scratch. Shows how the concepts apply to all levels in the organization, for both workers and management.
Hirano, Hiroyuki. *J.I.T. Factory Revolution: A Pictorial Guide to Factory Design of the Future.* Cambridge, Mass.: Productivity Press, 1989. An encyclopedic picture book of just-in-time practices. Shows how to set up each area of a plant and provides many useful ideas for implementation. Simply, easy-to-read text. Pictures provide a vivid depiction of work in a just-in-time environment.
Japan Management Association, ed. *Kanban and Just-in-Time at Toyota: Management Begins at the Workplace.* Translated by David J. Lu. Rev. ed. Cambridge, Mass.: Productivity Press, 1989. Based on seminars at Toyota, one of the best practical introductions to just-in-time procedures. Explains every aspect in clear and simple terms. Discusses the underlying rationale, system setup, getting everyone involved, and refining the system once in place.
Merli, Giorgio. *Total Manufacturing Management.* Cambridge, Mass.: Productivity Press, 1990. Provides a thorough comparison of Western and Japanese management approaches and cultural distinctions. Develops a model for production organization and integrates the tools and methods

that support this model. Lays out the principles and steps for just-in-time practices and offers a powerfully integrated strategy and implementation plan.

Ohno, Taiichi. *Toyota Production System: Beyond Large-Scale Production.* Cambridge, Mass.: Productivity Press, 1988. Written to enable people to understand the system correctly and implement it successfully in their own plants. The emphasis is on concepts, with only a few case studies. Based on the knowledge and experience of one of the originators of just-in-time procedures.

Shingo, Shigeo. *A Study of the Toyota Production System from an Industrial Engineering Viewpoint.* Cambridge, Mass.: Productivity Press, 1989. Written by one of the inventors of the just-in-time system. Explains the philosophy, highlights the system's important aspects, provides additional information, and criticizes weaknesses. Aims to treat the subject in such a way that special features will stand out.

Kambiz Tabibzadeh

Cross-References

Ford Implements Assembly Line Production (1913); The U.S. Government Reforms Child Product Safety Laws (1970's); Nader's *Unsafe at Any Speed* Launches a Consumer Movement (1965); CAD/CAM Revolutionizes Engineering and Manufacturing (1980's); Electronic Technology Creates the Possibility of Telecommuting (1980's).

CAD/CAM REVOLUTIONIZES ENGINEERING AND MANUFACTURING

CATEGORY OF EVENT: Manufacturing
TIME: The 1980's
LOCALE: The United States

Computer-Aided Design (CAD) and Computer-Aided Manufacturing (CAM) enhanced flexibility in engineering design, leading to higher quality and reduced time for manufacturing

Principal personages:

PATRICK HANRATTY, a General Motors Research Laboratory worker who developed graphics programs

JACK ST. CLAIR KILBY (1923-), a Texas Instruments employee who first conceived of the idea of the integrated circuit

ROBERT NOYCE (1927-1990), an Intel Corporation employee who developed an improved process for manufacturing integrated circuits on microchips

DON HALLIDAY, an early user of CAD/CAM who created the Made-in-America car in only four months by using CAD and project management software

FRED BORSINI, an early user of CAD/CAM who demonstrated its power

Summary of Event

Computer-Aided Design (CAD) is a technique whereby geometrical descriptions of two-dimensional (2-D) or three-dimensional (3-D) objects can be created and stored, in the form of mathematical models, in a computer system. Points, lines, and curves are represented as graphical coordinates. When a drawing is requested from the computer, transformations are performed on the stored data, and the geometry of a part or a full view from either a two- or a three-dimensional perspective is shown. CAD systems replace the tedious process of manual drafting, and computer-aided drawing and redrawing that can be retrieved when needed have improved drafting efficiency. A CAD system is a combination of computer hardware and software that facilitates the construction of geometric models and, in many cases, their analysis. It allows a wide variety of visual representations of those models to be displayed.

Computer-Aided Manufacturing (CAM) refers to the use of computers to control, wholly or partly, manufacturing processes. In practice, the term is most often applied to computer-based developments of numerical control technology; robots and flexible manufacturing systems (FMS) are included in the broader use of CAM systems. A CAD/CAM interface is envisioned as a computerized database that can be accessed and enriched by either design or manufacturing professionals during various stages of the product development and production cycle.

In CAD systems of the early 1990's, the ability to model solid objects became widely available. The use of graphic elements such as lines and arcs and the ability to create a model by adding and subtracting solids such as cubes and cylinders are the basic principles of CAD and of simulating objects within a computer. CAD systems enable computers to simulate both taking things apart (sectioning) and putting things together for assembly. In addition to being able to construct prototypes and store images of different models, CAD systems can be used for simulating the behavior of machines, parts, and components. These abilities enable CAD to construct models that can be subjected to nondestructive testing; that is, even before engineers build a physical prototype, the CAD model can be subjected to testing, and the results can be analyzed. As another example, designers of printed circuit boards have the ability to test their circuits on a CAD system by simulating the electrical properties of components.

During the 1950's, the U.S. Air Force recognized the need for reducing the development time for special aircraft equipment. As a result, the Air Force commissioned the Massachusetts Institute of Technology to develop numerically controlled (NC) machines that were programmable. A workable demonstration of NC machines was made in 1952; this began a new era for manufacturing. As the speed of an aircraft increased, the cost of manufacturing also increased because of stricter technical requirements. This higher cost provided a stimulus for the further development of NC technology, which promised to reduce errors in design before the prototype stage.

The early 1960's saw the development of mainframe computers. Many industries valued computing technology for its speed and for its accuracy in lengthy and tedious numerical operations in design, manufacturing, and other business functional areas. Patrick Hanratty, working for General Motors Research Laboratory, saw other potential applications and developed graphics programs for use on mainframe computers. The use of graphics in software aided the development of CAD/CAM, allowing visual representations of models to be presented on computer screens and printers.

The 1970's saw an important development in computer hardware, namely the development and growth of personal computers (PCs). Personal computers became smaller as a result of the development of integrated circuits. Jack St. Clair Kilby, working for Texas Instruments, first conceived of the integrated circuit; later, Robert Noyce, working for Intel Corporation, developed an improved process for manufacturing integrated circuits on microchips. Personal computers using these microchips offered both speed and accuracy at costs much lower than those of mainframe computers.

Five companies offered integrated commercial computer-aided design and computer-aided manufacturing systems by the first half of 1973. Integration meant that both design and manufacturing were contained in one system. Of these five companies—Applicon, Computervision, Gerber Scientific, Manufacturing and Consulting Services (MCS), and United Computing—four offered turnkey systems exclusively. Turnkey systems provide design, development, training, and implementation for each customer (company) based on the contractual agreement; they are meant to be used as delivered, with no need for the purchaser to make significant adjustments or perform programming.

The 1980's saw a proliferation of mini- and microcomputers with a variety of platforms (processors) with increased speed and better graphical resolution. This made the widespread development of computer-aided design and computer-aided manufacturing possible and practical. Major corporations spent large research and development budgets developing CAD/CAM systems that would automate manual drafting and machine tool movements. Don Halliday, working for Truesports Inc., provided an early example of the benefits of CAD/CAM. He created the Made-in-America car in only four months by using CAD and project management software. In the late 1980's, Fred Borsini, the president of Leap Technologies in Michigan, brought various products to market in record time through the use of CAD/CAM.

In the early 1980's, much of the CAD/CAM industry consisted of software companies. The cost for a relatively slow interactive system in 1980 was close to $100,000. The late 1980's saw the demise of minicomputer-based systems in favor of Unix workstations and PCs based on 386 and 486 microchips produced by Intel. By the time of the International Manufacturing Technology show in September, 1992, the industry could show numerous CAD/CAM innovations including tools, CAD/CAM models to evaluate manufacturability in early design phases, and systems that allowed use of the same data for a full range of manufacturing functions.

Impact of Event

In 1990, CAD/CAM hardware sales by U.S. vendors reached $2.68 billion. In software alone, $1.42 billion worth of CAD/CAM products and systems was sold worldwide by U.S. vendors, according to International Data Corporation figures for 1990. CAD/CAM systems were in widespread use throughout the industrial world. Development lagged in advanced software applications, particularly in image processing, and in the communications software and hardware that tie processes together.

A reevaluation of CAD/CAM systems was being driven by the industry trend toward increased functionality of computer-driven numerically controlled machines. Numerical control (NC) software enables users to graphically define the geometry of the parts in a product, develop paths that machine tools will follow, and exchange data among machines on the shop floor. In 1991, NC configuration software represented 86 percent of total CAM sales. In 1992, the market shares of the five largest companies in the CAD/CAM market were 29 percent for International Business Machines, 17 percent for Intergraph, 11 percent for Computervision, 9 percent for Hewlett-Packard, and 6 percent for Mentor Graphics.

General Motors formed a joint venture with Ford and Chrysler to develop a common computer language in order to make the next generation of CAD/CAM systems easier to use. The venture was aimed particularly at problems that posed barriers to speeding up the design of new automobiles. The three car companies all had sophisticated computer systems that allowed engineers to design parts on computers and then electronically transmit specifications to tools that make parts or dies.

CAD/CAM technology was expected to advance on many fronts. As of the early 1990's, different CAD/CAM vendors had developed systems that were often incompatible with one another, making it difficult to transfer data from one system to another. Large corporations, such as the major automakers, developed their own interfaces and network capabilities to allow different systems to communicate. Major users of CAD/CAM saw consolidation in the industry through the establishment of standards as being in their interests.

Resellers of CAD/CAM products also attempted to redefine their markets. These vendors provide technical support and service to users. The sale of CAD/CAM products and systems offered substantial opportunities, since demand remained strong. Resellers worked most effectively with small and medium-sized companies, which often were neglected by the primary sellers of CAD/CAM equipment because they did not generate a large volume of business. Some projections held that by 1995 half of all CAD/CAM systems would be sold through resellers, at a cost of $10,000 or less for each system. The CAD/CAM market thus was in the process of dividing into two markets: large customers (such as aerospace firms and automobile manufacturers) that would be served by primary vendors, and small and medium-sized customers that would be serviced by resellers.

CAD will find future applications in marketing, the construction industry, production planning, and large-scale projects such as shipbuilding and aerospace. Other likely CAD markets include hospitals, the apparel industry, colleges and universities, food product manufacturers, and equipment manufacturers. As the linkage between CAD and CAM is enhanced, systems will become more productive. The geometrical data from CAD will be put to greater use by CAM systems.

CAD/CAM already had proved that it could make a big difference in productivity and quality. Customer orders could be changed much faster and more accurately than in the past, when a change could require a manual redrafting of a design. Computers could do automatically in minutes what once took hours manually. CAD/CAM saved time by reducing, and in some cases eliminating, human error. Many flexible manufacturing systems (FMS) had machining centers equipped with sensing probes to check the accuracy of the machining process. These self-checks can be made part of numerical control (NC) programs. With the technology of the early 1990's, some experts estimated that CAD/CAM systems were in many cases twice as productive as the systems they replaced; in the long run, productivity is likely to improve even more, perhaps up to three times that of older systems or even higher. As costs for CAD/CAM systems concurrently fall, the investment in a system will be recovered more quickly. Some analysts estimated that by the mid-1990's, the recovery time for an average system would be about three years.

Another frontier in the development of CAD/CAM systems is expert (or knowledge-based) systems, which combine data with a human expert's knowledge, expressed in the form of rules that the computer follows. Such a system will analyze data in a manner mimicking intelligence. For example, a 3-D model might be created from standard 2-D drawings. Expert systems will likely play a pivotal role in CAM applications. For example, an expert system could determine the best sequence of machining operations to produce a component.

Continuing improvements in hardware, especially increased speed, will benefit CAD/CAM systems. Software developments, however, may produce greater benefits. Wider use of CAD/CAM systems will depend on the cost savings from improvements in hardware and software as well as on the productivity of the systems and the quality of their product. The construction, apparel, automobile, and aerospace industries have already experienced increases in productivity, quality, and profitability through the use of CAD/CAM. A case in point is Boeing, which used CAD from start to finish in the design of the 757.

Bibliography

Choobineh, Fred, and Suri Rajan, eds. *Flexible Manufacturing Systems.* Norcross, Ga.: Industrial Engineering and Management Press, Institute of Industrial Engineers, 1986. This book begins with a discussion of programmable automation technologies, including CAD/CAM, and covers planning, design, operation, and control issues involved in flexible manufacturing systems.

Groover, Mikell P., and Emory W. Zimmers, Jr. *CAD/CAM: Computer-Aided Design and Manufacturing.* Englewood Cliffs, N.J.: Prentice-Hall, 1984. A textbook for CAD/CAM theory and practice; also a good source for learners of CAD/CAM.

Henderson, Breck W. "CAD/CAM Systems Transform Aerospace Engineering." *Aviation Week and Space Technology* 136 (January 22, 1992): 49-51. Describes use of computer-aided design and computer-aided manufacturing in the aerospace industry, where it is widely accepted. New tools have eliminated costly design steps and made product development faster and cheaper. Data generated by sophisticated CAD/CAM systems have allowed rapid prototyping and conversion of CAD data directly into solid models of complex parts in a matter of hours and for a fraction of the cost of traditional methods.

Jurgen, Ronald K. *Computers and Manufacturing Productivity.* New York: Institute of Electrical and Electronics Engineers, 1987. Devoted exclusively to a discussion of productivity and automation. Full of illustrations, data, and issues, presented in an easy-to-read format.

Machover, Carl, and Robert E. Blauth, eds. *The CAD/CAM Handbook.* Bedford, Mass.: Computervision Corporation, 1980. A fairly comprehensive book on CAD/CAM. Serves both general and advanced readers.

Medland, A. J., and Piers Burnett. *CAD/CAM in Practice.* New York: John Wiley & Sons, 1986. A well-written manager's guide to understanding and using CAD/CAM. Does not assume any knowledge of CAD/CAM on the part of the reader. Illustrations are clear and concise.

Zhang, Hong-Chao. *Advanced Tolerancing Techniques.* New York: Wiley, 1997.

Jay Nathan

Cross-References

Firms Begin Replacing Skilled Laborers with Automatic Tools (1960's); AT&T and GTE Install Fiber-Optic Telephone Systems (1977); American Firms Adopt Japanese Manufacturing Techniques (1980's); Electronic Technology Creates the Possibility of Telecommuting (1980's); IBM Introduces Its Personal Computer (1981).

DEFENSE CUTBACKS DEVASTATE THE U.S. AEROSPACE INDUSTRY

CATEGORY OF EVENT: Foundings and dissolutions
TIME: The 1980's
LOCALE: The United States

The end of the Cold War and the decline of defense spending led to a decline in the U.S. aerospace industry

Principal personages:

GEORGE BUSH (1924-   ), the president of the United States, 1989-1993

RICHARD CHENEY (1941-   ), the secretary of defense under President Bush

RONALD REAGAN (1911-   ), the president of the United States, 1981-1989

RICHARD H. TRULY (1937-   ), the administrator of NASA

CASPAR WEINBERGER (1917-   ), the secretary of defense under President Reagan

Summary of Event

Early in his presidency, Ronald Reagan began an across-the-board rearmament program for the United States, with additional new spending running at $140 billion a year. His intent—more political than military—was to show the Soviet Union that it could not keep up in the economic and technological arms races. Efforts began with the deployment of cruise missiles in Europe and the expansion of numerous weapons programs at home. The expansion program reached a peak of sorts with Reagan's 1983 speech stating his administration's intention to pursue a Strategic Defense

Initiative (SDI), popularly known as "Star Wars." After that, the Soviet Union found itself unable to compete, either technologically or economically, in the Cold War. Internal pressures soon forced the Soviet Union to abandon Communism and to renounce goals of world conquest.

In the United States, American politicians quickly started to speak of a "peace dividend," wherein the savings from decreases in previously high levels of defense spending would be transferred to the civilian economy. Quickly, however, the "peace dividend" evaporated as the effects of layoffs worked their way through government contractors. A number of defense contractors found themselves in trouble and issued pink slips to thousands of highly paid, well-trained workers.

The defense budget rose from $81 billion in 1970 to $296 billion in 1990, but as a share of gross national product it actually fell by almost 4 percent during that period. In comparison, the Social Security and Medicare budgets grew from $36 billion to $345 billion. Although every aspect of the defense industry felt distress, the aerospace industry suffered acutely. Not only did orders for new aircraft tail off, but entire planned programs, such as the Navy's AX (Attack Experimental) aircraft, the modifications to Grumman's F-14 Tomcat, the V-22 Osprey, and a number of missile, experimental, and SDI-related projects, were canceled outright, were delayed, or had funding greatly reduced. In addition, the National Aeronautics and Space Administration (NASA), another client of the aerospace firms, saw its budgets constrained. During the late 1980's, virtually all of NASA's budget went for the fleet of existing space shuttles and toward development of Space Station Freedom. For contractors not involved in those projects, NASA provided little employment.

Competition in the aerospace companies' civilian/commercial market also weakened their position. By the late 1980's, the European Airbus airliner had cut deeply into sales of U.S. firms, both domestically and internationally. New planned aircraft, such as the McDonnell Douglas 80, faced delays in entering the highly competitive market.

Defense cuts rather than commercial sluggishness constituted the major problem for many aerospace contractors. Ironically, the 1980's drawdown in defense was the smallest of any in recent history. The difference in defense expenditures between the peak and the low point, as a percentage of gross domestic product, was only 2.9 percent in the post-1986 reductions, compared with 4.8 percent after the Vietnam War, 4.3 percent after the Korean War, and 35.6 percent after World War II. Moreover, the decline was more gradual. After World War II, the reductions averaged 8.9 percent annually, but the post-1986 reductions averaged only .26 percent. At the peak of World War II, annual spending on defense exceeded $885 billion (in 1993 dollars), while the post-1986 annual reductions totaled only $354 billion. Comparisons of this nature showed apparent inconsistency with the relatively serious problems many companies faced.

McDonnell Douglas, for example, was one of the leading aerospace companies, producing military and commercial aircraft as well as space vehicles. The McDonnell and Douglas companies had merged in 1967 to offset swings in the defense industry with swings in the commercial aircraft industry. In the late 1980's, as the world's largest defense contractor, McDonnell Douglas found itself teetering on the brink of unprofitability despite a huge backlog of orders. McDonnell Douglas had orders for the F/A-18 Hornet with the Navy and the F-15 Eagle and C-17 cargo aircraft with the Air Force, in addition to helicopter, space, and missile work. Nevertheless, its corporate investment in programs such as the Advanced Tactical Fighter had proved a drain, and McDonnell Douglas had the next to worst return on assets of any major aerospace contractor, trailing only General Dynamics. Its return on equity was third worst. In 1989, the company announced a radical restructuring to deal with its worst financial quarter since the merger. McDonnell Douglas forced five thousand mid-level managers to resign their titles and compete for half that number of jobs. A year later, McDonnell Douglas laid off twenty-two thousand employees.

General Dynamics (GD) was one of the few companies doing worse than McDonnell Douglas. It took a $639 million loss in 1990 and had the worst return on assets and return on equity of any of the nine major aerospace contractors. Only Grumman had a poorer bond rating. Unlike the relatively healthy Boeing Company, GD had virtually all of its work, 85 percent, in defense. In 1992, GD started to move out of aerospace by selling its fighter production program, mostly focused on production of the F-16 Fighting Falcon, to Lockheed Corporation, another industry giant. Lockheed had only about one-third the sales ($9 billion) of industry leader Boeing, but it had good earnings per share and an acceptable bond rating. It also had a recent success, production of the famous F-117 Stealth fighter, effectively used in the Gulf War of 1990. It maintained a large budget for "black," or secret, programs.

Despite Lockheed's production record, it had severe problems in its Trident D-5 missile production program. That, combined with its inability to break into commercial airline manufacturing (with the exception of the L-1011), made the company vulnerable to Air Force budget cuts. Only Boeing, with its almost $30 billion in sales and its twenty-year backlog in orders, was able to postpone the effects of the defense downturn. Even Boeing, however, found itself feeling the decline in defense production. In

1993, the Washington-based aircraft manufacturer joined the other companies by announcing significant planned layoffs.

Impact of Event

In 1990, Iraq's invasion of Kuwait and the subsequent U.S. military action led many to think that the defense cuts might not be as harsh as expected, or might be slower than expected. The election of Bill Clinton to the presidency in 1992 brought defense policy statements during his early tenure that suggested that the cuts would be worse than expected. At the same time, NASA's fragile budget came under fire because of the ballooning expense of Space Station Freedom, the failure to develop a reliable follow-on to the expensive space shuttles, and the performance errors of some NASA technology, such as the Hubble Space Telescope. Those events led some experts to predict another round of defense industry mergers, such as those that had occurred in the 1960's and 1970's.

By 1990, world events had caused some policymakers to reevaluate the sensibility of drastically downsizing the Department of Defense and the "military-industrial complex." The Gulf War proved, or at least greatly reinforced, the notion that the United States could build "high-tech" weapons that worked. That was true especially during the first six months after the war, when the claims for success of weapons such as the cruise and Patriot missiles were exaggerated by the media and the military. More significant, the threats posed by the Iraqi-launched Scud missiles on civilian populations greatly boosted the desirability of missile interception systems, which formed the basis of the Strategic Defense Initiative. Thus, one of the most expensive, "high-tech" sectors in the defense budget received an unexpected lift from a Middle Eastern despot with "low-tech" weapons.

After the first round of glowing reports on the Patriot and cruise missiles, however, a revisionist analysis claimed less effective performances from the weapons than once thought. Those criticisms arrived at a time when the budget deficit was growing and legislators were searching for ways to cut government spending. After all, if the weapons did not work, why spend additional money maintaining and improving them? Subsequent studies revised the critics' analysis, showing that most weapons performed at the highest standards ever attained in modern war. For example, American aircraft in the Gulf War flew more than twenty-nine thousand sorties with a loss of only fourteen aircraft, the lowest percentage of losses in any American war and barely half the loss rate in the Vietnam War. Another measure, the mission capability rates (the rate at which aircraft were maintained) actually exceeded the peacetime rate in eleven major lines of aircraft used in the Gulf. The comparison is blurred because typically under peacetime conditions aircraft might be held out for repair or maintenance for problems that would be repaired overnight under war conditions. Four of the aircraft attained mission capability rates of more than 95 percent.

Excellent performance did not change budget realities, however, and a number of firms by the late 1980's found themselves in the position of being out of business as a result of elimination of a single weapon. Grumman, for example, fought desperately to have the F-14 Tomcat upgraded for attack missions. Without the upgrades, Grumman would close. In the late 1980's, the Navy leaned heavily toward the AX (Attack Experimental) aircraft, but that program was canceled in 1990 after budget overruns and poor management. Grumman hung on. General Dynamics, on the other hand, had to sell its F-16 production line after the elimination of other fighter airplanes.

By 1990, most of the major airframe and propulsion contractors had concluded that the only way to survive was for them to join in consortia or "teams" to bid on expensive projects. That defeated the intent of the competitive bid contracts in some programs, while two or more "teams" competed for other contracts, as in the case of the Advanced Tactical Fighter (ATF, won by a Lockheed-led team and renamed the F-22). Other projects that saw teams either compete for the contracts or be formed in order to receive the entire contract award included the National Aero-Space Plane (General Dynamics, McDonnell Douglas, Rockwell, Rocketdyne, and Pratt & Whitney); the Light Helicopter Experimental (LHX) team of Boeing and Sikorsky, plus the engine team made up of a pairing of Allison and Garrett; and a variety of international teams, each featuring a U.S. contractor, for the new joint service trainer contract. The impetus toward sharing resources and knowledge gained ground in the late 1980's and early 1990's, but the evidence was far from conclusive on which investment and procurement practices were the most effective. A study by Jacques Gansler, a defense industry expert, showed that national and international cooperative efforts have taken longer and cost more than if each country had produced the weapon itself. A 1983 General Accounting Office document reported no teaming efforts that resulted in satisfied participating services and actual savings. If assessed solely on the variable of cost, teaming or joint programs generally resulted in higher costs to the taxpayer. Moreover, a spate of critics of corporate combinations produced work that showed that the most successful industries were the most highly competitive and the least reliant on government support, two traits that characterized few aircraft manufacturers by 1990.

Supporters of the consortia concept argued that the United States had fallen behind Europe with its Airbus airliner, funded in 1969 at a meeting in which Germany and France, as well as the Hawker-Siddeley company, agreed to unite to keep the market from the American aircraft manufacturers. The success of Airbus remains a matter of debate. It captured more than 20 percent of the world market, for the first time taking Boeing's share of the world market below 60 percent. Airbus, however, devoured more than $7 billion in taxpayers' money, and Europe did not create a single net new job from 1970 to 1981, the time during which the Airbus was being built in Europe to keep jobs from going overseas. Other forces certainly were at work regarding employment, but the evidence on Airbus was not unequivocal. Naturally, American aircraft manufacturers clamored for assistance from the U.S. government based on their perception that the Europeans gave their companies an unfair advantage.

The final, most obvious impact of the decline of the American aerospace industry came in the human terms of unemployment. White collar workers, engineers, and high-tech workers all faced unprecedented levels of layoffs, especially in California, where the economy started to stagnate for the first time in the post-World War II period. Defense cutbacks came at a time when Los Angeles had just become the nation's leading manufacturing center as well as one of the top high-tech regions in the United States. The effects on the California economy were felt in the real estate market, where growth in prices slowed to 5 percent per year—virtual stagnation in California terms. In some areas, housing prices fell, and homes stayed on the market far longer than in the past. Outmigration of companies started in earnest in the early 1990's. Neighboring states such as Arizona and Nevada, seeing their opportunity to attract defense giants, offered special tax breaks or other incentives to relocate. Lockheed relocated some of its factories to Georgia in response to an attractive deal offered by that state's government. Smaller defense companies left the Golden State in droves. How far the defense decline would go, and its ultimate effects on the aerospace industry, remained unknown by 1993. Les Aspin, Clinton's secretary of defense, made it clear that he supported still deeper cuts in the defense budget. At the same time, an international economic slowdown had caused many nations to cancel their purchases of American commercial aircraft, exacerbating the troubles from the defense side of the economy.

Bibliography

Gansler, Jacques. *Affording Defense*. Cambridge, Mass.: MIT Press, 1989. A follow-up to his *The Defense Industry* (1980). Ganlser details the problems and pitfalls of weapons procurement in an age in which legislators were determined that contractors would not get away with "fraud and abuse." In reality, as Gansler shows, the system was pregnant with barriers to efficiency that only served to drive up costs. Rules that required competition in all lines of weapons often caused two or more unhealthy companies to limp along, growing increasingly dependent on the military.

Hallion, Richard P. *Storm over Iraq: Air Power and the Gulf War.* Washington, D.C.: Smithsonian Institution Press, 1992. More than a history of the Gulf War. Hallion provides a synopsis of air power theory, a review of trends in procurement and production, a superior technical appraisal of tactics and technologies, and an overall thorough assessment of the role of aircraft in modern warfare.

Morrocco, John D. "Defense Conversion Panel Urges Dramatic Changes." *Aviation Week and Space Technology* 138 (January 25, 1993): 64-65. Provides a critical comparison of defense drawdowns, those following World War II, the Korean War, and the Vietnam War and that of the 1980's. Invaluable statistics include spending relative to gross domestic product, average change per year, and difference between high points and low points.

Puth, Robert C. *American Economic History.* 3d ed. New York: Dryden Press, 1993. A general survey useful for trends in government, defense, and civilian budgets in the 1980's, as well as a review of employment and investment statistics relevant to the defense industry.

Weinberger, Caspar. *Fighting for Peace: Seven Critical Years in the Pentagon.* New York: Warner Books, 1990. Contains a detailed insider's discussion of the buildup during the Reagan years.

Larry Schweikart

Cross-References

Roosevelt Signs the Emergency Price Control Act (1942); Roosevelt Signs the G.I. Bill (1944); The U.S. Service Economy Emerges (1960's); The United States Plans to Cut Dependence on Foreign Oil (1974).

ELECTRONIC TECHNOLOGY CREATES THE POSSIBILITY OF TELECOMMUTING

CATEGORIES OF EVENT: Labor and business practices
TIME: The 1980's
LOCALE: The United States and other industrial nations

Developments in electronic office equipment installed in people's homes enabled business employees to work at home as telecommuters

Principal personages:
ALVIN TOFFLER (1928-   ), a futurist who predicted the rise of telecommuting
THOMAS W. MILLER, the director of the National Work at Home Survey
PATRICIA LYON MOKHTARIAN, a researcher who chronicled advances in telecommuting
JACK M. NILLES, a consultant to the California Telecommuting Pilot Project in the late 1980's

Summary of Event
In the early 1980's, key improvements were made in both the power and the affordability of electronic office equipment. These developments enabled many business employees to work all or part of the week at their places of residence. The personal computer was the centerpiece of the modern gadgetry. With a modem, a printer, a fax machine, a telephone with special features, and, a few years later, a small copy machine, a home-based white-collar worker could put together a "virtual office" with links to the

Telecommuting has made possible a revolution in lifestyles for many workers. (PhotoDisc)

company office to enable transfer of information in either direction.

The term "telecommuters" was adopted for home-based workers connected to their employers by electronic equipment. The pioneers of such work practices were a few isolated individuals with unusual levels of specialized technological expertise who set up arrangements of their own design. In the early 1980's, the technology became accessible to large numbers of typical businesspeople. By 1984, about two hundred companies had made some experiments with telecommuting, and about thirty had set up programs.

Companies with employees working at home were initially concerned about productivity. Soon, however, some insurance companies, such as Blue Cross and Blue Shield of South Carolina, were able to report improvements in output when workers stayed at home. Employees were initially interested in flexibility in the ways of combining work and home obligations. Many other advantages of telecommuting were gradually recognized, and futurists surmised that the way work is done in society could be transformed. Some projected that by the middle of the 1990's, there could be twenty million telecommuters.

Technical developments in home-installed electronic equipment connected to equipment at the corporate office offered new possibilities in the flexibility of working arrangements. The developments included portable telephones and other devices that allowed workers to contact employers when on the road, held up in traffic, or on commuter trains. By the early 1990's, fax machines that could be used in cars were on the market.

In most cases, the equipment for telecommuters was provided by employers. There were some individuals, however, whose enthusiasm to set up home-working arrangements led them to buy their own equipment.

With a personal computer at home, a worker can produce letters, reports, budgets, sales projections, forecasts, and other documents in exactly the same way as in the corporate office. Necessary data could come via modem, and finished documents could go back the same way. The machine at home, together with its software, needed to be compatible with that at the office. For some years, there were problems of information exchange between Apple and International Business Machines (IBM) systems and between personal computers and mainframes. Translatability and conversion features were built into the systems as manufacturers recognized that users were increasingly linking machines.

When a modem is used in conjunction with a computer, access to data stored elsewhere becomes possible, and a conduit for communication is established. This makes available a whole range of information and business support services, including electronic mail service. These capacities reduce the isolation that would otherwise be the condition of workers at home.

Worker mobility increased with the advent of laptop computers. These small machines are powered by rechargeable batteries. They are light enough to be carried around, but many were nearly as powerful as some personal computers by the early 1990's.

Improvements in computer printer technology also benefited telecommuters. Many printer manufacturers offered several versions of their products, intended for various levels of use and different levels of quality. Printers for home use need not be different from those attached to computers in offices, but cost savings could be realized by using a printer designed for less strenuous or exacting work.

The facsimile machine established itself as an indispensable piece of office equipment. The word "fax" became part of the English language, as both a noun and a verb. A fax machine sends a copy of a document to another machine, using telephone lines. Falling costs and increasing use of the machines made them affordable for home offices and allowed workers to reach a large proportion of the business world without leaving home.

Developments in telephone technology are often mentioned in the context of telecommuting. A worker dealing with routine claims processing for an insurance company, for example, may need nothing more than basic telephone service. Others may need a line separate from their personal telephone, together with a message system or voice mail. Still others may need cellular telephones, which can be taken on the road. Cellular telephones made long commutes more productive and allowed offices to keep in touch with traveling employees.

People who switched to working at home could get some benefits from advanced technology even without purchasing equipment. For documents not suitable for fax or modem delivery, and for people without these devices, improved services of the United States Postal Service, United Parcel Service, and Federal Express were available. Businesses, particularly copy shops, began offering fax service to customers.

For a time, the major weakness in the telecommuter office was the lack of a copier. Home-based workers in the 1980's regularly used the services of local copy centers as a useful supplement to the home office. This was expensive in terms of time, if not in charges for copies. Copy machines were large, heavy, and expensive, and so not suitable for use in the home. Responding to the needs of home-based workers, manufacturers began producing inexpensive desk-top copiers. With this addition, home offices took on the characteristics of corporate offices.

Impact of Event

Telecommuting has had effects on individuals who work at home, their employers, and society as a whole. Telecommuters spend less time, or no time, traveling to and from work. This reduces both the unproductive use of time and expenditures for gasoline and vehicle maintenance. Telecommuters also enjoy flexibility in organizing their work, being less constrained by office hours. In the case of parents, the chance to work at home permits combining paid work and child-care responsibilities. Many parents found it possible to look after children while putting in a normal day's work. In some cases, parents from different families shared child-minding duties while maintaining, among themselves, the required attention to computer terminals.

Parents who decide to stay home to provide childcare can ease their transition back to the office by finding employment as telecommuters or in other home-based work. Telecommuting offers a solution to the conflicting pressures of work and family. Telecommuting also enables a gradual return to work for convalescents not yet ready for five-day-a-week rigor. Persons rendered immobile through an injury such as a broken hip or a permanent disability can be productive even though unable to travel to work. Telecommuting thus offered new possibilities for disadvantaged workers.

The disadvantages of telecommuting primarily flow from the isolation of being at home. Many employees who have known the ways of the office become acutely aware of what they are missing when they stay at home: the informal communication and social interaction of the office. Some worry that their reduced visibility will limit their promotion prospects. The value of face-to-face contact as part of the communication that supports work activities is missed when working at home. These concerns are mitigated when the employee goes to the office for part of the working week.

Motivation can be affected in either direction by telecommuting. Those who need the stimulation of rapport with others will be less motivated at home. Others may enjoy the feeling of enhanced competence when they discover that they can find a way to meet a challenge without recourse to the help of the worker at the next desk. Although human oversight is diminished, home- based workers can still be given production goals. Some computer software allows monitoring of the amount of work performed.

The situation for disabled workers is delicate and complex. Special efforst to use new home-based technology to bring house-bound people into the workforce can either liberate them from the feeling of being unproductive or reinforce their sense of isolation. Companies may decide that it is less expensive to keep a worker at home than to redesign the office to meet his or her needs.

Regarding the impact on companies, a primary concern is the productivity of employees working at home. Without acceptable productivity, no company is likely to permit telecommuting. The verdict from diverse companies is that responsible and mature employees generally show an increase in productivity when working from home. Companies that had instituted telecommuting programs by the 1990's included those in banking, insurance, publishing, business services, computers, catalog retailing, and stock brokerage. All found that telecommuting had the potential to increase productivity.

There are legitimate concerns regarding whether a person working at home will be distracted by various elements of the home environment and thus deflected from work. The office itself has distractions, however, and many workers find it easier to concentrate and keep on task at home. Although not everyone may be temperamentally suited to working at home, many peo-

The development of increasingly powerful and compact laptop computers during the 1980's and 1990's further expanded the freedom of telecommuters to work wherever they please. (PhotoDisc)

ple are more productive. The company office can maintain links and can telephone or fax a telecommuter to keep a check. At the other extreme, some people increase the length of their workday because there is no longer a point in the day when they leave the work environment. Their work is in their homes and may be difficult to ignore.

Aside from gains in worker productivity, companies benefit through economies in office space, parking, and other overhead expenses. More subtle effects include enhancement of communicative skills of managers, since more precision is needed to convey instructions to people who are not physically present; development of different methods of project management to allow workers who do not physically meet to bring parts of a project together; and development of judicious schemes of goals and rewards for people working outside the office. All these gains can translate into better use of traditional, office-based employees.

Some companies with telecommuting employees are faced with problems of monitoring and security. In most cases, the requirement that work be done to specification and by a certain deadline are the only control criteria necessary. In some cases, a business might be worried about home employees using company equipment for freelance work or about the use of proprietary information by employees who could undertake work for competitor companies or sell information.

The impact of telecommuting on society as a whole is potentially enormous, as it reduces the distinctions between work and home. Tax law has had to adapt to workers who are neither office-based nor self-employed, or who work part of each week at an office outside the home. At the local level, laws that restrict use of the home for commercial purposes were challenged.

Another consideration for society is the matter of pollution and fuel consumption resulting from the familiar types of commuting. As travel becomes more expensive, inconvenient, and time-consuming, the benefits of telecommuting increase. Telecommuting reduces the burdens on those forced to travel and on society in general by reducing traffic congestion and pollution.

Regarding questions of distributive economics, the impact of telecommuting may well include both bad and good. Organized labor has warned of the increasing use of employees who, because they are dispersed, are unlikely to become part of a collective unit that protects their interests. Labor unions warn of home-based sweatshop labor. On the positive side, there is evidence that in Great Britain, home-based workers' pay is better than average. It is conceivable that the hiring of home-based people in low-income neighborhoods by companies in the suburbs could be encouraged as a public policy for reducing geographic disparities in income. The technology that supports telecommuting has both liberating and isolating tendencies. Its long-term impact will depend on how business and workers choose to act on the possibilities that the technology creates.

Bibliography

Arden, Lynie. *The Work-at-Home Sourcebook*. 4th ed. Boulder, Colo.: Live Oak, 1992. Gives practical information about many aspects of telecommuting and other home-based work. Indicates the kinds of work that lend themselves to home work and includes directories of companies that have telecommuting programs. Helpful for anyone searching for a telecommuting job or other home-based employment.

Bernardino, Adriana. *Telecommuting: Modeling the Employer's and the Employee's Decision-Making Process*. New York: Garland, 1996.

Best, Fred. "Technology and the Changing World of Work." *The Futurist* 18 (April, 1984): 61-66. Deals with the many issues associated with working at home, including skill requirements, displacement of workers, and management of decentralized systems. Includes speculation about a future home-based economy.

Hamilton, Carol-Ann. "Telecommuting." *Personnel Journal* 66 (April, 1987): 90-111. A guide for setting up telecommuting programs in a company. Recognizes various factors affecting employees, including security, employee benefits, career development, equipment, and insurance. Useful for companies considering a telecommuting program.

Kanarek, Lisa. *Organizing Your Home Office for Success: Expert Strategies That Can Work for You*. New York: Penguin, 1992. A practical guide to organizing the office at home. Includes material on choosing the location for the office, filing systems, planning, time management, handling information, and choosing printers. Contains useful lists of suppliers of equipment.

Kinsman, Francis. *The Telecommuters*. New York: John Wiley & Sons, 1987. A study of telecommuting in Great Britain. Describes specific company schemes in detail and reports high productivity and good earnings among telecommuters. Interesting and futuristic.

Wolfgram, Tammara H. "Working at Home: The Growth of Cottage Industry." *The Futurist* 18 (June, 1984): 31-34. Offers a perspective about the future of work. The trend toward work at home is noted. States that some issues need to be faced, including the changing of laws that restrict home-based work.

Richard Barrett

Cross-References

Nixon Signs the Occupational Safety and Health Act (1970); AT&T and GTE Install Fiber-Optic Telephone Systems (1977); IBM Introduces Its Personal Computer (1981); A Home Shopping Service Is Offered on Cable Television (1985); *Time* magazine Makes an E-commerce Pioneer Its Person of the Year (1999).

CONGRESS DEREGULATES BANKS AND SAVINGS AND LOANS

CATEGORY OF EVENT: Finance
TIME: 1980-1982
LOCALE: Washington, D.C.

Deregulation in the banking and thrift industries redefined the roles of financial institutions and encouraged intense competition in financial markets

Principal personages:
PAUL A. VOLCKER (1927-   ), the chairman of the Federal Reserve Board, 1979-1987
JAKE GARN (1932-   ), a senator from Utah, chairman of the Senate Banking Committee from 1975 to 1984
FERNAND ST. GERMAIN (1928-   ), a congressman from Rhode Island, chairman of the House Banking Committee from 1980 to 1988
JIMMY CARTER (1924-   ), the president of the United States, 1977-1981
RONALD REAGAN (1911-   ), the president of the United States, 1981-1989

Summary of Event

Early in the 1980's, the United States Congress passed two pieces of legislation that represented the most significant movement toward depository institution reform since the 1930's. The Depository Institutions Deregulation and Monetary Control Act of 1980 (DIDMCA) and the Depository Institutions Act of 1982 (Garn-St. Germain Act) signaled the resolve of two presidential administrations to create a financial marketplace that would be more adaptable to changing economic conditions.

The U.S. government traditionally has held that regulation of the banking and thrift industries is vital to the safety and stability of the economy. Thus, when the banking system nearly collapsed in the 1930's, a number of regulations were introduced that restructured the industry. These regulations met most of their objectives for several decades because the system operated well in the prevailing environment of relatively stable prices and interest rates.

The status quo was overturned, however, by two disruptive forces. First, in the 1960's, the United States attempted to simultaneously fight both domestic poverty and a war in Southeast Asia. The economy expanded tremendously, and demand for credit increased. Eventually, unprecedented high interest rates and inflation resulted. Second, in the 1970's development of computer and communications technology created an ability to establish accounting and fund transfer systems that early bankers would have envied. These systems were easily accessible to nondepository institutions wishing to offer products and services comparable to those offered by banks and savings and loans. In some respects, nonbanks had a competitive edge because they were not regulated as heavily. By the late 1970's, some regulations were seen as being detrimental to the financial industry's health.

At this time, both banks and thrifts were restricted in the interest they could pay to depositors by Regulation Q of the Federal Reserve Act. Whenever market interest rates rose higher than Regulation Q ceilings, depositors removed funds from banks and thrifts. Money market mutual funds were highly successful in drawing funds away from banks and thrifts simply because they could offer higher returns. This draining of funds, called disintermediation, restricted the lending activities of banks and thrifts.

Savings and loans had an especially difficult time in this environment of high interest rates because of their financial structures. The bulk of their assets consisted of long-term fixed-rate mortgages at interest rates below the market rates of the time. On the other hand, most liabilities were in the form of deposits that could be withdrawn almost immediately. Any increases in interest rates that the Federal Reserve Board allowed under Regulation Q immediately affected the institutions' interest expenses, or the cost of funds. Consequently, as rates rose in response to competition, profit margins narrowed. Institutions that did not increase the rates paid to depositors, by choice or because of regulation, found their sources of funds drying up and therefore were unable to make new loans to take advantage of higher interest rates.

During the late 1970's, the banking industry experienced another challenge. Many banks that were members of the Federal Reserve System (the Fed) gave up their memberships. Members were required to hold reserves (a fraction of deposits, meant to ensure that banks could meet depositors' withdrawals) in noninterest-bearing accounts at the Fed. Nonmembers also were required to maintain reserves, but their reserves could be held at correspondent banks, where they could be traded for "free services." As interest rates increased, the free services offered also increased and member fallout from the Fed increased critically.

Early in 1980, bankers lobbied for decontrol of interest rates on deposits and elimination of restrictions imposed on loan rates by state usury laws. Paul A. Volcker, chairman of the Federal Reserve Board, emphasized the seriousness of the Fed membership problem and warned of a crisis if action was not taken quickly. The Senate and House banking committees began holding joint meetings in March, 1980. Near the end of March, a compromise reform bill was presented to Congress and passed quickly. The Depository Institutions Deregulation and Monetary Control Act of 1980 (DIDMCA) was signed into law by President Jimmy Carter on March 31, 1980.

The primary objective of DIDMCA was to create a more competitive environment for the depository institutions. The secondary objective was to improve the Fed's power to control the money supply. In the most important provision, Regulation Q was phased out over a six-year period. Savings and loans were granted expanding lending powers, primarily the capability to invest in consumer loans. State usury laws were overridden for all federally insured lenders. Interest-bearing checking accounts were authorized for all depository institutions. Mutual savings and loans were allowed to convert more easily to a stock structure. In addition, deposit insurance coverage was raised to $100,000 per account.

The Fed membership problem also was addressed in an attempt to promote the Fed's control of the money supply. All depository institutions would be required to meed the same reserve requirements. Moreover, they could meet those requirements only by holding their reserves in the vaults or at the Fed. This removed the advantage nonmembers previously enjoyed. At the same time, the Fed was required to offer its services to nonmembers. These provisions reversed the tide of Fed membership losses.

The objective of creating a more competitive environment was only partially met. The problem was that market rates were so high that competition with nondepository institutions was an unprofitable undertaking. For the thrifts in particular, it became increasingly difficult to avoid losses. By the end of 1980, about 36 percent of the thrift industry was losing money, despite DIDMCA. In 1981, that proportion rose to 80 percent.

In 1981 and 1982, various bills were introduced in Congress to assist the thrifts with their problem. After months of compromising, new legislation was signed by President Ronald Reagan on October 15, 1982. Its official title was the Depository Institutions Act of 1982; it has become popularly known as the Garn-St. Germain Act after its sponsors, Senator Jake Garn and Congressman Fernand St. Germain.

The Garn-St. Germain Act sought to rescue and support the thrifts and to reform the basic function of the industry. Among the major provisions of the act was authorization of money market deposit accounts for banks and thrifts. Savings and loans were granted expanded powers. They were authorized to make commercial loans, more nonresidential real estate loans, and more consumer loans. The act also made it easier for troubled thrifts to be acquired. The Federal Savings and Loan Insurance Corporation (FSLIC) and the Federal Deposit Insurance Corporation (FDIC) were authorized to purchase "net worth certificates" from floundering thrifts or banks to keep them from failing. The act also overrode state restrictions on due-on-sale clauses, allowing lenders to adjust the rate on mortgage loans that were assumed by property buyers.

Impact of Event

The larger, more aggressive thrifts welcomed DIDMCA. They saw potential profit in the ability to include shorter term consumer loans in their portfolios. Disintermediation was their biggest threat, so the demise of Regulation Q was welcomed. Not all smaller banks and thrifts were happy with DIDMCA. Many were not anxious to compete for high-cost funds and then enter into unfamiliar loan arrangements. There was another group of DIDMCA "losers"—banks that were not members of the Federal Reserve System. They were forced to place reserves into noninterest-bearing accounts. In return, they received the authority to purchase services from the Fed. They saw this as a poor trade.

In the first year after passage of DIDMCA, interest rates remained extremely high. This was a poor environment for institutions to test their new competitive powers. Consequently, the problems of disintermediation and thrift losses did not improve. Even the more extensive lending powers provided by the Garn-St. Germain Act did not have an immediate effect. One tool that did have an impact fairly quickly was the provision allowing money market depository accounts (MMDAs). Money market mutual funds had amassed more than $230 billion in accounts by 1982, mainly at the expense of banks and thrifts. At the end of 1982, depository institutions began attracting many of these funds back through MMDAs. By the end of 1983, MMDAs represented about 16 percent of the total deposits at banks and thrifts. Total deposits in MMDAs overtook deposits in money market mutual fund accounts.

There was a negative side to this "success." The legacy of deregulation will be that it created an era of expensive funds at depository institutions. Deregulation made it possible for banks and thrifts to compete, but shrinkage of margins between lending and borrowing rates made institutions vulnerable to failure. In the years following Garn-St. Germain, the number of bank and thrift failures was unprecedented.

From 1983 to 1986, unrelated to deregulation, inflation subsided and interest rates fell. The business climate improved, and the real estate market boomed. Thrifts made extensive use of their new power to make nonresidential loans. This prosperity turned around in just a few years. By the late 1980's, problems in the oil industry and an overbuilt real estate market led the economy downward. The FSLIC could not handle the drain on its resources caused by numerous failures of thrifts. In response, Congress enacted the Financial Institutions Rescue, Recovery, and Enforcement Act (FIRREA) in August, 1989. In some respects, FIRREA was the counterpoint to Garn-St. Germain. FIRREA put the clamps back on the thrift industry. It provided funds to support the industry, but it also imposed provisions to return the industry to its residential mortgage roots.

There are several implications to be drawn from events since deregulation. First, individual institutions have made changes in their functions and in the products and services they offer. Different types of institutions are becoming more alike; there is a blurring of function among the various depository institutions. Second, greater competition has meant more competitive pricing and shrinking profit margins. Few banks and thrifts can afford to offer free or underpriced services as benefits to customers. This is likely to be a permanent feature of the industry. Third, shrinking profit margins have resulted and likely will continue to result in bank and thrift failures. This trend appears to be leading to an industry of fewer, but larger, institutions. Fourth, the increased incidence of failure has led to further government intervention. This re-regulation is apparent in some of the provisions of FIRREA. Fifth, deregulation led some government analysts to the conclusion that there was regulatory overlap in the system. The FDIC absorbed the FSLIC through FIRREA. More such consolidations are probable.

One of the implications of deregulation for consumers is that they can expect to find market rates offered on financial services. Borrowers will pay market rates to obtain funds and may be asked to absorb more of the risk of changes in interest rates through variable-rate loan arrangements. Borrowers who had locked in low rates benefited tremendously in the 1970's and early 1980's. Depositors will seek market rates on the funds they invest in banks and thrifts. Consumers have become more sophisticated about the financial markets and will continue to show interest rate sensitivity in making deposit choices. In addition, consumers will be given more options through increased competition. Deregulation has brought about a proliferation of alternative financial services. Consumers should be able to tailor financial services to their needs.

Not all the implications of deregulation are positive. It is clear, however, that the impact of deregulation has been extensive and long-lasting. The structure of the financial markets has been changed profoundly. The roles of the banks and thrifts and the manner in which they conduct business have been revolutionized.

Bibliography

Bowden, Elbert V., and Judith L. Holbert. *Revolution in Banking*. 2d ed. Reston, Va.: Reston, 1984. Provides detailed analysis of changes occurring in the financial services industry during the early 1980's and an outlook for the system from that era's point of view. Represents an early attempt at putting deregulation of depository institutions into perspective. Includes numerous suggested readings on the topic.

Cargill, Thomas F., and Gillian G. Garcia. *Financial Deregulation and Monetary Control*. Stanford, Calif.: Hoover Institution Press, 1982. Presents the DIDMCA from a historical perspective. Written prior to completion of the deregulation process; presents an interesting foretelling of events yet to come. Emphasizes the impact of DIDMCA on the financial system, with an excellent review of the implications for governmental monetary policy.

Cooper, Kerry, and Donald R. Fraser. *Banking Deregulation and the New Competition in Financial Services*. Cambridge, Mass.: Ballinger, 1986. Extensive academic review of the literature concerning the revolution in financial services. Reviews and analyzes financial change; assesses the forces and events that forged the new structure. Describes the nature of changes as they existed and offers insights into possible future directions of the industry.

Dickens, Ross N. *Contestable Markets Theory, Competition, and the United States Commercial Banking Industry*. New York: Garland, 1996.

Lash, Nicholas A. *Banking Laws and Regulations: An Economic Perspective*. Englewood Cliffs, N.J.: Prentice-Hall, 1987. A comprehensive but nontechnical review of the major laws and regulations influencing the banking/thrift systems. Completely describes the evolution and demise of Regulation Q. Clearly states the major provisions of both DIDMCA and Garn-St. Germain.

Roussakis, Emmanuel N. *Commercial Banking in an Era of Deregulation*.

New York: Praeger, 1989. Examines commercial banking in the framework of the entire U.S. financial services industry. Emphasizes the changes experienced by the industry at large, stressing the transformation of roles of various depository institutions. Examines the forces that shaped new trends in the financial markets. Places greatest emphasis on the management challenges of the new competition.

Victor J. LaPorte, Jr.

Cross-References

The Federal Reserve Act Creates a U.S. Central Bank (1913); The Banking Act of 1933 Reorganizes the American Banking System (1933); The Banking Act of 1935 Centralizes U.S. Monetary Control (1935); The Kennedy-Johnson Tax Cuts Stimulate the U.S. Economy (1964); Bush Responds to the Savings and Loan Crisis (1989).

THE CABLE NEWS
NETWORK DEBUTS

CATEGORY OF EVENT: New products
TIME: June 1, 1980
LOCALE: Atlanta, Georgia

CNN altered the customary format of television programming by introducing a twenty-four-hour daily schedule of in-depth newscasting and live transmission to a global audience

Principal personages:
ROBERT EDWARD "TED" TURNER III (1938-   ), the founder of the
    Turner Broadcasting System, the parent company of CNN
KIRK KERKORIAN (1917-   ), a motion picture entrepreneur
WYATT THOMAS "TOM" JOHNSON, JR. (1941-   ), the third president
    of CNN, beginning in 1990

Summary of Event

The advent of the Cable News Network (CNN) changed the nature of television production and news programming. The innovative quality of CNN's programming arose from the application of satellite technology to news production and distribution across national frontiers. CNN revolutionized the strategy and structure of mass communication with the inception of around-the-clock transmission of news to a global audience. CNN's global scope and live coverage of the news brought visual instancy to international events and reconfigured the contextual perception of international relations.

The history of CNN is inseparable from the entrepreneurial genius of Robert Edward "Ted" Turner III, the builder of the organization. Turner broke into the leadership ranks of the competitive mass communication industry, and CNN owes its success to his objective definitions and uncompromising self-confidence. The history of CNN is an account of the entrepreneurial restlessness of its founder and the eventual transformation of a fledgling family venture into a transnational corporate outfit.

After the death of his father, Turner inherited the Turner Advertising Company, which specialized in billboards. Turner, through some ingenious reordering of rights and liabilities, extricated the billboard enterprise, conservatively valued at more than $1 million, from contractual problems, thus retaining control of it. He proceeded to expand the company through the acquisition of other billboard companies.

Turner's interest in mass communication went beyond outdoor advertising. By 1969, he was ready to diversify his holdings, which included a number of radio stations he had acquired as part of a strategic marketing approach. He had placed the billboard firm in stable and profitable order and seemed resolved to apply his skills and profits to a higher level of enterprise. He entered into negotiations with Rice Broadcasting, the proprietors of WTSG-Channel 17, a small ultrahigh frequency (UHF) television broadcaster based in Atlanta, Georgia. Turner bought Channel 17 for $3 million. Its weak transmission signal and a number of regulatory constraints contributed to $689,000 in operational losses in Turner's first year of ownership.

Despite a string of losses in the new venture, Turner did not slip into bankruptcy. He had successfully transformed the billboard company from a family-based unit into the organizational basis of a public company, the Turner Broadcasting System. That company remained profitable and churned out financial support for Turner's television efforts, which included a subsequent acquisition in North Carolina, Charlotte's Channel 36. By 1973, Turner had combined business strategy, hard work, and a dash of luck to push up his Atlanta station's ratings. Channel 17, now called WTBS, began running comedies, wrestling, sports, and films. Turner's billboards adver-

Ted Turner, founder of CNN. (George Bennett)

tised the station and proudly publicized upcoming broadcasts of Atlanta Braves baseball games on Channel 17.

Wrestling was well received and boosted Channel 17's share of the viewing audience. The viewership further expanded after Turner secured a five-year right, for $2.5 million, to screen Atlanta Braves baseball games. Channel 17 also took over from the local WSB-TV, then an affiliate of the National Broadcasting Company (NBC), the carriage of some NBC network programs. The expansion in programming increased the audience and visibility of Channel 17.

The mid-1970's saw pivotal changes for Turner Broadcasting. The deregulation of cable access by the Federal Communications Commission enabled private broadcasters such as WTBS and John Kluge's Metromedia to explore opportunities in satellite technology. Turner Broadcasting, following in the steps of Home Box Office (HBO), took advantage of a satellite facility, SAT COM I, previously considered for telephonic application by the Radio Corporation of America, to transmit signals to Earth receivers. In 1976, Turner's WTBS Channel 17, using a national cable format, transmitted to receivers in almost every state.

WTBS signals went via satellite to cable receivers nationwide. The unorthodox venture into national cable networking proved successful and potentially expandable. At the same time, Turner further diversified his holdings to expand the input sources for WTBS programming. The expansion in program sources was necessary to sustain a twenty-four-hour daily output. Turner bought the Atlanta Braves baseball and Atlanta Hawks basketball teams in 1976 and acquired rights to show Atlanta Flames hockey games on the WTBS network. WTBS aired a variety of news and entertainment shows but gave precedence to the latter. News broadcasting, however, would turn out to be the structural hinge and competitive strategy of the company in the 1980's and beyond.

On June 1, 1980, four years after inaugurating its national cable programming, the Turner Broadcasting System launched the Cable News Network (CNN), the first around-the-clock cable news service. Its initial audience consisted of 1.7 million U.S. homes. That year, CNN recorded $7 million in revenue and $16 million in operating losses. Even after five consecutive years of losses, Turner did not abandon his vision. The founder of CNN had major plans to extend the day-long format of broadcasting in a new direction. At midnight on December 1, 1981, he launched CNN2, which offered a condensed edition of the news in thirty-minute slots and updates. CNN2 was renamed CNN Headline News in August, 1983, having absorbed its only competitor, the Satellite News Channel. The 1980's, a decade of consolidation and expansion at CNN, took the network on a prodigious path of innovative growth, with profound effects on global news production, distribution, and consumption.

Impact of Event

The founding of CNN brought innovation to the structure and strategy of competition in the mass communication industry, particularly in cable programming. CNN's daily offerings around the clock revolutionized the scope and content of news production. Television viewers with cable access no longer had to wait for prime-time broadcasts for news delivery. The network's live coverage and in-depth analysis of events introduced a new dimension to news distribution and consumption, offering free and instant flow of information across national boundaries by satellite.

Turner's internationalist outlook underscored the orientation and performance of CNN. CNN won the right in April, 1982, to be on a footing with the major network organizations in White House press pooling. It initiated the first live television broadcast since 1958 from Cuba to the United States. The "International Hour," a world-events documentary covering events in more than a hundred nations, debuted on CNN in March, 1984. In April, CNN received the George Foster Peabody Broadcasting Award, the first of many awards for program quality and excellence. In September, 1985, CNN International was launched as a twenty-four-hour global news service. Its signal initially went to Europe, then by 1989 to Africa, Asia, and the Middle East via Soviet satellite. By 1993 it served more than thirty million subscribers worldwide.

CNN's rapid development finally paid off in profits. Five years of operating losses, partly the result of reinvested returns, ended in 1985, which saw $123 million in total revenue and $13 million in profit. The turnaround was remarkable, given an operating loss of $20 million for the preceding year. By 1985, the network had unquestionably established a respectable presence in a cutthroat media market. CNN offered a national audience a live glimpse of the *Challenger* space shuttle explosion in 1986. The network's camera was present in North Africa for instantaneous coverage of U.S. aerial bombardment of Libya in April, 1986. CNN received the Overseas Press Club Award for that coverage. The Turner Broadcasting System acquired a vast film library in 1986 through a deal with Kirk Kerkorian.

CNN's approach to news marketing and consumption was path-breaking. Aside from enhancing the political consciousness of the public by broadcasting world events, CNN positioned viewers in a make-believe situation of participant-observer. Viewers watched live events unfolding across the globe. For example, for two months in 1987, the public watched the Iran-Contra investigation in Congress. Two years later, the world watched as students and activists confronted government forces in China. Beginning in 1987, the *CNN World Report* collected and collated, without censorship, news reports from different parts of the world. In May, 1988, Noticiero Telemundo-CNN was launched as a Spanish-language news service for viewers in the United States and Latin America.

The increasing sophistication and coverage of the network were obvious. In 1988, CNN received a second George Foster Peabody Broadcasting Award for its analytical focus on the 1987 stock market plunge. In 1991, CNN and CNN Headline News together claimed 34.5 percent of the national news audience, by households, compared with 23.8 percent for the American Broadcasting Company (ABC), 21.0 percent for the Columbia Broadcasting System (CBS), and 20.0 percent for the National Broadcasting Company (NBC). In 1992, CNN telecasts reached almost sixty million American homes and about thirty million foreign households in 130 nations. By January, 1992, a daily average of 190,000 viewers watched CNN's editorial briefs on Headline News.

The string of awards conferred on CNN since 1984 reflects the quantitative and qualitative content of the medium's output as well as the industry's recognition of the network's distinctive influence on mass communication. The recognitions accorded to CNN include the Golden Cable ACE, DuPont Silver Baton, Clarion, Silver Gavel, National Headliner, Edward R. Murrow, and the New York International Television and Film Festival awards. In 1991, *Time* magazine recognized CNN's founder, Ted Turner, as its "Man of the Year." An ACE award in 1992 recognized CNN's distinctive live coverage of the Persian Gulf War.

By 1992, the network had accumulated five George Foster Peabody Broadcasting Awards. Critics of television programming and production have suggested that the effectiveness and popularity of CNN arise from the network's capacity to move far beyond the parochial limits of soap operas and situation comedies into the more realistic realms of humanity and social conditions. Supporters point to Turner's sponsorship of the Goodwill Games in Moscow as well as the commitment of the Turner Broadcasting System to the causes of global peace, conservation, nuclear order, public education, and impartial reporting.

The Turner Broadcasting System and its subsidiaries responded to a variety of interests. At selected airport terminals and supermarkets, travelers and shoppers could watch the Airport and Checkout channels aired by the Turner Private Networks. For the business community, CNN provided *Business Day, Business Morning, Moneyline,* and *Your Money.* CNN International aired *Business Asia, Business News,* and *World Business Today.* Sports fans got daily reports. *Newsroom* served as a classroom teaching aid.

CNN Radio offered both network and closed circuit services to domestic and international radio listeners. CNN's *Larry King Live* provided a serious yet casual talk show, and *Special Report* offered investigative journalism.

Ted Turner demonstrated the relevance of satellite technology to mass communication. He successfully combined broadcast and nonbroadcast services for domestic and international consumption. His experiments in news broadcasting proved the voracious appetite of the American public for up-to-the-minute coverage of events worldwide.

Bibliography

Brenner, Daniel L., and Monroe E. Price. *Cable Television and Other Nonbroadcast Video: Law and Policy.* New York: Clark Boardman, 1986. Presents the regulatory and deregulatory framework of cable television and carriage, and includes a comprehensive overview of the Cable Communication Policy Act of 1984, FCC rulings, and judicial decisions. Of technical value to researchers as well as general readers.

Denisoff, R. Serge. "Ted Turner's Crusade: Economics Versus Morals." *Journal of Popular Culture* 21 (Summer, 1987): 27-42. An interesting discussion of programming constraints and choices in television. Describes a balance between financial competitiveness and philosophical imperatives.

Media Institute. *CNN Versus the Networks—Is More News Better News? A Content Analysis of the Cable News Network and the Three Broadcast Networks.* Washington, D.C.: Author, 1983. The brief analysis examines the news content and competitive context of programming.

Sherman, Stratford P. "Ted Turner: Back from the Brink." *Fortune* 114 (July 7, 1986): 24-31. The issue's cover story, a profile of the man and the institutions he built. The writer portrays Turner as cocky, shrewd, and "wildly unorthodox."

Smith, Perry M. *How CNN Fought the War: A View from the Inside.* New York: Carol Publishing Group, 1991. Discusses television broadcasting, both foreign and domestic, at CNN. The network's coverage of the Persian Gulf War receives particular attention. General discussion of the competition for news in television and in the press.

Volkmer, Ingrid. *News in the Global Sphere: A Study of CNN and Its Impact on Global Communications.* Lutton: University of Lutton Press, 1999.

Whittemore, Hank. *CNN: The Inside Story.* Boston: Little, Brown, 1990. Examines the pattern and scope of CNN's television broadcasting, including insightful glimpses at the competitive strategy and organizational structure of the network. Not without a few ungrounded generalizations.

Satch Ejike

Cross-References

Station KDKA Introduces Commercial Radio Broadcasting (1920); The A. C. Nielsen Company Pioneers in Marketing and Media Research (1923); Congress Establishes the Federal Communications Commission (1934); The 1939 World's Fair Introduces Regular U.S. Television Service (1939); Murdoch Extends His Media Empire to the United States (1976); A Home Shopping Service Is Offered on Cable Television (1985); Cable Television Rises to Challenge Network Television (mid-1990's).

REAGAN PROMOTES SUPPLY-SIDE ECONOMICS

CATEGORY OF EVENT: Government and business
TIME: 1981
LOCALE: Washington, D.C.

By passing the Economic Recovery Tax Act of 1981, the U.S. Congress enacted supply-side tax cuts to stimulate the economy and enhance revenues

Principal personages:
ARTHUR LAFFER (1940-   ), the economist who pioneered the concept of supply-side economics and advised lawmakers such as Jack Kemp
RONALD REAGAN (1911-   ), the president of the United States, 1981-1989
JACK KEMP (1935-   ), the congressman who spearheaded efforts to pass the Economic Recovery Tax Act of 1981
GEORGE GILDER (1939-   ), an economic analyst who provided ideas to implement the supply-side philosophy

Summary of Event
The Economic Recovery Tax Act of 1981 had its origins in a movement called supply-side economics that gained momentum in the early 1970's. Arthur Laffer, a young economist out of the University of Chicago, had worked as a budget analyst for the Office of Management and Budget and made a set of daring economic predictions based on incentives in the tax system. He introduced the "Laffer Curve" to President Gerald Ford. The ideas represented by the curve are both simple and irrefutable: At a 0 percent tax rate a government will receive no revenue, and at a 100 percent tax rate a government will receive no revenue, because no one will work if all

wages go to the government. Therefore, there must be some tax rate between 0 and 100 percent that maximizes tax revenues.

Laffer estimated that the tax rate that would maximize revenues was about 15-20 percent for the top income earners, much lower than the rates of 40-60 percent then in place. He pointed out that his theory supported the tax cuts enacted by President John F. Kennedy in the early 1960's. Those tax cuts were associated with increased revenues. Most important to Laffer were effects in two distinct areas. First, the wealthy paid a much higher share of total taxes after the cuts (both under Kennedy and in the 1920's after the Coolidge-Mellon tax cuts of the same nature). Second, in both cases the tax cuts had dramatic positive effects on the economy. The business community stood to benefit most from the cuts. Businesses would benefit directly from the decreased rates and indirectly from the overall improvement in the economy likely to come as a result of the cuts. Because businesses and workers could keep a larger portion of their incomes, they would supply increased effort to productive endeavors; hence the term "supply-side" economics.

Laffer was made into the "father" of the supply-side tax cuts by editorial writer Jude Wanniski. In 1976, Congressman Jack Kemp met with Laffer and Wanniski. He subsequently fleshed out Laffer's proposals to cut taxes and introduced the ideas as legislation in Congress. At the same time, a powerful grass-roots revolt against higher taxes in California had culminated with the passage of Proposition 13, which limited the taxes that could be imposed without direct approval of the taxpayers.

The federal budget started to grow dramatically during the presidency of Jimmy Carter. The federal budget deficit as a share of gross national product (GNP) also increased, from .3 percent in 1970 to 2.8 percent by 1980. Budget pressures acted to increase the rates of inflation and unemployment. Ronald Reagan won election as president in 1980 on his promise to cut taxes, relieve the burden on business, and "get government off the backs of the people."

Kemp and other Republicans in Congress already had started to forge a tax reduction package, but their efforts had been blocked by Carter. Early in 1979, however, the Joint Economic Committee, under the leadership of Senator Lloyd Bentsen (D-Texas) and Congressman Clarence Brown (R-Ohio), endorsed a supply-side policy in its economic report.

The drain on the economy caused by high tax rates was clear to Reagan, who had been a Democrat until the 1960's. Reagan's familiarity with the Kennedy tax cuts (and his personal witnessing of the effects of the Coolidge-Mellon cuts) convinced him that reducing marginal tax rates would accomplish two objectives. First, it would give individuals more money to invest.

Reagan believed that individuals could make better decisions than could the government concerning investment. Second, lowering tax rates would reduce the government's claim on individuals' resources in relative terms. Even though his economic advisers pointed out that individuals' tax payments might increase in dollar amount, the proportion of income devoted to government would in most cases decline.

Upon election, Reagan immediately pushed for a Kemp-type tax cut of 30 percent, to be implemented in 1981. Even before the economic proposals could be presented, budget director David Stockman voiced opposition. He feared effects on the deficit. The Treasury Department already had compromised and proposed tax cuts of 10 percent per year for three years, rather than an immediate 30 percent cut. Stockman called for reducing the 1981 tax cut to 5 percent and delaying it until October. Eventually his proposal was enacted. Tax rates for the highest income levels were reduced from 50 percent to 33 percent.

Laffer and other supply-side advocates noted that the main effects of the tax cuts would not occur immediately. The tax cuts were expected to affect investment, and investment plans take time to formulate and implement. In addition, some businesses might be prompted to postpone some of their new investment to take advantage of the even lower tax rates to come.

Impact of Event

Measuring the effects of the tax cuts on business is difficult because many factors influence business activity and such activity can be measured in various ways. Several statistics, however, are indicative of the success of the tax cuts. Real GNP (GNP adjusted for inflation) rose 3.6 percent in 1983, the first year that the full tax cut went into effect, and 6.8 percent in 1984. The rate of inflation, which was in the high teens during the Carter years, fell to 3.2 percent in 1983 and 4.3 percent in 1984. The unemployment rate dropped from 7.1 percent in 1980 to 5.5 percent by the end of Reagan's term. The employment effects from the tax cuts were more impressive than the unemployment rate reflected, since millions of women had entered the workforce in the 1980's. The decreased unemployment rate reflected those millions of people finding jobs in addition to previously unemployed people going back to work.

As predicted in George Gilder's *Wealth and Poverty* (1981), virtually all the impact of the tax cuts was on new businesses and small businesses, which accounted for all net job growth since 1980. Small business incorporations stood at record levels in the 1980's, with no corresponding increase in business failures. Small businesses, in net, had produced most of the fourteen million new positions. Critics contended that the tax cuts produced part-time "burger flipper" jobs, but studies by several government agencies revealed that the service-sector jobs that had made up the majority of job creation during that period paid on average more than $10 an hour, more than double the minimum wage and enough to put workers into the middle class.

Per capita after-tax income rose by approximately 25 percent from 1980 to 1988, even including the effects of the 1982 recession. Real GNP rose from $3.1 trillion to $4 trillion during the same period. The average level of prices, which almost doubled during the four years of the Carter Administration, rose approximately 20-40 percent (depending on the measure used) during Reagan's eight years in office.

Critics attempted to claim that such astounding improvements were "consumption driven" and that American industrial capability had suffered, refuting the notion that the tax cuts on the wealthy had resulted in investments in plant and equipment. That claim was refuted by American productivity increases, especially in manufacturing. U.S. industries such as steel used the 1980's to downsize as well as to invest in new plant and equipment to replace outdated machinery.

Critics of the Reagan tax cuts and supply-side philosophy argued that an economic boom would have occurred even without the policy changes. Economic indicators, however, showed improvements beyond those typical in a recovery. Clearly, the business community approved of and responded to the tax cuts.

Supply-side economics changed the American economy in the 1980's, essentially rescuing it from a decade of complacency and high-tax malaise. It also restored the role of investment and incentives to center stage in the economic debate. The success of supply-side tax cuts was questioned by liberals, who traditionally were opposed to smaller government and lower taxes, and even by some conservatives. Reagan's vice president, George Bush, termed the notion that tax cuts could increase revenues "voodoo economics."

The primary criticism against the performance of the economy after the supply-side tax cuts focused on federal deficits, which reached record levels (before being adjusted for inflation), and the national debt, which by 1990 exceeded $4 trillion. Reagan was assailed as being the architect of the "twin towers of debt," namely the domestic debt and the foreign trade deficit, which rose during the 1980's. Critics maintained that the United States was borrowing to finance consumption and that the supply-side cuts had ushered in a rash of leveraged buyouts on Wall Street and the popularity of junk bonds. Businesses, they claimed, used the tax cuts as incentives not to invest in real plants and equipment but instead to make paper profits through buying and selling existing companies.

Laffer's primary theory concerning tax cuts related to revenues. It is irrefutable that the wealthiest taxpayers paid significantly more in taxes and reported more capital gains (profits on investments) than they had at the higher tax rates. The share of all taxes paid by the top income earners rose.

At the height of the war in Vietnam and as the Great Society programs peaked, federal spending stood at 19.8 percent of GNP. Ten years later, as Reagan took office, the federal government's spending as a share of GNP had risen to more than 22 percent, and at the time the tax cuts went into effect, the figure had risen to almost 24 percent. Spending, rather than decreases in tax revenue, apparently caused rising government budget deficits. In addition, each year after 1983, the deficit as a proportion of GNP fell. Increases in the deficit reflected the fact that the American economy had grown and prices had risen; removing those factors showed that the relative burden of the deficit was smaller. By the time Reagan left office, the federal deficit as a share of GNP was smaller than it was in 1975 by almost 1 percent and almost exactly what it was when Reagan took office in 1980.

Another criticism of the supply-side tax cuts' effect on business held that the United States had become a net importer of foreign capital, which was used by Americans to finance a consumption binge rather than to invest in U.S. businesses. Evidence against that argument shows that the supply-side cuts made investing in American business and manufacturing so rewarding that banks and individual investors kept their money home for the first time in a decade. Banks, however, began to write off loans to Argentina, Mexico, and other Latin American nations. This caused changes in the capital account, but the real events behind those changes actually had been occur- ring over a long period of time. Thus, the trade deficit was illusory, and to the extent that a capital inflow existed, it occurred only because U.S. investors, like everyone else, realized that the tax cuts had made the United States a much more profitable place to do business.

The last area in which the supply-side tax cuts were criticized came in the appellation "decade of greed." Critics suggested that the tax cuts encouraged personal consumption at the expense of charitable giving, since the tax deduction for a charitable contribution of a given size now reduced taxes by a smaller amount than previously. Charitable contributions by individuals actually grew faster in the 1980's than in the late 1970's.

In short, the achievements of the supply-side tax cuts were clear and substantial. The American economy showed its greatest boom since the 1920's, employment soared, small businesses thrived, American manufac- turing staged a resurgence, and the wealthy paid more in taxes, invested more, and gave away more than in the previous decade or under higher tax regimes. Analyses of government budgets showed that total tax revenues rose after the cuts, especially after the third installation of the cut. Nevertheless, the incentives created by lower tax rates raised U.S. productivity to its highest levels in a decade, levels that matched those of America's closest foreign competitors.

Lost in the debates were the increases in the tax burden for most Americans in the tax "reform" package of 1986 and the "deficit reduction package" of 1990. The net effect of the two groups of laws was to increase the actual taxes most Americans had to pay. The 1986 laws eliminated numerous tax deductions, and the subsequent deficit reduction package increased taxes on a variety of items. Overall, the negative effects of the two tax increases dampened the economy to such an extent that full-fledged recession set in by 1990 and had not been alleviated by 1992. Further "deficit reduction plans" only promised higher levels of taxes, suggesting that the favorable business climate that had existed in the 1980's had all but disappeared by 1993.

Bibliography

Fink, Richard H., ed. *Supply-Side Economics: A Critical Appraisal.* Frederick, Md.: University Publications of America, 1982. A collection of essays by proponents and opponents of supply-side tax cuts. Contains debates on most of the crucial issues but does not address any of the economic effects of the Reagan program.

Gilder, George. *Wealth and Poverty.* New York: Basic Books, 1981. The "bible" of early supply siders. Incoming president Ronald Reagan reportedly handed out copies of this book to his entire staff as a guide for public policy. Gilder is perceptive and clear in his analysis yet has been dismissed by some supply-side writers (as has Arthur Laffer) who call his work "journalistic" or "unscholarly."

Nau, Henry R. *The Myth of America's Decline.* New York: Oxford University Press, 1990. A thorough and convincing, if somewhat restrained, analysis of American economic performance since 1960. Nau, a former State Department official, offers an insider's view of policy-making while applying his economic and quantitative skills to issues of international growth. He concludes that the resurgence of the U.S. economy during the 1980's resulted from policies enacted between 1982 and 1985.

Puth, Robert C. *American Economic History.* 3d ed. Fort Worth, Tex.: Dryden Press, 1993. A standard and useful economic history that covers the modern period. It repeats some of the deficit/debt fallacies.

Raboy, David G., ed. *Essays in Supply Side Economics.* Washington, D.C.:

Institute for Research on the Economics of Taxation, 1982. A set of scholarly essays by economists and historians. The essays examine various aspects of supply-side economics such as the rational expectations model, the theoretical heritage of supply side, and the distortions of taxation and savings that can develop.

Roberts, Paul Craig. *The Supply-Side Revolution: An Insider's Account of Policymaking in Washington.* Cambridge, Mass.: Harvard University Press, 1984. Written by a former Kemp adviser who served in the Treasury Department under Reagan, this book provides an excellent insider history of the tax cut battle. Roberts criticizes Laffer and those in the administration who had broader goals for the economic program.

Wanniski, Jude. *The Way the World Works: How Economies Fail—and Succeed.* New York: Basic Books, 1978. One of the earliest published advocacy pieces for supply-side tax cuts, Wanniski's book also provides one of the first published analyses of the causes of the Great Depression that links the Smoot-Hawley Tariff to the stock market crash. A clear and persuasive discussion of the positive effects of low tax rates.

Larry Schweikart

Cross-References

The Kennedy-Johnson Tax Cuts Stimulate the U.S. Economy (1964); Defense Cutbacks Devastate the U.S. Aerospace Industry (1980's); Insider Trading Scandals Mar the Emerging Junk Bond Market (1986); Drexel and Michael Milken Are Charged with Insider Trading (1988); Mexico Renegotiates Debt to U.S. Banks (1989).

FEDERAL REGULATORS AUTHORIZE ADJUSTABLE-RATE MORTGAGES

CATEGORY OF EVENT: Finance
TIME: March, 1981
LOCALE: Washington, D.C.

Adjustable-rate mortgages enabled banks to hedge against inflation while offering borrowers low initial interest rates

Principal personages:
JAY JANIS (1932-   ), the president of the Federal Home Loan Bank Board, 1979-1980
JOHN H. DALTON (1941-   ), the president of the Federal Home Loan Bank Board, 1980-1981
RICHARD T. PRATT (1937-   ), the president of the Federal Home Loan Bank Board, 1981-1983
JOHN G. HEIMANN (1929-   ), the comptroller of the currency, 1977-1981
WILLIAM POINDEXTER IV (1944-   ), the chairman of the U.S. Senate Banking Committee in 1981

Summary of Event

Adjustable-rate mortgages (ARMs) are loans for which the mortgage rate fluctuates along with the market interest rate. This type of mortgage instrument is an alternative to the traditional fixed-rate mortgage (FRM). The interest rate on an ARM usually is tied to a reference interest rate. ARM contracts include several other stipulations, including the frequency of interest rate changes, the maximum permissible change in monthly payments, and the low initial rate. ARMs are also referred to as variable-rate mortgages.

ARMs were introduced in California as early as 1975. Four years later, the Federal Home Loan Bank Board (FHLBB), which oversaw the activities of savings and loans institutions (S&Ls) nationwide, authorized ARMs on a national scale. The move was spearheaded by Jay Janis, the president of the FHLBB at the time. These early ARMs were subject to substantial limitations with respect to changes in their interest rates. In 1981, FHLBB president John Dalton and Comptroller of the Currency John G. Heimann authorized nationwide use of ARMs with all restrictions removed, despite earlier criticism by the Senate Banking Committee, chaired by William Poindexter IV. Their decision was prompted by a sharp increase in interest rates that hindered housing sales and construction. Variability allowed in interest rates on the new ARMs was to be determined by the individual borrowers and lenders.

One way to simplify discussion of ARMs is to think of them as series of short-term mortgages, each with a maturity equal to the length of the adjustment period. The interest rate at a given time is the sum of two elements: an index of market interest rates and a fixed margin. A borrower's monthly payments therefore would change as a result of fluctuations in the interest rate index. The two most popular market indexes are the interest rate on one-year Treasury bills and the Eleventh District Cost of Funds. The latter is a weighted average of interest rates on deposits for S&Ls located in California, Arizona, and Nevada. Despite being specific to only one region, over time this index has mirrored the national average of interest rates on deposits. Each ARM is matched with an index of corresponding maturity. For example, a six-month ARM (one with interest rate adjustments every six months) is pegged to the interest rate on Treasury bills with a maturity of six months, a one-year ARM to the rate on Treasury bills maturing in one year, and so on.

ARM frequencies of adjustment typically varied between six months and five years in the early 1990's. (All examples will be for that time period unless otherwise stated.) The most popular is the one-year ARM. The shorter the adjustment period, the more frequent the fluctuations in monthly payments, with ARMs having longer adjustment periods resembling fixed-rate mortgages. An adjustment takes place following a change in the ARM interest rate index. The most common way to adjust the monthly payments is by an amount proportional to the change in the index.

In order to limit the increase in monthly payments, ARMs are subject to periodic caps and lifetime caps. Periodic caps limit the amount that the interest rate can increase or decrease at each adjustment. The periodic caps vary with the frequency of the adjustment periods. A typical periodic cap on a one-year ARM is 2 percent.

Lifetime caps and floors limit the range of change in the interest rate over the entire course of the loan. The lifetime cap is expressed as a change from the mortgage's initial rate. A typical lifetime cap or floor is 5 percent. For example, if a one-year ARM has an initial rate of 8 percent, a periodic cap of 2 percent, and a lifetime cap of 5 percent, then the interest rate will be between 6 and 10 percent in the second year and will never fall below 3 percent or rise above 13 percent.

To make ARMs more appealing than fixed-rate mortgages, lenders often offer initial rates that are lower than the prevailing market mortgage rate. These are called teaser rates and are temporary. At the first adjustment, the teaser rate is replaced by the market interest rate index plus the margin. There is no general rule for how attractive teaser rates should be. Generally, teasers vary inversely with the loan origination fees, commonly called points. Lenders vary in the points charged to borrowers. The higher the points, the more attractive the teaser rate is likely to be. Borrowers have to look for the best combination of interest rates and fees.

Although ARMs provide several benefits to borrowers, including low initial rates and the ability to benefit from falling interest rates without refinancing, their features are complex and can hide surprises. For example, a mere 2 percent increase in interest rates could raise monthly payments by 25 percent under reasonably likely conditions. This can occur because the first few payments on a loan are almost entirely interest payments, with little payment of principal. A rise of 2 percent in the interest rate with an initial rate of 8 percent thus would cause payments to rise by about 25 percent. The borrower's ability to pay may not increase by the same proportion. For example, interest rates may rise in response to expected inflation that has not yet caused higher wages.

Another disadvantage with ARMs is that although their initial rate is tempting, borrowers have a difficult time comparing them with their FRM counterparts. Because the value of an ARM changes frequently with market interest rates, a borrower is forced to guess the future trend in mortgage rates before making a choice between an ARM and an FRM. As a result, borrowers often select an FRM because they know that the monthly payment will never change.

Impact of Event

The core business of savings and loan associations is the issuance of home mortgages. S&Ls raise funds by offering their customers checkable and time deposits. Traditionally, most of their assets consisted of fixed-rate thirty-year mortgages, whereas their liabilities were typically short-term certificates of deposit with a maximum maturity of five years.

Because of the nature of their business, raising funds short term and lending long term, S&Ls are particularly vulnerable to interest rate risk. For example, if market interest rates rise, S&Ls would be forced to raise deposits on the open market by paying high deposit rates while earnings from fixed-rate mortgages remained stagnant. Falling interest rates benefited S&Ls, but borrowers had the option of paying back their mortgages and refinancing at lower rates.

Interest rate risk posed only small problems as long as rates were relatively stable. The period from 1976 through 1982, however, was marked by the most volatile interest rates in modern U.S. economic history. FRM rates rose sharply from 9 percent in 1976 to 16 percent in 1982, driving many S&Ls out of business. This increase was a result in part of tight monetary policy pursued by the Federal Reserve System in a long effort to fight inflation. The crucial role of ARMs during that period was their fundamental feature of shifting interest rate risk to borrowers. On the traditional fixed-rate mortgages, the lender bore the entire risk from interest rate increases.

After 1982, a combination of volatile interest rates, a deregulatory political environment, and widespread mismanagement compounded the problems of S&Ls. By 1989, the S&L industry required a $150 billion rescue plan. The 1989 bailout legislation, known as the Financial Institutions Rescue, Recovery, and Enforcement Act (FIRREA), rescinded investment powers that many S&Ls had abused. A notable example was the right to invest in highly speculative "junk" bonds. Many S&Ls had invested in junk bonds to increase earnings as a way of paying the higher interest rates on deposits. When issuers of junk bonds defaulted, those S&Ls faced losses and even bankruptcy.

Perhaps the major shortcoming of FIRREA is that it failed to address the gap in maturity between S&L assets (mortgages) and liabilities (deposits). That gap was at the root of the interest rate risk that resulted in disaster. The problems of the S&Ls could have been alleviated by avoiding FRMs and issuing primarily ARMs. S&Ls, however, use their fixed-rate mortgages to speculate on the future course of interest rates. If interest rates are expected to fall, S&Ls will issue fixed-rate rather than variable-rate mortgages, hoping to lock in the currently high rates. S&Ls did not want to give up an instrument that enabled them to bet on the trend of future rates, with enormous rewards for correct predictions. It is the riskiness of long-term mortgages that makes them unsuitable for thrift institutions, which ideally should be averse to risk. Although the odds of an interest rate increase or decline are equal on average, their impact on thrifts is asymmetric because borrowers have the option to refinance their mortgages when rates fall.

A fundamental difficulty in evaluating mortgages lies in the prepayment option that a borrower can exercise and how it is affected by changes in interest rates. When interest rates go down, borrowers rush to refinance their existing mortgages at lower rates in order to reduce their monthly payments. This poses a problem for the S&L lender, because it causes an early redemption of principal that will have to be reinvested at a lower market interest rate. Conversely, when rates increase, borrowers delay prepayment. This often takes the form of continuing to live in a current home rather than selling, prepaying the mortgage, and getting a new mortgage on a new home. For example, a borrower would take into consideration the cost of giving up a below-market mortgage at 8 percent on a current home and getting a new one at 12 percent on a new house. At the same time, a rise in interest rates reduces S&L profits because existing assets are earning a below-market rate of return.

Mortgage refinancing on ARMs is less significant than on fixed-rate counterparts primarily because an ARM's interest rate mimics the movement in the market interest rate. That is not to say that ARMs are immune from prepayment. Borrowers often prepay on existing ARMs in order to substitute others at lower initial rates.

Soon after they were introduced, ARMs accounted for 40 percent of all mortgage originations. In 1984, more than 65 percent of all new residential mortgages issued by S&Ls were ARMs. By mid-1987, however, as interest rates started to decline, many S&Ls returned to FRM lending, and the share of ARMs fell. The mortgage expansion during that period triggered by a strong housing sector led to a large increase in the dollar amount of ARMs in lenders' portfolios. By 1992, the share of ARMs had stabilized at about 25 percent. As both the level and volatility of mortgage interest rates declined, FRMs regained their lost appeal.

It is unclear how the real estate market would be affected if S&Ls stopped issuing FRMs altogether. Most economists argue that the impact on housing demand would be minimal, primarily because ARMs are subject to restrictions on how much their monthly payments can adjust in a given year. An analysis of the period preceding the introduction of ARMs shows that housing starts were significantly inversely related to mortgage rates: The higher the mortgage rates, the smaller the volume of housing starts. After 1982, this relationship became weaker as a result of the ARMs' low initial interest rates. Despite high mortgage rates during that period, housing starts were brisk as home buyers switched to the cheaper ARMs. After 1986, the relationship between housing starts and FRM interest rates was much weaker, since borrowers could choose low initial rates through ARMs. When rates began to drop after 1989, home buyers switched back to FRMs to lock in low rates. It thus appears that ARMs ease the impact of high mortgage rates on the housing sector and complement the role of FRMs in mortgage lending. Equally important is the growth in housing caused by the introduction of ARMs. Because of their low initial rates, homeowners unable to qualify under the guidelines of FRMs may very well be able to qualify for ARMs with lower initial monthly payments. This important feature made housing affordable to a larger share of the population, as evidenced by the explosive growth in housing sales from 1982 to 1984. Housing starts grew by almost 85 percent during that period. The introduction of ARMs made the housing sector more resilient to economic slowdowns and less sensitive to changes in interest rates.

Bibliography

Jaffee, Dwight M. *Money, Banking, and Credit.* New York: Worth, 1989. An intermediate text in money and banking. Well written by a distinguished professor of economics. Using simple examples, the author discusses how ARMs can reduce interest rate risk.

Kamerschen, David R. *Money and Banking.* 7th ed. Cincinnati, Ohio: South-Western, 1980. A standard textbook in money and banking. Accessible to the beginning reader.

Mayer, Thomas, James S. Duesenberry, and Robert Z. Aliber. *Money, Banking, and the Economy.* 4th ed. New York: Norton, 1990. Includes updated material on the relationship between ARMs and the S&L crisis. Easy to read.

Mishkin, Frederic S. *The Economics of Money, Banking, and Financial Markets.* 5th ed. Reading, Mass.: Addison-Wesley, 1998.

Smith, Gary. *Money, Banking, and Financial Intermediation.* Lexington, Mass.: D.C. Heath, 1991. A primer in this area. Helpful examples show how changes in interest rates affect a homeowner's monthly payments. Provides a discussion of loan eligibility criteria.

White, Lawrence J. *The S&L Debacle.* New York: Oxford University Press, 1991. Written for a nonacademic audience. Traces the origins of the S&L crisis to the fixed-rate mortgage instrument. Detailed discussion of events preceding and following introduction of ARMs.

Sam Ramsey Hakim

Cross-References

The Federal Reserve Act Creates a U.S. Central Bank (1913); The Banking Act of 1933 Reorganizes the American Banking System (1933);

The Banking Act of 1935 Centralizes U.S. Monetary Control (1935); Roosevelt Signs the G.I. Bill (1944); Congress Deregulates Banks and Savings and Loans (1980-1982); Bush Responds to the Savings and Loan Crisis (1989).

AIR TRAFFIC CONTROLLERS OF PATCO DECLARE A STRIKE

CATEGORY OF EVENT: Labor
TIME: August 3, 1981
LOCALE: The United States

In an effort to win labor contract disputes, the Professional Air Traffic Controllers Organization (PATCO) declared an illegal work stoppage on August 3, 1981, to bring nationwide air traffic to a halt

Principal personages:
RONALD REAGAN (1911-   ), the president of the United States, 1981-1989
ROBERT E. POLI (1936-   ), the president of PATCO, 1980-1981
GARY W. EADS (1945-   ), the president of PATCO beginning in 1982
ANDREW LEWIS (1931-   ), the U.S. secretary of transportation, 1981-1983
WILLIAM CLAY (1931-   ), a U.S. congressman

Summary of Event

On August 3, 1981, the Professional Air Traffic Controllers Organization (PATCO), under the direction of Robert E. Poli, union president, declared an illegal nationwide strike of 14,500 members. Approximately 11,500 members walked off their jobs because of contract disputes with the Federal Aviation Administration (FAA). PATCO's illegal work stoppage temporarily left thousands of passengers stranded at airports throughout the world and caused the cancellation of thousands of scheduled flights. This unprecedented move came as a surprise, since a strike of federal employees against the government of the United States was illegal. The reaction to the illegal strike by President Ronald Reagan's administration was also unprecedented. An ultimatum was handed down demanding that the controllers return to work within forty-eight hours. Those who refused would be fired from their jobs. Labor negotiations faltered, and the strikers maintained their walkout past the deadline. The strikers were summarily fired from their jobs and ultimately were banned from ever working as federal air traffic controllers again.

Events leading to the drastic action of PATCO members and the federal government's response went back several years. During the early 1960's, working relations between controllers and FAA management and supervisors gradually deteriorated. Controllers felt overwhelmed by working conditions, the wage negotiations process, and the general lack of management support. In 1968, a core of frustrated New York City controllers formed a professional association known as the Professional Air Traffic Controllers Organization (PATCO). F. Lee Bailey, a renowned criminal lawyer, agreed to draft the association's charter and assumed directorship of the association until June, 1970. At the June, 1970, PATCO convention in Las Vegas, Nevada, the PATCO board of directors elected John F. Leyden as the union's second president. Leyden would serve as PATCO's president from 1970 to 1980. In 1970, PATCO also filed with the Department of Labor for official recognition as an affiliate of the American Federation of Labor-Congress of Industrial Organizations (AFL-CIO) and was so certified.

During PATCO's formative years, the association flexed its newly recognized organizational muscle and challenged its supervising body, the FAA. Only seven months after organization, controllers initiated a "work by the book" slowdown (following all regulations precisely, thus working at a slowed pace) in New York City after they decided that air traffic congestion had reached critical proportions. In March, 1970, three thousand controllers struck for twenty days after the FAA tried to carry out an involuntary transfer of four controllers from Baton Rouge, Louisiana. The FAA fired fifty-two striking controllers, of whom forty-six were later reinstated to their positions, and suspended nearly one thousand more controllers for a short period of time. In June, 1978, a federal court judge fined PATCO $100,000 for a "work by the book" slowdown aimed at specific airlines that had refused to allow controllers free rides overseas on jump seats for "familiarization training."

This rather militant history of job actions and FAA challenges led some PATCO members to feel disenchanted with the leadership of John Leyden. In January, 1980, Leyden submitted his resignation and left an opening for a more activist member, Robert E. Poli. In April, 1980, after a tough and mean-spirited election, Poli was elected as PATCO's third president.

It was within this charged environment that PATCO began efforts to campaign for enhanced contract negotiations. In early 1980, Congressman William Clay (D-Missouri) drafted H.R. 1576, the Air Traffic Controllers Act of 1981. Under the bill's provisions, PATCO members would have won the following job concessions: a higher wage scale than the one that applied to government workers generally, a cost-of-living provision, compensation for "unusual or strenuous hours of work," reduction of work from forty hours a week to thirty-two, a retirement plan that "objectively recognizes the unusual occupational hazards of such employment," a substantial increase in the number of controllers, and the clarification of FAA obligations in the bargaining process.

After introduction of Congressman Clay's bill, the Congressional Budget Office concluded that the bill would cost $13 billion over a five-year period. The media quickly publicized objections to the cost, and Poli was put on the defensive even before the scheduled FAA-PATCO contract negotiations began. In mid-February, 1981, negotiations began between the FAA and PATCO. Poli opened the bargaining session with a list of ninety-six demands and made it clear that three of PATCO's demands were major concerns of his 14,500 members. First, he requested a $10,000 across-the-board annual pay increase for all controllers, along with a twice-a-year cost-of-living increase that would be one and one-half times the rate of inflation and a new maximum salary of $73,420, up from $49,229. Second, the union requested a reduction in the five-day, forty-hour week to a four-day, thirty-two-hour schedule. Third, Poli asked for a liberalization of provisions for retirement.

After fruitless negotiations, PATCO's working contract expired on March 15, 1981. At the PATCO convention in May, 1981, Poli announced that PATCO would strike on June 22, 1981, if labor demands were not met. Just before the June 22 deadline, Andrew Lewis, the new U.S. secretary of transportation, made PATCO a counteroffer. The FAA package included $40 million in improvements, complete with a 10 percent pay hike for controllers who also acted as instructors, an increase in the pay differential for night work to 15 percent, and a guaranteed thirty-minute lunch period. In addition, Poli negotiated a "responsibility differential" whereby controllers would earn time-and-a-half pay after thirty-six hours worked in a week. Medically disqualified controllers would be eligible for the Second Career Program and extra training benefits. Poli got acceptance for this FAA proposal from his executive board.

Ten days later, however, upon taking the negotiated proposal to the general membership, Poli met with resistance. Put to a membership vote, the tentative contract collapsed by a margin of twenty to one. On July 31,

Poli called a news conference. He emphasized again that if the government would not agree to the union's three principal demands—the $10,000 raise, the thirty-two-hour week, and improved retirement benefits—the controllers would strike on August 3, 1981. The FAA raised its offer to a $50 million package with various conditions. Poli rejected the conditions, and PATCO officially went out on strike on the morning of August 3, 1981.

Impact of Event

The illegal PATCO work stoppage on August 3, 1981, was an attempt to bring nationwide air traffic to a halt and thereby put pressure on governmental negotiators. President Reagan's response to the strike effort was swift and decisive. On the day that it began, he declared the PATCO strike as illegal and replied with a stiff ultimatum to strikers—get back to work within forty-eight hours or be fired. In a Rose Garden presentation, President Reagan repeated an oath that Congress required all federal employees to take: "I am not participating in any strike against the Government of the United States or any agency thereof, and I will not so participate while an employee of the Government of the United States or any agency thereof."

Approximately 11,300 PATCO members remained off the job. The president remained firm in his demands, and the striking controllers were summarily fired for their lifetimes from their jobs as air traffic controllers. Although the initial shock of the strike was significant, within three days the level of air traffic was approximately three-fourths of what it had been prior to the strike. PATCO's plan of bringing the air traffic control system to a halt simply was not realized. This is not to imply that there was no loss of revenues or severe hardships during this period. The airlines estimated that they lost anywhere from $30 to $35 million per day as a result of canceled flights and fewer passengers willing to risk the chance of suffering cancellations or delays in their airline travel. The Air Transport Association (ATA) estimated losses during the first two weeks of the strike at $210 to $315 million.

Financial losses aside, however, PATCO leaders made four strategic errors that all but doomed their strike from the very start. First, they underestimated the ability of the FAA to continue operations without the aid of the striking controllers. The FAA was able to rely on approximately 5,275 managers and supervisors, 3,225 nonstriking PATCO members, and an initial force of 500 military air traffic controllers to maintain air traffic control throughout the country. In addition, the FAA had secretly devised an emergency flight control plan (known as the 75-50 Flow Control Plan) that would reduce air traffic to a manageable level. Specifically, only one-half of the regularly scheduled flights at twenty-two of the nation's largest airports were allowed to fly for a period of at least a month. The airlines had the jurisdiction to cancel the flights they thought were appropriate. In addition, the FAA closed sixty smaller control towers and spaced flights further apart in both distance (from five to twenty miles for jets on the same route) and time.

Second, PATCO overrated the value of its campaign endorsement in 1980 to then-presidential candidate Ronald Reagan. PATCO was one of the few unions to endorse Ronald Reagan during the campaign. A letter from Reagan to Poli was misread to imply total and unyielding support. In the letter, Reagan commented on "the deplorable state of our nation's air traffic control system" and assured Poli that "if I am elected President, I will take whatever steps are necessary to provide our air traffic controllers with the most modern equipment available, and to adjust staff levels and workdays so they are commensurate with achieving the maximum degree of public safety." He also pledged that his administration would pursue a spirit of cooperation between the president and the air traffic controllers.

Although Ronald Reagan began his political career as a labor leader himself, he was completely unsympathetic to the PATCO leaders' call for a strike. (White House Historical Society)

Third, PATCO ignored Reagan's often-voiced revulsion to strikes by federal employees and the length to which he was prepared to go in retaliation. Reagan's contention was that there was no strike. Federal law (Title 5, Section 7311 of the U.S. Code) states that a federal civil servant may not continue to hold his or her job if he or she takes part in a strike against the government. Reagan therefore was adamant that if the controllers walked off their jobs, they had quit. Such a philosophy did not go unnoticed by other federal unions.

Fourth, PATCO failed to gain the support of other unions and the public. The union hoped that this support would bring additional pressures against the Reagan Administration. Prior to the strike, Poli did not inform or seek advice from other union leaders. The walkout caught AFL-CIO president Lane Kirkland and United Auto Workers president Douglas Fraser off guard and unprepared to assist. Although both unions paid supporting lip service to the PATCO strike, both unions refused to fully back the strike or provide financial support. Public support was also blatantly missing from the PATCO strike. Gallup polls from August 6 and 7, 1981, showed 52 percent support for the government and only 29 percent for the controllers. In addition, 67 percent of respondents thought PATCO was wrong in breaking the federal oath not to strike against the government.

On October 22, 1981, the Federal Labor Relations Authority (FLRA) voted to decertify PATCO. This was the first time the authority had stripped a government workers' union of its bargaining rights. The three-member FLRA panel stipulated that PATCO had called, participated in, and condoned a strike. This was a clear violation of federal laws forbidding strikes by government employees. On December 31, 1981, Poli resigned as PATCO president. He was replaced by PATCO's fourth president, Gary W. Eads, on January 1, 1982. In July, 1982, the Circuit Court of Appeals upheld the PATCO decertification decision of the FLRA, and PATCO was officially terminated. The termination sent a strong message to other unions of federal employees that strike behavior would not be tolerated.

Bibliography

Alter, Jonathan. "Featherbedding in the Tower: How the Controllers Let the Cat Out of the Bag." *The Washington Monthly* 13 (October, 1981): 22-27. Contends that PATCO's air traffic controllers were actually over-staffed and that the union was "featherbedding" members in the towers, keeping employment unnecessarily high. Alter discloses that before the strike, nineteen thousand controllers and supervisors handled air traffic. After the strike began, nine thousand workers handled 75 percent of normal traffic.

Kilpatrick, James J. "They Struck a Blow for Tyranny." *National Review* 33 (October 2, 1981): 1132-1137. Discusses the PATCO strike and its blatant violation of federal law. He acknowledges that the strike caused financial losses but notes that it may also have resulted in gains beyond the price in awakening the nation to the perils of public employee unionism.

Magnuson, Ed. "The Skies Grow Friendlier." *Time* 118 (August 24, 1981): 14-16. Discusses the chronology of events following the PATCO strike on August 3, 1981. Emphasizes President Reagan's firm reaction to the strike and the imposed firing of striking controllers. Also explains how the FAA was able to maintain air traffic control at ever-increasing levels.

_____. "Turbulence in the Tower." *Time* 118 (August 17, 1981): 14-21. Discusses the initial impact of PATCO's job walkout across the country and the FAA's emergency procedures implemented to maintain air traffic control in the initial hours of the strike.

Meadows, Edward. "The FAA Keeps Them Flying." *Fortune* 104 (December 28, 1981): 48-52. Discusses the FAA's reaction to the PATCO strike. The article discusses regulations implemented to handle diminished air traffic with fewer controllers as well as the plans for replacing PATCO members who were fired because of their strike participation.

Morganthau, Tom. "Who Controls the Air?" *Newsweek* 98 (August 17, 1981): 18-24. Provides an excellent summary of the events leading up to the PATCO strike against the FAA. Also discusses the FAA's emergency response to the strike as well as the Reagan Administration's immediate and severe reaction to the striking controllers.

Nagy, David. "How Safe Are Our Airways?" *U.S. News and World Report* 91 (August 24, 1981): 14-17. Provides an excellent chronology of the PATCO strike. Explains in detail why the PATCO strike had little chance of success.

Nordlund, Willis J. *Silent Skies: The Air Traffic Controllers' Strike.* Westport, Conn.: Praeger, 1998.

Shostak, Arthur, and David Skocik. *The Air Controllers' Controversy.* New York: Human Sciences Press, 1986. Shostak, a union researcher and consultant, and Skocik, a fired PATCO member, provide an extremely detailed account of the PATCO strike. Although at times biased, the book provides excellent insight into the birth, growth, and final demise of PATCO.

John L. Farbo

Cross-References

The DC-3 Opens a New Era of Commercial Air Travel (1936); Amtrak Takes Over Most U.S. Intercity Train Traffic (1970); Carter Signs the Airline Deregulation Act (1978).

IBM INTRODUCES ITS PERSONAL COMPUTER

CATEGORY OF EVENT: New products
TIME: August 12, 1981
LOCALE: Armonk, New York

After other companies had pioneered in the production and sale of personal computers, IBM entered the product area in 1981 and for a while seemed likely to dominate the field

Principal personages:
PHILIP DON ESTRIDGE (1938-1985), the IBM executive in charge of the company's personal computer strategy and production
FRANK CARY (1920-), a chairman and chief executive officer of IBM
STEVEN JOBS (1955-), a cofounder of Apple Computer
JOHN AKERS (1934-), the chairman of IBM who presided over the decline of the IBM PC program

Summary of Event

The computer revolution, which began shortly after the end of World War II, seemed to have reached a state of maturity by the late 1960's. At that time, International Business Machines (IBM) dominated the field, producing large machines called mainframes used primarily by government agencies and major corporations. IBM's chief rivals in the mainframe business were Burroughs, Univac, National Cash Register, Control Data, Honeywell, Radio Corporation of America, and General Electric. On the horizon were such significant Japanese companies as NEC, Fujitsu, and Hitachi. The industry's attention was concentrated on IBM, its rivals, and mainframes.

A small number of hobbyists became interested in much smaller machines. These could be assembled from parts and were inexpensive enough to be used by individuals rather than corporations and government agencies. The movement toward smaller machines began in 1971 with Marcian Edward "Ted" Hoff, Jr., who worked at Intel, an electronics manufacturer. Hoff designed and then created the first microprocessor, or computer on a chip. The 4004 was little more than a curiosity, but even then Hoff knew that it could become the heart of a small computer.

Ted Hoff holds one of the computer chips he invented while with Intel in 1971. (Intel Corporation)

Scientists at the small, New Mexico-based electronics firm of Instrument Telemetry Systems had the same realization. In 1975, they created the Altair, a $400 kit from which could be assembled a small computer that contained the 8080 microprocessor. Peripheral equipment costing about $2,000 would allow a hobbyist to assemble a complete small computer.

Other kits followed, most sold from small stores catering to hobbyists.

The market for small computers then developed through other channels. In the late 1970's, Commodore International came out with the PET, a pre-assembled computer. Heath offered computer equipment through catalogs, and Radio Shack, a chain store, offered the TRS-80 computer, which sold for $499.

The real breakthrough, however, came from another firm, Apple Computer. Founders Steven Jobs and Stephen Wozniak had produced the Apple I, a relatively weak machine, and then went on to create the Apple II, which was demonstrated at the West Coast Computer Fair in 1977. Apple took orders for the small machine and was surprised by the demand. The company grew rapidly, achieving $2.5 million in revenues in 1977, then $117 million in 1980. Other companies also made their mark, among them Kaypro and Osborne. By the late 1970's, it appeared that the small computer was an established part of the market.

Observing all of this was IBM Chairman Frank Cary, who was in the midst of revamping the corporation by attempting to shed its traditional, slow-moving, bureaucratic structure. Those efforts had met with limited success, but Cary had introduced an element of flexibility into the firm. The key was the restructuring of the General Systems Division. Important new facilities were created far from the Atlanta, Georgia, headquarters. By the end of the 1970's, installations in Boulder, Colorado, and San Jose, California, were filled with bearded, sandaled young men who were far different from what the public had come to expect from IBM.

Cary selected Philip Don Estridge, a middle manager, to head a team that would create a small computer that would be IBM's entry into the product area. Estridge and his associates were based in a ramshackle building in Boca Raton, Florida. Cary ordered that Estridge was to work undisturbed by the IBM bureaucracy. Estridge and his team created the PC, which was designed to run on the DOS (Disk Operating System) that Bill Gates of Microsoft had purchased for $75,000.

The computer, known as the IBM PC, was introduced on August 12, 1981. It was an instant hit; IBM could not produce enough of the product to keep up with demand. Unlike Apple, IBM did not insist on retaining patent or other rights to software. This meant that Microsoft, Lotus, and other vendors were free to offer it to other PC manufacturers. Nor did IBM attempt to prevent Intel, which provided the PC's chips, from dealing with rivals. The approach all but ensured that the IBM machines would become the standard for the industry and that "clone" manufacturers would proliferate. Soon came the creation of Compaq, Columbia, Corona, Dell, and many more manufacturers producing machines intended to emulate the IBM PC. Wang came out with a dedicated word processor that soon became the class of the industry. In time, Japanese, Korean, Dutch, and British computers came to market as well.

Even so, in the beginning IBM led the pack, primarily because of the company's financial clout and reputation. In the early 1980's, most computer purchasers had little notion of the machines' capabilities or even the names of the clone manufacturers. They had heard of IBM, one of the most honored and trusted nameplates in the business machines market. They purchased the IBM PC, even though it cost more than the others, because of that reputation.

The PC was a huge success, far greater than IBM anticipated it would be. At the time, IBM sold or leased about 2,500 mainframes a year. The company sold about 200,000 PCs in the first year that the product was on the market. Soon the company was selling that many a month. The profit

The original IBM PC/XT computer. (International Business Machines Corporation)

margins were lower than for mainframes, but the returns were still gratifying.

Estridge did not rest on his laurels. One of the few people at IBM who had a thorough knowledge of the personal computer industry and who recognized that rapid change would be the rule, he appreciated that the PC soon would become obsolete. He rushed the introduction of the XT, with a hard disk, and then the PC AT (advanced technology), a faster machine. These products were released in 1983. The XT and AT duplicated the original PC's success. By then, IBM had 75 percent of the personal computer business.

Impact of Event

It was then that the company took the first of several missteps. Aiming at a home market for computers that did not develop until the late 1980's, it released the IBM PCjr in 1983. IBM was fearful of cutting into the XT market and so designed the new machine with low power and a smaller keyboard. It was unable to run the Lotus 1-2-3 spreadsheet, one of the most popular programs of the period, and customers complained that the keyboard was difficult to use.

Expected sales failed to materialize, and within months it was clear that IBM had stumbled badly. The company cut prices, added features, offered to replace keyboards on previously purchased machines, and stepped up advertising. Nothing worked. In 1985, IBM announced that the PCjr would "fulfill its manufacturing schedules," meaning that it would be killed. By then, Estridge was more involved in IBM's internal politics and in the process of being edged out of the operation. In 1985, he died in an airplane crash, and others took over the PC operation.

Other blunders followed. In 1982, Compaq had come out with a transportable personal computer. Although it was the size and weight of a suitcase, it could be carried from place to place. It was not the first portable computer, but the Kaypro best-seller was not IBM-compatible, as it used the CP/M system. IBM followed Compaq's lead, but its product was a disaster. By the time IBM produced an acceptable transportable computer, the public demanded laptop computers. After further stumbles, IBM produced an acceptable laptop, but by that time the public wanted even smaller notebook computers. It was not until the 1990's that IBM turned out acceptable versions, but by then its cachet had been lost.

Early on, Bill Gates had realized that PCs were only vehicles to run software; software would become the paramount consideration for users. In contrast, IBM thought that the machine itself was central to the sale. Gates knew that in time PC users would educate themselves about software applications and not require the kind of technical support IBM had provided for mainframe users. IBM talked of the nation becoming computer literate; Gates knew that the trick was to make software so simple such literacy would not be required.

Steven Jobs of Apple also had that insight. Even IBM could not provide all the technical support that some users would desire; the trick was to build technical support into the software and make it as simple to use as possible. Given its history and traditions, IBM was unable to accept this truism. Steve Armstrong, a key player in the IBM PC business, noted that the IBM philosophy was that prevailing in PCs would be no different from prevailing in the rest of the computer business.

That philosophy was the basis of many of IBM's problems. The company was comfortable dealing with mainframes and their users, but customers were being drawn to simpler programs and smaller machines. Corporate clients would spend millions of dollars on IBM equipment because, as the saying went, "No one ever got fired for using IBM." Years later, some writers would reveal the IBM "golden screwdriver," a good example of the company's arrogance. A customer would be sold a computer, but IBM would ship a machine twice as powerful as the one requested, with a few lines of software added to block some of its capabilities. Then, when the customer invariably required a faster machine with more memory, an IBM technician would arrive and, with the golden screwdriver, erase the redundant software and make a few other changes. Soon after, the customer would receive a large bill for the improvements.

In the early 1980's, IBM seemed to believe that its magic initials on a machine were worth hundreds or thousands of dollars to writers, students, office managers, and other potential purchasers of PCs. At first, IBM's reputation did carry the market, but consumers proved to be more informed and perceptive buyers than were corporate purchasing agents who, after all, were not spending their own money. They wanted value, so they learned to shun high-priced IBM PCs and opt for machines from young companies such as Apple and Kaypro, then later Dell, Compaq, and other "clone" manufacturers. Steve Wozniak, an Apple cofounder, once told a reporter that Apple was successful because he and Jobs had never manufactured computers before and so were not encumbered by the kind of ideology that blinded IBM.

IBM failed to take advantage of several opportunities. It could have controlled Microsoft, which would have died without IBM's early patronage. As late as 1986, Gates was willing to sell IBM a major interest in his company. IBM had taken a 20 percent stake in Intel in 1983 and could have expanded that share at will to 30 percent or perhaps more. Lotus and Borland, two software manufacturers, would have gone nowhere without

IBM's patronage; they too would have sold out to IBM. After dismissal of an antitrust action against IBM in 1981 and given the probusiness stance of the government at the time, IBM might have made these acquisitions with ease and might have been able to maintain control in the computer market. The 1980's were cluttered with IBM's lost opportunities.

Much of IBM's failure resulted from a lack of vision. Cary's successor, John Opel, was the quintessential company man. John Akers followed Opel and resigned in disgrace in 1993. Under Akers, IBM instituted a large-scale layoff program, cut spending and stock dividends, and showed signs of revival in the PC area. By the time Akers left, to be succeeded by Louis Gerstner, the first outsider to head the company, its personal computers and notebook computers were as good as rivals' machines and priced competitively. IBM remained the industry's leading company, but the old mystique was gone, possibly forever. The mystique was killed not by Japanese competitors in mainframes, where the challenge seemed to be at the beginning of the 1980's, but by scores of much smaller American competitors, software companies, and chip manufacturers that became the major forces in this stage of the computer revolution.

Unwilling to give up on what was the industry's fastest-growing segment, in 1990 IBM released the PS/1 line of computers. These quickly gained the reputation of being underpowered and overpriced. The line limped along until early 1993, when IBM gave the division more independence. Now free to experiment and innovate, engineers revamped the PS/1s, and prices were slashed. Sales increased by more than 300 percent within half a year, offering hope that the IBM mystique would return.

Bibliography

Carroll, Paul. *Big Blues: The Unmaking of IBM*. New York: Crown, 1993. Carroll covered the IBM story for *The Wall Street Journal* and based this book on his observations and interviews with IBM rivals, particularly those at Microsoft. The best book on the subject of how IBM's culture weakened it in the struggle for domination of the industry.

Chposky, James, and Ted Leonsis. *Blue Magic: The People, Power, and Politics Behind the IBM Personal Computer*. New York: Facts on File, 1988. A good chronological study of the making and unmaking of the personal computer project at IBM. A good introduction to the subject.

DeLamarter, Richard. *Big Blue: IBM's Use and Abuse of Power*. New York: Dodd, Mead, 1986. Written before IBM's failures were well known. DeLamarter was convinced that IBM had the power to crush all rivals. This book offers insights into how students of the industry misread the signs of failure.

McKenna, Regis. *Who's Afraid of Big Blue?* Reading, Mass.: Addison-Wesley, 1989. McKenna was one of the first to realize the weaknesses in IBM's strategies regarding the personal computer. Somewhat dated, but useful.

Manes, Stephen, and Paul Andrews. *Gates: How Microsoft's Mogul Reinvented an Industry.* New York: Doubleday, 1993. A study of Bill Gates of Microsoft, with an explanation of why the personal computer industry demanded strategy and tactics different from those used by IBM in gaining the lion's share of the mainframe market.

Moritz, Michael. *The Little Kingdom: The Private Story of Apple Computer.* New York: Morrow, 1984. An early history of Apple Computer. Describes in detail Steve Jobs's view of the personal computer, different from IBM's.

Pugh, Emerson W. *Building IBM: Shaping an Industry and Its Technology.* Cambridge, Mass.: MIT Press, 1995. Useful history, both as a case study of IBM and as an overview of the computer industry generally. Contains an extensive bibliography and an index.

Rodgers, F. G. *The IBM Way: Insights into the World's Most Successful Marketing Organization.* New York: Harper & Row, 1986. Rodgers was a longtime IBM executive, mostly in sales and promotion. In this book, he attempts to explain IBM's success. Careful readers will realize that he is also explaining weaknesses that would surface in the computer wars.

Rose, Frank. *West of Eden: The End of Innocence at Apple Computer.* New York: Viking, 1989. A detailed account of the computer wars, told from the Apple point of view. An update of the Moritz book, showing how Apple made a series of errors in the fight with IBM.

Slater, Robert. *Saving Big Blue: Leadership Lessons and Turnaround Tactics of IBM's Lou Gerstner.* New York: McGraw-Hill, 1999.

Robert Sobel

Cross-References

IBM Changes Its Name and Product Line (1924); Jobs and Wozniak Found Apple Computer (1976); Electronic Technology Creates the Possibility of Telecommuting (1980's); *Time* magazine Makes an E-commerce Pioneer Its Person of the Year (1999); Dow Jones Adds Microsoft and Intel (1999); The Y2K Crisis Finally Arrives (2000).

AT&T AGREES TO BE BROKEN UP AS PART OF AN ANTITRUST SETTLEMENT

CATEGORY OF EVENT: Monopolies and cartels
TIME: January 8, 1982
LOCALE: Washington, D.C.

An agreement between AT&T and the federal government brought competition to long distance telecommunications and freed AT&T from government regulations concerning its expansion into new areas of business

Principal personages:
WILLIAM SAXBE (1916-   ), a former senator from Ohio, responsible for filing the suit against AT&T
WILLIAM F. BAXTER (1929-1998), the assistant attorney general in charge of the antitrust division of the Justice Department
HAROLD H. GREENE (1923-   ), a judge on the U.S. District Court for the District of Columbia who watched over all aspects of the agreement
WILLIAM J. MCGOWEN (1927-   ), a venture capitalist and early investor in MCI
CHARLES L. BROWN (1921-   ), the chief executive officer of AT&T, responsible for changing the company's course regarding the wisdom of divesting the operating companies

Summary of Event

On November 20, 1974, the U.S. Department of Justice filed suit against the American Telephone and Telegraph Company (AT&T), alleging that it had monopolized and attempted to monopolize various telecommunications markets. The suit asked that Western Electric, AT&T's manufacturing arm, be divested, along with some or all of the Bell Operating Companies (BOCs). Although some of the charges against AT&T had been made earlier and had been settled in a consent decree in 1956, they had become relevant again because of technological advances achieved in the 1960's and early 1970's, coupled with the appearance of a competitor, MCI Communications Corporation, in the business of supplying long distance telecommunications service.

MCI had begun as Microwave Communications, Incorporated, a small debt-laden company supplying communications services between Chicago and St. Louis. Soon thereafter, it had solicited and received a capital infusion from William J. McGowen, a venture capitalist. He soon insinuated himself into company leadership and used his position to attack the hitherto impregnable AT&T. The upstart company quickly expanded its horizons and despite its heavy debt load was able to make inroads into AT&T's monopoly position in the field of long distance communications.

Led by McGowen, MCI quickly became a scourge of "Ma Bell," filing antitrust suits alleging monopolization while at the same time attempting to extend its services to cover the most lucrative markets. This became known as "skimming the cream." As MCI's success became evident, other companies joined the fray. Regulated by the Federal Communications Commission (FCC), AT&T was unable to protect itself from such incursions. Its rates were set; it could not offer discounts in response to the lower charges of the new competitors.

At first, the progress of the government's antitrust case appeared to parallel that of the action against International Business Machines Corporation, as the health of the presiding judge, Joseph Waddy, steadily deteriorated. The situation quickly changed with the appointment of his replacement, activist Harold H. Greene, who was determined that there be no further unnecessary delays in reaching a settlement—preferably one that was court adjudicated. Scheduling the trial to begin on January 15, 1981, he allowed a brief window of time for appointees in the new administration of President Ronald Reagan to have input in attempting to work out a consent decree along lines suggested by the outgoing negotiators, led by Assistant Attorney General Sanford Litvack. When the two sides were unable to come to an agreement, the trial began.

The new assistant attorney general in charge of the antitrust division, William F. Baxter, was interested in reaching a settlement, but upon different grounds. Instead of seeking a piecemeal divestiture, he wanted to split the regulated parts of AT&T from those endeavors that were unregulated. That way, there would be no possibility of "cross-subsidization," in which the regulated portions might subsidize initiatives in the competitive arena. Any other type of solution would be punitive and, as he stated, "lacking in theory."

Within a surprisingly short period of time, the government and the telecommunications giant reached a consent agreement that included the divestiture of all the BOCs but not any manufacturing or research facilities. Further, the BOCs were to provide local, and not long distance, service. In return, the 1956 consent decree prohibition on AT&T against involvement in nontelecommunications endeavors was removed, allowing it to expand into the computer business. Although the agreement was framed as a modification of the 1956 decree, Judge Greene empowered himself to rule on subsequent changes. The agreement was reached on January 8, 1982, but Greene did not approve it until August, after some modifications had been made.

As a result of the agreement, AT&T was to divest itself of seven distinct corporate entities comprising all of its local operations throughout the United States. These companies and their areas of operation were Nynex Corporation, New York and New England; Bell Atlantic Corporation, New Jersey, Pennsylvania, Delaware, Maryland, Virginia, West Virginia, and the District of Columbia; BellSouth Corporation, Alabama, Florida, Georgia, Kentucky, Louisiana, Mississippi, North and South Carolina, and Tennessee; American Information Technologies Corporation (Ameritech), Illinois, Indiana, Michigan, Ohio, and Wisconsin; Southwestern Bell Corporation, Arkansas, Kansas, Missouri, Oklahoma, and Texas; U.S. West, Incorporated, Arizona, Colorado, Idaho, Iowa, Minnesota, Montana, Nebraska, New Mexico, North and South Dakota, Oregon, Utah, Washington, and Wyoming; and Pacific Telesis Group, California and Nevada. Some of these companies adopted names describing the location of their primary service interest; others were more imaginative and tried to project a forward-looking image. New York and New England Telephone added an "x" to the initial letters of its service area to become Nynex; "telesis" means intelligently managed progress.

Impact of Event

On January 1, 1984, AT&T ceased offering local service. The responsibility for this class of service was transferred to the successor companies listed above. AT&T continued to offer long distance service, but now consumers had choices of other long distance carriers. In addition to AT&T, entities such as MCI, Sprint, and Rochester Telephone offered long distance service. Each user had the option of choosing a primary long distance provider. No one picking up a telephone receiver would have been able to detect any difference in service. Not every area was directly affected. Other independent operating companies, such as General Telephone and Electronics, Rochester Telephone, and independent Bell companies, continued to serve their territories as before. Their customers would shortly gain similar opportunities to choose among long distance carriers.

When AT&T was providing all services, costs were not equally apportioned. Long distance service had subsidized local service, and benefits to consumers such as information operators had been supported by cash-generating sources. With the advent of competition in the long distance market, it was no longer possible to cross-subsidize other services. Everything had to be on a pay-as-you-go basis; the cost of local calls therefore rose relative to other charges. Ironically, the government decree precluded AT&T from continuing a progressive rate structure. Low-income people place more local calls relative to long distance than do high-income people, and as a result their expenditures rose while those of the more wealthy declined as competition among providers forced long distance rates to fall.

There were minor growing pains as the seven divested companies were forced to work out various unexpected complications. Nevertheless, compared to some of the difficulties experienced in the late 1970's by AT&T, and especially taking into account the immensity of the reorganization of the entire telecommunications system, the troubles were small and quickly overcome. Each of the BOCs quickly set out to establish its own identity by concentrating on certain areas. Several became involved in cable television, and all came to have interests in cellular telephony. They were enjoined, however, from such activities within the geographic area of their regulated endeavors. Some of the BOCs invested in foreign telecommunications systems. Bell Atlantic, BellSouth, and Pacific Telesis established office equipment sales and leasing subsidiaries. Of all the BOCs, Southwestern Bell expanded the most broadly. It bought an interest in a local professional basketball team, the San Antonio Spurs, and also became deeply involved in publishing, attempting to expand upon its highly profitable Yellow Pages franchise. All the BOCs began to seek ways to escape from some of the strictures imposed on them by the settlement. Pacific Telesis has been the most innovative, planning to split itself into two separate parts, replicating the philosophy behind the 1982 agreement. Many of the unregulated tasks would be transferred to the new entity, while the regulated operations would remain with the slimmed down operating company.

Perhaps the biggest corporate change took place at AT&T. Freed from the shackles of the 1956 decree, it was able to expand into all aspects of the computer industry. Not only did it begin the manufacture of computers themselves, but it also became involved in software and network design.

Despite the intensity of its efforts, however, the company was not able to become the market force that it wished until its daring takeover of NCR Corporation, a leader in the industry. Early results indicated that the amalgamation was a success. As the telecommunication needs of the United States and the rest of the world become more sophisticated, technology involving computers will be inexorably involved, making the NCR takeover appear to be a logical move.

The changes in corporate structure since the breakup were matched by the variety of options offered to telephone users. Vigorous competition occurred in pricing and services. Each of the long distance providers endeavored to persuade callers to use its system. They resorted to various pricing strategies, heavy advertising, and various incentives in the struggle. This price and service competition benefited consumers. On the negative side, many consumers complained of being switched to new companies against their will. Overzealous salespeople were found to be making unauthorized service changes.

The evolution of the telecommunications industry is by no means complete. Competition may emerge on the local level as technology makes it possible to bypass the local service provider. In this scenario, local "MCI-like" companies would compete for local service in specific areas. As of 1993, one of the independents, Rochester Telephone, already had decided to split itself into two parts so as to be able to benefit from this possibility. It was likely that at least one of the BOCs would follow suit. The Pacific Telesis plan may well be amended to achieve this end. In the field of cellular communications, it is very easy to bypass the local BOC. AT&T acquired a large stake in McCaw Cellular, a leading provider of this type of service. Almost immediately, the BOCs protested that the transaction violated the 1982 agreement, which precluded AT&T's involvement in local service. The telecommunications industry is still growing and evolving. It is impossible to predict the direction that the industry will take, but it is clear that the breakup of AT&T and emergence of competitors set the stage for service far different from and much more flexible than that offered prior to the breakup.

Bibliography

Allen, Robert E. *When the Whole Becomes Less than the Sum of Its Parts: The Story Behind the AT&T Breakup.* St. Louis, Mo.: Center for the Study of American Business, Washington University, 1996. Brief paper on the effects of the breakup of AT&T.

Coll, Steve. *The Deal of the Century: The Breakup of AT&T.* New York: Atheneum, 1986. A popularly oriented—bordering on the sensational—treatment of the story.

Henck, Fred W., and Bernard Strassburg. *A Slippery Slope: The Long Road to the Breakup of AT&T.* Westport, Conn.: Greenwood Press, 1988. Offers a very good treatment of the activities of the various regulatory bodies prior to the breakup.

Kahaner, Larry. *On the Line: The Men of MCI—Who Took on AT&T, Risked Everything, and Won!* New York: Warner Books, 1986. A good popular history that provides a fine treatment of the early years of MCI.

Kovaleff, Theodore P. "For Whom Did the Bell Toll? A Review of Recent Treatments of the American Telephone and Telegraph Divestiture." *The Antitrust Bulletin* 34 (Spring, 1989): 437-450. A bibliographical essay on the subject.

Krauss, Constantine Raymond, and Alfred W. Duerig. *The Rape of Ma Bell: The Criminal Wrecking of the Best Telephone System in the World.* Secaucus, N.J.: Lyle Stuart, 1988. A poorly written and extremely partisan treatment of the topic.

Peritz, Rudolph J., Jr. *Competition Policy in America, 1888-1992: History, Rhetoric, Law.* New York: Oxford University Press, 1996. History of federal government policies relating to antitrust issues. Includes a substantial bibliography and index.

Stone, Alan. *Wrong Number: The Breakup of AT&T.* New York: Basic Books, 1989. An attempt to explain the rationale for breaking up the company. Stone gives good insights into the intricacies of regulatory politics.

Temin, Peter, and Louis Galambos. *The Fall of the Bell System: A Study in Prices and Politics.* New York: Cambridge University Press, 1987. The definitive work on the background to the AT&T breakup.

Theodore P. Kovaleff

Cross-References

Congress Passes the Clayton Antitrust Act (1914); Congress Establishes the Federal Communications Commission (1934); AT&T and GTE Install Fiber-Optic Telephone Systems (1977); Federal Court Rules That Microsoft Should Be Split into Two Companies (2000).

COMPACT DISCS REACH THE MARKET

CATEGORY OF EVENT: New products
TIME: 1983
LOCALE: Worldwide

The introduction of the compact disc opened a new era in sound recording and revitalized the recording industry

Principal personages:
AKIO MORITA (1921-1999), a Japanese physicist and engineer who was a cofounder of Sony
WISSE DEKKER (1924-   ), a Dutch businessman who led the Philips company
W. R. BENNETT (1904-1983), an American engineer who was a pioneer in digital communications and who played an important part in the Bell Laboratories research program

Summary of Event
The digital system of sound recording, like the analog methods that preceded it, was developed by the telephone companies to improve the quality and speed of telephone transmissions. The system of electrical recording introduced by Bell Laboratories in the 1920's was part of this effort. Even Edison's famous invention of the phonograph in 1877 was originally conceived as an accompaniment to the telephone. Although developed within the framework of telephone communications, these innovations found wide application in the entertainment industry.

The basis of the digital recording was a technique of sampling the electrical waveforms of sound called PCM, or Pulse Code Modulation. PCM measures the characteristics of these waves and converts them into numbers. This technique was developed at Bell Laboratories in the 1930's to transmit speech. At the end of World War II, engineers of the Bell System began to adapt PCM technology for ordinary telephone communications. The problem of turning sound waves into numbers was that of finding a method that could quickly and reliably manipulate millions of them. The answer to this problem was found in electronic computers, which used binary code to handle millions of computations in a few seconds. The rapid advance of computer technology and the semiconductor circuits that gave computers the power to handle complex calculations provided the means to bring digital sound technology into commercial use. In the 1960's, digital transmission and switching systems were introduced to the telephone network.

Pulse coded modulation of audio signals into digital code achieved standards of reproduction that exceeded even the best analog system, creating an enormous dynamic range of sounds with no distortion or background noise. The importance of digital recording went beyond the transmission of sound because it could be applied to all types of magnetic recording in which the source signal is transformed into an electric current. There were numerous commercial applications for such a system, and several companies began to explore the possibilities of digital recording in the 1970's.

Researchers at the Sony, Matsushita, and Mitsubishi electronics companies in Japan produced experimental digital recording systems. Each developed its own PCM processor, an integrated circuit that changes audio signals into digital code. It does not continuously transform sound but instead samples it by analyzing thousands of minute slices of it per second. Sony's PCM-F1 was the first analog-to-digital conversion chip to be produced. This gave Sony a lead in the research into and development of digital recording.

All three companies had strong interests in both audio and video electronics equipment and saw digital recording as a key technology because it could deal with both types of information simultaneously. They devised recorders for use in their manufacturing operations. After using PCM techniques to turn sound into digital code, they recorded this information onto tape, using not magnetic audio tape but the more advanced video tape, which could handle much more information. The experiments with digital recording occurred simultaneously with the accelerated development of video recording technology and owed much to the enhanced capabilities of video recorders. At this time, videocassette recorders were being developed in several corporate laboratories in Japan and Europe. The Sony Corporation was one of the companies developing video recorders at this time. Its U-matic machines were successfully used to record digitally. In 1972, the

741

Nippon Columbia Company began to make its master recordings digitally on an Ampex video recording machine.

There were powerful links between the new sound recording systems and the emerging technologies of storing and retrieving video images. The television had proved to be the most widely used and profitable electronic product of the 1950's, but with the market for color television saturated by the end of the 1960's, manufacturers had to look for a replacement product. A machine to save and replay television images was seen as the ideal companion to the family TV set. The great consumer electronics companies—General Electric and RCA in the United States, Philips and Telefunken in Europe, and Sony and Matsushita in Japan—began experimental programs to find a way to save video images.

RCA's experimental teams took the lead in developing an optical videodisc system, called Selectavision, that used an electronic stylus to read changes in capacitance on the disc. The greatest challenge to them came from the Philips company of Holland. Its optical videodisc used a laser beam to read information on a revolving disc, in which a layer of plastic contained coded information. With the aid of the engineering department of the Deutsche Grammophon record company, Philips had an experimental laser disc in hand by 1964.

The Philips Laservison videodisc was not a commercial success, but it carried forward an important idea. The research and engineering work carried out in the laboratories at Eindhoven in Holland proved that the laser reader could do the job. More important, Philips engineers had found that this fragile device could be mass produced as a cheap and reliable component of a commercial product. The laser optical decoder was applied to reading the binary codes of digital sound. By the end of the 1970's, Philips engineers had produced a working system.

Ten years of experimental work on the Laservision system proved to be a valuable investment for the Philips Corporation. Around 1979, it started to work on a digital audio disc (DAD) playback system. This involved more than the basic idea of converting the output of the PCM conversion chip onto a disc. The lines of pits on the compact disc carry a great amount of information: the left- and right-hand tracks of the stereo system are identified, and a sequence of pits also controls the motor speed and corrects any error in the laser reading of the binary codes.

This research was carried out jointly with the Sony Corporation of Japan, which had produced a superior method of encoding digital sound with its PCM chips. The binary codes that carried the information were manipulated by Sony's sixteen-bit microprocessor. Its PCM chip for analog-to-digital conversion was also employed. Together, Philips and Sony produced a commercial digital playback record that they named the compact disc. The name is significant, as it does more than indicate the size of the disc—it indicates family ties with the highly successful compact cassette. Philips and Sony had already worked to establish this standard in the magnetic tape format and aimed to make their compact disc the standard for digital sound reproduction.

Philips and Sony began to demonstrate their compact digital disc (CD) system to representatives of the audio industry in 1981. They were not alone in digital recording. The Japanese Victor Company, a subsidiary of Matsushita, had developed a version of digital recording from its VHD video disc design. It was called Audio High Density Disc (AHD). Instead of the small CD disc, the AHD system used a ten-inch vinyl disc. Each digital recording system used a different PCM chip with a different rate of sampling the audio signal.

The recording and electronics industries' decision to standardize on the Philips/Sony CD system was therefore a major victory for these companies and an important event in the digital era of sound recording. Sony had found out the hard way that the technical performance of an innovation is irrelevant when compared with the politics of turning it into an industrywide standard. Although the pioneer in videocassette recorders, Sony had been beaten by its rival, Matsushita, in establishing the video recording standard. This mistake was not repeated in the digital standards negotiations, and many companies were convinced to license the new technology. In 1982, the technology was announced to the public. The following year, the compact disc was on the market.

Impact of Event

The compact disc represented the apex of recorded sound technology. Simply put, here at last was a system of recording in which there was no extraneous noise—no surface noise of scratches and pops, no tape hiss, no background hum—and no damage was done to the recording as it was played. In principle, a digital recording will last forever, and each play will sound as pure as the first. The compact disc could also play much longer than the vinyl record or long-playing cassette tape.

Despite these obvious technical advantages, the commercial success of digital recording was not ensured. Several other advanced systems had not fared well in the marketplace, and the conspicuous failure of quadrophonic sound in the 1970's had not been forgotten within the industry of recorded sound. Historically, there were two key factors in the rapid acceptance of a new system of sound recording and reproduction: a library of prerecorded music to tempt the listener into adopting the system and a continual decrease in the price of the playing units to bring them within the budgets of more buyers.

By 1984, about a thousand titles were available on compact disc in the United States; that number had doubled by 1985. Although many of these selections were classical music—it was naturally assumed that audiophiles would be the first to buy digital equipment—popular music was well represented. The first CD available for purchase was an album by popular entertainer Billy Joel.

The first CD-playing units cost more than $1,000, but Akio Morita of Sony was determined that the company would reduce the price of players even if it meant selling them below cost. Sony's audio engineering department improved the performance of the players while reducing size and cost. By 1984, Sony had a small CD unit on the market for $300. Several of Sony's competitors, including Matsushita, had followed its lead into digital reproduction. Several compact disc players were available in 1985 for less than $500. Sony quickly applied digital technology to the popular personal stereo and to automobile sound systems. Sales of CD units increased roughly tenfold from 1983 to 1985.

When the compact disc was announced in 1982, the vinyl record was the leading form of recorded sound, with 273 million units sold annually compared to 125 million prerecorded cassette tapes. The compact disc sold slowly, beginning with 800,000 units shipped in 1983 and rising to 53

Among the important products made possible by compact disc technology are CD-ROM drives that enable computer users to access large volumes of program software, sound and image files, and other information from compact and inexpensive disks. (PhotoDisc)

million in 1986. By that time, the cassette tape had taken the lead, with slightly fewer than 350 million units. The vinyl record was in decline, with only about 110 million units shipped. Compact discs first outsold vinyl records in 1988. In the ten years from 1979 to 1988, the sales of vinyl records dropped nearly 80 percent. In 1989, CDs accounted for more than 286 million sales, but cassettes still led the field with total sales of 446 million. The compact disc finally passed the cassette in total sales in 1992, when more than 300 million CDs were shipped, an increase of 22 percent over the figure for 1991.

The introduction of digital recording had an invigorating effect on the recorded sound industry, which had been unable to fully recover from the slump of the late 1970's. Sales of recorded music had stagnated in the early 1980's, and an industry accustomed to steady increases in output became eager to find a new product or style of music to boost its sales. The compact disc was the product to revitalize the markets for both recordings and players. During the 1980's, worldwide sales of recorded music jumped from $12 billion to $22 billion, with about half of the sales volume accounted for by digital recordings by the end of the decade.

The success of digital recording served in the long run to undermine the commercial viability of the compact disc. This was a play-only technology, like the vinyl record before it. Once users had become accustomed to the pristine digital sound, they clamored for digital recording capability. The alliance of Sony and Philips broke down in the search for a digital tape technology for home use. Sony produced a digital tape system called DAT, while Philips responded with a digital version of its compact audio tape called DCC. Sony answered the challenge of DCC with its Mini Disc (MD) product, which can record and replay digitally.

The versatility of digital recording has opened up a wide range of consumer products. Compact disc technology has been incorporated into the computer, in which CD-ROM readers convert the digital code of the disc into sound and images. Many home computers have the capability to record and replay sound digitally. Digital recording is the basis for interactive audio/video computer programs in which the user can interface with recorded sound and images. Philips has established a strong foothold in interactive digital technology with its CD-I (compact disc interactive) system, which was introduced in 1990. This acts as a multimedia entertainer, providing sound, moving images, games, and interactive sound and image publications such as encyclopedias. The future of digital recording will be broad-based systems that can record and replay a wide variety of sounds and images and that can be manipulated by users of home computers.

Bibliography

AT&T Bell Laboratories. *A History of Engineering and Science in the Bell System: Communications Sciences (1925-1980)*. New York: Author, 1984. A thorough account of the early research in digital recording, from the viewpoint of Bell Laboratories. Although often highly technical, this is the most comprehensive account of the history of this technology.

Copeland, Peter. *Sound Recordings*. London: British Library, 1991. An up-to-date account of the development of sound recording technology. Covers the research into and introduction of digital recording. Written for the layperson, with some useful illustrations.

Graham, Margaret B. *RCA and the VideoDisc*. New York: Cambridge University Press, 1986. A scholarly account of the research into video digital technology, also covering the competition of several leading international companies and their race to develop a new line of electronics products.

Morita, Akio, Edwin Reingold, and Mitsuko Shimomura. *Made in Japan: Akio Morita and Sony*. New York: Dutton, 1986. A personal account of the history of the Sony Corporation from the end of World War II to the 1980's. Includes Morita's account of the development of digital recording.

Nathan, John. *Sony: The Private Life*. Boston: Houghton Mifflin, 1999. Study of the inner workings of the giant corporation.

Schlender, Brenton R. "How Sony Keeps the Magic Going." *Fortune* 125 (February 24, 1992): 81. An overview of the Sony Corporation, with an emphasis on its latest products based on digital technology. Provides information about the corporate culture and its style of research and development.

Andre Millard

Cross-References

IBM Introduces Its Personal Computer (1981); Sony Purchases Columbia Pictures (1989); Cable Television Rises to Challenge Network Television (mid-1990's); Dow Jones Adds Microsoft and Intel (1999).

FIREFIGHTERS V. STOTTS UPHOLDS SENIORITY SYSTEMS

CATEGORY OF EVENT: Labor
TIME: June 12, 1984
LOCALE: Memphis, Tennessee, and Washington, D.C.

The U.S. Supreme Court ruled that labor agreements could use seniority as a criterion for layoffs even when that use would oppose the goals of affirmative action programs

Principal personages:
CARL STOTTS, a black firefighting captain in Memphis
BYRON WHITE (1917-   ), the U.S. Supreme Court justice who delivered the decision
HARRY BLACKMUN (1908-1999), a dissenting Supreme Court justice
LYNDON B. JOHNSON (1908-1973), the U.S. president who urged passage of the 1964 Civil Rights Act
EMANUEL CELLER (1888-1981), a New York congressman who supported Title VII of the 1964 Civil Rights Act
EVERETT DIRKSEN (1896-1969), an Illinois senator who questioned provisions of the 1964 Civil Rights Act
POTTER STEWART (1915-1985), a Supreme Court justice who upheld seniority systems in a 1977 decision

Summary of Event

Reflecting broad public concerns and controversies about a gamut of civil liberties, a combination of liberals and conservatives in Congress, goaded by President Lyndon B. Johnson, fought for passage of the 1964 Civil Rights Act. Title VII of the act delineated a series of formal and informal remedial procedures designed to end employment discrimination based on race, color, religion, sex, or national origin. The objective of Title VII was to pave the way for equal employment opportunity for all Americans.

Ultimately, the constitutionality of the act's major sections would be tested by the U.S. Supreme Court as litigation relating to the act reached the Court on appeal or came to the justices for review. While Earl Warren was chief justice of the United States (1953-1969), the Court gave expansive interpretations to a wide range of civil liberties. The Court's decisions in these cases, as was frequently noted, often amounted to additional "legislation." In regard to labor law, decisions of the Warren Court were characterized by their focus on intergovernmental relationships. It found few occasions to define the rights of individuals in the workplace and no occasions to strike down employment discrimination based on sex.

Beginning in 1969, those two tasks were undertaken by the Court under Earl Warren's successor, Warren E. Burger, despite pundits' predictions that Burger would lead a conservative reaction in the field of civil rights. On the contrary, the Burger Court broke new ground in labor law by delineating the rights of individuals in the workplace, often in the light of provisions of the 1964 Civil Rights Act.

It was in this context that the case of *Firefighters Local Union No. 1784 v. Stotts et al.* came to argument before the Court on December 6, 1983. The case questioned the legality of using job seniority as a criterion for layoffs. As legal scholars noted, along with issues associated with affirmative action and so-called "reverse discrimination," seniority problems were among the most sensitive and bitterly contested in the realm of antidiscrimination legislation embodied in provisions of Title VII of the 1964 Civil Rights Act. Moreover, the American Federation of Labor-Congress of Industrial Organizations (AFL-CIO), which had played a major role in mustering political support for passage of the 1964 act, had battled consistently to preserve the integrity of seniority systems. Black workers, notoriously among those "last hired and first fired," however, perceived established seniority systems as additional racial roadblocks to their advancement and job security.

Carl Stotts, a black captain in the Memphis, Tennessee, fire department, joined others in a class action suit invoking Title VII of the 1964 Civil Rights Act. They alleged that city officials displayed a pattern of racial discrimination in their hiring and promotion practices in the fire department. Entering a consent decree with the courts, the city accordingly evinced its willingness to reform the department's hiring and promotion policies, but broader considerations intervened. Fiscal difficulties soon thereafter required a budget reduction that, in turn, meant employee layoffs.

At this juncture, a district court prohibited the city from following its seniority system in effecting the layoffs on grounds that proposed reductions would have a racially discriminatory effect. Modifications in the city's system thereafter resulted in the layoffs of white employees who had more seniority than black employees who were retained, in compliance with the district court's wishes.

The district court was following what it believed to be the direction confirmed by many lower court rulings, namely that established seniority systems must be struck down if they perpetuated the effects of past discrimination, regardless of whether these systems had been designed to discriminate intentionally. This line of ruling obviously contradicted the intent of Congress. In enacting the 1964 Civil Rights Act, Congress, under pressure from the AFL-CIO and other organizations, had made every effort to ensure that Title VII would in no way upset established seniority plans. Nevertheless, grudgingly and at considerable expense, unions and management thereafter were forced to comply with court rulings or face costly litigation.

In 1977, this situation was reversed by the Supreme Court's decision, drafted by Justice Potter Stewart, in *Teamsters v. United States.* Stewart, returning to what he believed to be the intent of Congress, declared that bona fide seniority plans, even if discriminatory in their past or present effects, were immunized by provisions of Title VII, specifically its Section 703(h).

Such was the situation when Justice Byron White delivered the heart of the *Firefighters* decision, namely, that the district court had erred in mandating that white employees be laid off by the City of Memphis when otherwise its established seniority system would have called for the layoff of black employees with less seniority. Justice White, noting the *Teamsters* ruling, declared that Section 703(h) permitted "the routine application of a seniority system absent proof of an intention to discriminate." Memphis had, in White's estimate, a bona fide seniority system before the district court ruled and the consent decree causing modification in the city's plan went into effect. Section 703(h) seemed clear enough to him in declaring it legal employment practice for an employer "to apply different standards of compensation, or different terms, conditions, or privileges of employment" in establishing or maintaining a "bona fide seniority or merit system," provided these differences were not the result of intentional discrimination based on race, color, sex, religion, or national origin.

Seniority systems had been cherished by labor because they provided objective standards for what otherwise might have been arbitrariness or favoritism on the part of management or unions in respect to job security.

The *Firefighters* decision reinforced seniority systems even if they adversely affected minority groups.

Impact of Event

The so-called "White Rule," announced by Justice Byron White in 1984, in practice meant that a bona fide seniority plan could not cause white workers to be laid off ahead of black workers with less seniority. This left Memphis' new affirmative action employees, all black, at the same risk of layoffs as all other workers. Thus affirmative action plans could prevent some whites from being hired, but they could not cause them to be fired. From the perspectives of black leaders and black workers, the rule perpetuated workplace policies that had placed them in the position of being the last hired and the first fired. It mattered little that such was not the intent of Justice White.

In 1986, although the specifics of the litigation differed from those in *Firefighters*, White cast a deciding vote reinforcing his views in *Wygant v. Jackson Board of Education*. A Jackson, Mississippi, school board and the Jackson Teachers Union had signed an agreement designed to prevent minority teachers hired under affirmative action plans from being laid off. The agreement stipulated that the minority teachers were to be protected even if tenured white teachers had to be laid off. White's ruling treated the results of the Jackson affirmative action plan as reverse discrimination. White teachers were being fired because of their race, and in his view no affirmative action scheme justified that result.

The decisions handed down by White and the Court's majority in conflicts arising between seniority plans and affirmative action policies from 1977 to 1986 represented an effort to reflect more accurately the intent of Congress in its enactment of the 1964 Civil Rights Act and the drafting of Title VII. Without directly overruling the Court's earlier decision in *Griggs v. Duke Power Company* (1971), a landmark adverse impact case that prohibited even unintentional discrimination, the Court had narrowed its interpretations of what constituted discrimination.

During the quarter century after passage of the 1964 Civil Rights Act, a number of important changes occurred in the business world, in organized labor, and in congressional attitudes. For example, caught between officially divergent interpretations of what constituted discrimination—that is, determinations of the will of Congress on one hand and Supreme Court decisions on the other—many of the nation's leading business interests and institutions receiving federal or state funds had begun implementing voluntary affirmative action plans. In some instances, these voluntary plans were structured around implicit "quotas" to be used in guiding minority hiring. Moreover, businesses' incentive to comply with nondiscriminatory practices was inspired less by fear of traditional collective bargaining with trade unions than it was by threats posed by potential suits filed by the Equal Employment Opportunity Commission (EEOC), by feminist groups, by civil rights organizations, by consumers' groups, and by the alleged victims of discrimination.

In addition, trade unionism of the traditional kind, which had fought for and won great gains for manufacturing and assembly line workers from the 1930's until the early 1950's, was dying. A new unionism was supplanting it. Because of rapid technological change and the diminishing importance of manufacturing in the American economy, the new unionism was heavily influenced by new breeds of workers. Among them were semiprofessional and white collar workers, who by 1980 accounted for more than half of the labor force, as well as rapidly expanding contingents of service workers. In addition, at the close of the 1980's more than half of all employees were women, most of whom were keenly aware of previous and present sex discrimination. Most semiprofessional and white collar workers were inclined to downplay the significance of seniority systems in regard to hiring, pay, promotions, retirement, and layoffs. Instead, in regard to these matters they favored the application of merit principles.

Structural and attitudinal changes such as these that developed through the 1970's and 1980's, as well as the direction taken by the Supreme Court between the *Griggs* decision and the ruling in *Firefighters*, led Congress to enact the Civil Rights Act of 1991. This new act followed the Court's ruling in *Ward's Cove Packing Co. v. Atonio* in 1989. The decision basically overruled *Griggs*, rejecting "business necessity" as the sole criterion justifying the maintenance of practices that had a disparate impact, that is, that were discriminatory. The Court lamented the fact that any employer with a racially imbalanced work force was likely to be hailed into court and forced to engage in costly and time-consuming defense of employment methods. Further, the Court recognized that the sole option available to employers was the adoption of racial quotas. In the spirit of the *Firefighters* decision, the Court held that constraining employers to move to this option was never intended by Congress in Title VII of the 1964 Civil Rights Act.

By 1991, congressional majorities viewed matters differently. Although the 1991 Civil Rights Act made no mention of quotas, it did nothing to curtail employer incentives to engage in race-conscious hiring; in fact, it encouraged the adoption of implicit quotas. The act of 1991 expanded the antidiscrimination interpretations of *Griggs* and broadened the scope of compensatory damages that could be collected by proven victims of discrimination. Employers could defend themselves against charges of discrimination by proving that their practices rested upon "business necessity."

Complainants bore the burden of proving that each particular challenged practice caused a disparate impact. The act likewise weakened the *Firefighters* decision by expanding rights to challenge discriminatory seniority systems. As Congress and the Supreme Court pursued different and often confusing paths in seeking to end discrimination with justice to all, some civil libertarians opined that civil rights acts had become the major threat to civil rights, while others denounced them for having achieved too little.

Bibliography

Epstein, Richard A. *Forbidden Grounds: The Case Against Employment Discrimination Laws.* Cambridge, Mass.: Harvard University Press, 1992. Scholarly evaluation of the substance and consequences of modern civil rights legislation and court decisions. Best in its field for a critical survey by a civil rights expert. Informative page notes, appendices, table of cases, extensive index.

Gould, William B. IV. *Agenda for Reform: The Future of Employment Relationships and the Law.* Cambridge, Mass.: MIT Press, 1993. Excellent, clear, and scholarly. Chapter 3 deals with the history of job security and seniority. Later chapters deal with racial and other forms of discrimination. Chapter 8 is a fine discussion of the 1991 Civil Rights Act, race, and discrimination.

Hacker, Andrew. *Two Nations: Black and White, Separate, Hostile, Unequal.* New York: Scribner's, 1992. A reflective, substantive analysis of the subject, including conflicts in the workplace over seniority and many other issues involved in discrimination. Offers a depressing picture, although critical balance is maintained.

Hall, Kermit L., ed. *The Oxford Guide to United States Supreme Court Decisions.* New York: Oxford University Press, 1999. Multiauthored collection of essays on more than four hundred significant Court decisions, with supporting glossary and other aids.

Heckscher, Charles C. *The New Unionism: Employee Involvement in the Changing Corporation.* New York: Basic Books, 1988. Extremely interesting and essential in taking account of changes in employee values, rights, organization, and relations with corporate employers.

McWhirter, Darien A. *Your Rights at Work.* New York: John Wiley & Sons, 1989. A crisp, reasonably accurate guide to civil rights as related to the workplace. Heavily based on court decisions. Well done, informative, and helpful.

Zimmer, Michael J. *Cases and Materials on Employment Discrimination.* 4th ed. New York: Aspen Law & Business, 1997.

Clifton K. Yearley

Cross-References

The Wagner Act Promotes Union Organization (1935); Roosevelt Signs the Fair Labor Standards Act (1938); The Taft-Hartley Act Passes over Truman's Veto (1947); The Civil Rights Act Prohibits Discrimination in Employment (1964); The Supreme Court Orders the End of Discrimination in Hiring, (1971); The Pregnancy Discrimination Act Extends Employment Rights (1978); The Supreme Court Rules on Affirmative Action Programs (1979); The Supreme Court Upholds Quotas as a Remedy for Discrimination (1986).

HOME SHOPPING SERVICE IS OFFERED ON CABLE TELEVISION

CATEGORY OF EVENT: Marketing
TIME: July 1, 1985
LOCALE: Clearwater, Florida

The Home Shopping Network offered television viewers the convenience of shopping from their own homes for a variety of products

Principal personages:
LOWELL W. "BUD" PAXSON (1935-   ), the founder and president of Home Shopping Network
ROY SPEER (1932-   ), the first chairman of Home Shopping Network
IRWIN JACOBS (1941-   ), the majority shareholder in COMB (Close-Out Merchandise Buyers)

Summary of Event

The advent of home shopping services was a watershed event in the history of marketing in the United States. The first such service at the national level was offered by Home Shopping Network (HSN) on July 1, 1985. The popularity of this concept has grown impressively since.

Lowell W. "Bud" Paxson, the founder and president of HSN, entered the business of home shopping almost by accident. As the owner of an AM radio station in Dunedin, a small town on the west coast of Florida, Paxson was faced with decreasing revenues at a time when popular stations were converting from AM to FM broadcast formats. One of Paxson's clients settled his advertising bills with some merchandise in lieu of money. Paxson attempted to sell this merchandise in a radio broadcast, at prices far below regular retail prices. Positive response from listeners helped this type of radio show evolve into a regular daily feature on Paxson's station. In a typical show, the sale merchandise was described, and interested customers would call the station later to conclude sales transactions.

Encouraged by the success of the radio shopping concept, Paxson extended it to cable television in July, 1982. Paxson's cable television channel 52, located in Clearwater, Florida, offered everything from $2 household items to expensive cruise vacations to viewers in two neighboring counties. This teleshopping service registered substantial growth. By the end of its third year, it was generating 190,000 orders a month from 130,000 members.

The success of this local-level television-based shopping approach encouraged Paxson to launch the national-level HSN, a live cablecast show that operated continuously. This show sold merchandise acquired in bulk from closeouts, bankruptcies, and liquidation sales. The strategy enabled HSN to use a value-based selling theme to attract customers by offering products at discounted prices. Initially, this cable network covered 462 multiple systems operators (MSOs) in the cable industry, representing five million homes. HSN paid 5 percent of sales generated to the MSOs as compensation for providing access to cable media.

At the outset, HSN employed ten on-air hosts, with each host working a shift of two to three hours. The host typically offered only one item for sale at a time and presented a persuasive sales pitch. Because shoppers did not have advance knowledge about when a particular product or type of product might be offered for sale, and because any product's sale offer was limited to the short interval (usually ten minutes) it was shown on television, home shopping was potentially an addictive experience for consumers in search of bargains. Viewers were encouraged to call a toll-free telephone number immediately to purchase the currently displayed item. First-time shoppers were given a $5 incentive to become members of the Home Shopping Club, which would assign them unique identification numbers on HSN's computer. These numbers facilitated quick subsequent sales transactions, circumventing the need for shoppers to convey detailed shipping instructions each time they shopped.

HSN's venture into cablecast shopping was very successful. In its first eight months of operation, HSN generated $63.9 million in revenues and $6.8 million in profits. These impressive results were well received by stock investors. When the company went public in May, 1986, at $18 a share, its stock rose almost immediately to $42 and stabilized in the following months around $75. Paxson and Richard Speer, chairman of HSN, owned most of the HSN stock.

For a variety of reasons, HSN achieved notable success in an area in which several earlier ventures had obtained less than spectacular results. First, unlike HSN, many of the shows launched in the 1980's operated for a relatively short duration. For example, the *Home Shopping Show* on Modern Satellite Network ran for a half hour, five times a week. Such shows failed to provide the "anytime shopping" convenience of HSN. Second, some of HSN's predecessors and local-level competitors did not sell merchandise at discount prices. Viewers may not have perceived any "value" advantage in such home shopping outlets. Third, HSN's format was the closest to interactive television-based shopping and facilitated objective information search on products. HSN shoppers could speak to the on-air host directly on the telephone and get ready answers to any specific product-related questions before making a purchase decision. A caller might ask the host, "What does the back of that belt look like?" and obtain an immediate audiovisual response on the television screen. In contrast, the only other teleshopping mode to offer anything approaching interactive at-home shopping was Cableshop, a joint venture of the Adams-Russell cable system and Soskin-Thompson Associates, a direct marketing subsidiary of the J. Walter Thompson advertising agency. Cableshop was a "video-on-demand" advertising service, as opposed to a live or scheduled shopping program. Shoppers first had to access a directory channel to choose specific advertising messages that interested them. They could later view these messages, specially prepared for the Cableshop service, after making a telephone request. A disadvantage was that viewers had to wait several minutes for a message to appear after making a request, a factor that could have discouraged extensive use of this home shopping service.

Finally, HSN aggressively sought to maintain shopper loyalty and interest with various promotional devices. These included sending anniversary and birthday cards to members of the Home Shopping Club, sweepstakes with attractive prizes, trivia contests, crossword puzzle games, and a magazine called *Bargaineer*. In addition, prizes were sometimes awarded without any prior announcement to make the program appear exciting and pleasantly unpredictable. Such efforts quickly led to a large base of loyal buyers who made an average of fifteen purchases in 1985.

Impact of Event

The success of HSN's entry into the cablecast shopping business rapidly stimulated further growth and competition in this new area. HSN launched an ambitious expansion program by acquiring several small broadcast stations. It also started a second network in March, 1986, called HSN II. It offered more upscale and more innovative items. The home shopping phenomenon also attracted some of the major firms in the cable industry.

For example, TeleCommunications Inc. (TCI, an MSO based in Denver) and Close-Out Merchandise Buyers (COMB, a Minnesota-based firm controlled by financier Irwin Jacobs) together launched the Cable Value Network (CVN), a national-level competitor to HSN. CVN positioned itself differently in the home shopping market. Unlike HSN, CVN telecasts involved more unusual items and included thematic shopping programs focusing on one type of merchandise at a given time. Similarly, Comp-U-Card and Financial News Network (FNN) together launched the Teleshop cable shopping program, which unlike CVN and HSN did not own the merchandise it offered for sale. This program merely facilitated sales of merchandise for the product sources it represented; the goods sold were shipped to consumers directly from the sources.

Since the advent of the Home Shopping Network, consumers have begun to order an ever-growing of array of products advertised on television. (PhotoDisc)

Will the growing popularity of cablecast shopping pitches carry negative implications for traditional retailers? Cable-based home shopping has the potential to expand impressively, and some of this growth may be at the expense of established retailers. The reasoning runs as follows: Cable shopping networks depend on discount prices (made possible by low procurement costs and relatively low overhead to create the perception of bargain shopping, which in turn should generate high sales volume; because the product's price is the basis of competition between such outlets and traditional retailers that charge full price for similar merchandise, the latter may risk losing business.

On the other hand, the reliance of cable shopping networks on opportunistic buying at deep discounts (from close-out sales, for example) could force them to sell an erratic supply of nonstandard merchandise. Because the products sold are not comparable to those sold by traditional retailers, the traditional retailers may remain relatively unaffected by the emergence of cable shopping networks. Further, an element of immediacy or time pressure surrounds purchase decisions on cable shopping networks; this characteristic, when combined with the lure of apparently attractive price discounts offered on such networks, may trigger impulse purchases unlikely to materialize in a traditional retail environment. Another argument is that home shopping is relatively new, and its success could be a passing fad.

The emergence of cable shopping networks has implications for consumer education and protection efforts. The United States Office of Consumer Affairs' *Draft Consumer Education Brochure on the Televised Shopping Industry in the United States* (1988) delineates several issues about cablecast shopping programs. Such programs often use a system of comparative pricing that appears deceptive. The offered price of a product is frequently compared with a baseline labeled the "retail" or "regular store" price. Cablecast programs offer merchandise that may not be available in typical stores, including "exclusive" lines, discontinued merchandise, and products from closeout sales. To the extent that such merchandise cannot realistically have a comparable retail price, the baseline "retail" or "regular" prices are misleading and deceptive. Other cost aspects of home shopping may be less than explicit. Many home shopping programs offer money-back protection to consumers wishing to return the merchandise purchased within a limited period, but it is sometimes unclear who bears the costs of return shipping in such cases. Attention to these and other consumer education and protection issues is likely to increase in the future as growth in penetration of cable technology substantially increases the number of households with access to cablecasts from shopping channels.

Television-based home shopping programs either exist at rudimentary levels or are nonexistent in most nations other than the United States. Although they were available in Japan and Germany in the early 1990's, no specific rules or laws concerning such programs existed in these countries. Canada had a significant teleshopping industry. The Canadian Home Shopping Network was the largest network in Canada in the early 1990's and served more than five million households, generating annual revenues of $40 million. Canada, however, lacked any direct regulations. In The Netherlands, no special rules applied to cablecast shopping programs if they reached other nations. A few other nations, including Denmark, Finland, and France, provided for a limited mandatory cooling-off period during which consumers could return goods purchased via home-shopping programs.

Cablecasts represent only one of several devices that provide home shopping convenience. Other devices include mail order sales (also called direct marketing), telemarketing (sales solicitation via telephone), and interactive videotex systems that integrate telephone, television, and computer technologies to enable consumer subscribers to retrieve data on products and services held in a central computer through a dialing device. The data are displayed on the consumer's television monitor. Mail ordering, and telemarketing have existed longer than has cable-based home shopping, and most countries have developed regulatory policies to protect consumer interests in these areas. Rules and regulations designed to protect the interests of cable shoppers had not fully evolved by the early 1990's even in the countries in which cablecast shopping had developed.

Bibliography

"Cable Shopping Channel Woos Viewers Via Direct Response." *Direct Marketing* 48 (June, 1985): 76-149. Presents an interview with Keith Halford, vice president of marketing for the Home Shopping Network. Discusses how the home shopping concept evolved from a radio show to local telecasting and later into a national cable network. Offers a detailed description of the day-to-day working of HSN's home shopping service.

Ciciora, Walter S., James Farmer, and David Large. *Modern Cable Television Technology: Video, Voice, and Data Communications.* San Francisco: Morgan Kaufmann Publishers, 1999.

Dagnoli, Judann. "Home Shopping Gets Push from Cable Systems." *Advertising Age* 57 (June 9, 1986): 64. Summarizes the competition scenario almost a year after HSN launched its cablecast home shopping service in the United States.

Ivey, Mark, and Patrick Houston. "Don't Touch That Dial—You Might Miss a Bargain." *Business Week*, June 2, 1986, 35-36. Discusses home shopping from the shopper's perspective, describing the range of products offered for sale and how such shows can become addictive.

Klokis, Holly. "Cable TV: A Retail Alternative?" *Chain Store Age Executive* 62 (August, 1986): 11-14. Analyzes how established retailers perceive and react to the home shopping phenomenon.

Organisation for Economic Co-Operation and Development. *New Home*

Shopping Technologies. Washington, D.C.: Author, 1992. Reviews developments and trends in electronic marketing (shopping via telephone, television, and interactive videotex systems) in several countries; delineates conditions that may benefit consumers by encouraging competition and expanding choice.

Strauss, Lawrence. *Electronic Marketing: Emerging TV and Computer Channels for Interactive Home Shopping*. White Plains, N.Y.: Knowledge Industry, 1983. Offers an exhaustive account of cablecast home shopping prior to HSN's nationwide launch of this concept. A good source for understanding why earlier efforts in home shopping were not very successful. Various forms of electronic marketing in the United States, including videotex and several direct marketing devices, also are discussed.

"Tele-buying." *The Economist* 301 (October 18, 1986): 76. Analysis of growth and competition in the home shopping industry. Discusses HSN's ambitious strategy to expand by buying several television broadcast stations and assesses possible implications from the perspective of cable operators.

U.S. Office of Consumer Affairs. *Draft Consumer Education Brochure on the Televised Shopping Industry in the United States*. Washington, D.C.: Government Printing Office, 1988. Probes implications of the home shopping industry for average shoppers. Focuses on reasons and circumstances under which home shopping can be deceptive to consumers.

Siva Balasubramanian

Cross-References

Station KDKA Introduces Commercial Radio Broadcasting (1920); The 1939 World's Fair Introduces Regular U.S. Television Service (1939); Cable Television Rises to Challenge Network Television (mid-1990's); *Time* magazine Makes an E-commerce Pioneer Its Person of the Year (1999).

THE SUPREME COURT UPHOLDS QUOTAS AS A REMEDY FOR DISCRIMINATION

CATEGORY OF EVENT: Labor
TIME: 1986
LOCALE: Washington, D.C.

The Supreme Court, in a number of decisions, defined the permissible extent of affirmative action programs

Principal personages:
WILLIAM J. BRENNAN, JR. (1906-1997), an associate justice of the Supreme Court who wrote the majority opinions in several affirmative action cases
WARREN BURGER (1907-1995), a justice of the Supreme Court who advocated an activist role for the court in fostering civil liberties
WILLIAM REHNQUIST (1924-   ), the chief justice of the United States following Burger's retirement
ANTONIN SCALIA (1936-   ), an associate justice of the Supreme Court

Summary of Event

Title VII of the Civil Rights Act of 1964, amended by the Equal Employment Opportunity Act of 1972, is intended to eliminate discrimination by employers and labor unions. In addition, Executive Order 11246 regulates employment practices of federal contractors and, in some cases, requires contractors to implement affirmative action programs to improve the opportunities of minorities and women. The implementation of these fair employment regulations led to considerable legal interpretation. In *United Steel-workers of America v. Weber* (1979), the Supreme Court set down norms for legitimate affirmative action programs. The Weber criteria are that any affirmative action program must be part of an overall plan, must be voluntary, must have an objective of remedying imbalances arising from discrimination, must be temporary, and must not trammel the interests of others.

Throughout the early 1980's, the Justice Department under President Ronald Reagan argued that the objective of civil rights legislation should be to rectify injustices done to specific individuals. Giving a preference to a minority group member who was not a proven victim of discrimination was considered to be a form of "reverse discrimination" against the majority. A number of Supreme Court decisions in the 1986 session served to expand the scope of permissible affirmative action programs.

In *Wygant v. Jackson Board of Education*, the Court supported by a five-to-four vote the concept of an affirmative action plan along the lines spelled out in *Weber* but opposed a provision in the plan that gave preference to black workers in layoff decisions. The plurality view of the Court was that when a person is laid off, the entire burden of the decision is borne by that employee. The rights of the laid-off worker are affected much more than in a case in which a person is not promoted. The effort to remedy discrimination imposes an excessive cost on a single person, the one laid off. In addition, the Court concluded that other remedies that imposed less cost might have been available. The view of the Court was that although seniority could be overridden in promotions and other job assignments, it should not be in layoffs.

In 1975, a New York district court found that the sheet metal workers union discriminated against nonwhite workers in its apprenticeship program. The court ordered an end to the discrimination and established a goal of 29 percent nonwhite membership, to be reached by July, 1981. The percentage was arrived at based on the nonwhite composition of the local New York City labor market. The union was subsequently fined for failing to meet the goal. Both the goal and the date for achieving it were changed. A district court and the court of appeals found the union in contempt for failing to reach the court-ordered revised goals. The union appealed to the Supreme Court. The union, along with the solicitor general of the United States, argued that the membership goal and the means prescribed to achieve it were in violation of Title VII of the Civil Rights Act, which implies that no court could order admission of an individual to a union if that individual was refused for reasons other than discrimination.

In *Local 28 Sheet Metal Workers International Association v. Equal*

Employment Opportunity Commission (1986), the Supreme Court by a five-to-four vote affirmed the decision of the district court against the union. Justice William J. Brennan, speaking for the Court, asserted that even though the individuals admitted to the apprenticeship program had not themselves been previously denied admission or discriminated against, the courts had the right to provide relief when the union had been guilty of egregious discrimination or discrimination had been endemic. Brennan concluded that unless courts have the right to require agencies to employ qualified minorities roughly in proportion to their number in the labor market, it may be impossible to provide the equal opportunity that is the intent of Title VII. Brennan made a subtle distinction regarding racial quotas. Although it is clear from congressional deliberations and Title VII that quotas should not be used simply because of the existence of racial imbalance in the workplace, this does not preclude the use of quotas by the courts to rectify racial imbalances in cases in which discrimination is proven to exist. The purpose of affirmative action is not to make whole the victims of discrimination but rather to provide relief to the group discriminated against. The recipients of relief need not have suffered themselves.

In *Local 93 International Association of Firefighters v. City of Cleveland* (1986), the Supreme Court by a six-to-three vote approved a consent decree to eliminate racial discrimination. An association of minority group members brought suit against the city of Cleveland, charging discrimination in the city's fire department. A federal district court approved a consent decree between the city and the firefighters' association to rectify the problem. The decree set forth a quota system for the promotion of minorities over a four-year period. The terms of the decree were arrived at by the parties to a lawsuit and were approved by the court. Local 93 was not a party to the initial suit, and it did not approve the decree. Local 93 appealed to the Supreme Court, arguing that public safety required that the most competent people be promoted. The Court again affirmed the right of the courts to prescribe corrective plans that benefit individuals who were not actual victims of discrimination. The majority of the Court further held that voluntary consent decrees can go beyond what the courts would have ordered to rectify the problem. The decision did recognize the right to challenge consent decrees in the courts. In the private sector, consent decrees arrived at with the Equal Employment Opportunity Commission could similarly be challenged as violations of collective bargaining agreements, Title VII, or the equal protection clause of the Fourteenth Amendment.

In the light of a 1984 Supreme Court decision, the Reagan Administration had advised cities to reexamine consent decrees, believing that less aggressive affirmative action plans might be acceptable. The administration now found itself uncertain as to which way the court was leaning. These 1986 decisions marked the end of the activist approach of the Court under chief Justice Warren Burger while at the same time making the more conservative approach of Chief Justice William Rehnquist more difficult to establish.

Impact of Event

Although the 1986 decisions applied specifically to minorities, it soon became clear that affirmative action programs similar to those approved by the Court could also be applied to women. In *Johnson v. Santa Clara County Transportation Agency* (1987), the Court, by a six-to-three vote, concluded that promoting a woman to the job of dispatcher ahead of more qualified men was acceptable under the provisions of a voluntary affirmative action program in the public sector. The agency was to consider sex as one factor in making promotion decisions for jobs in which women were underrepresented. The long-term objective was to have employment in the agency mirror the composition of the local labor market. No explicit quota was established, but the agency was to examine annually the composition of its work force and undertake the steps necessary to achieve its long-term goal.

The case arose when a woman was given the job of dispatcher over Paul Johnson, another candidate. He appealed to the Equal Employment Opportunity Commission. The EEOC granted the right to sue, and the lower court held that Johnson's rights under Title VII of the Civil Rights Act had been violated. The court ruled that gender had been the only factor in the promotion of the woman and that the agency program was not "temporary," as required by the Weber decision.

In the majority opinion of the Supreme Court, Justice Brennan was careful to avoid the pejorative implications of quotas. He concluded that there was a manifest imbalance in the representation of women in this job classification and that the agency program did not specify a strict number of women that should be hired, but rather set aspirations, subject to change and review. Hiring was not to be based solely on the basis of sex, but rather was to use sex as one factor. Justice Lewis Powell pointed out that there were seven candidates who were deemed qualified for the job, so Johnson did not have an unqualified right to the job in the absence of the preference granted to women. Although Johnson was denied promotion, he retained his position in the agency, so that an undue burden was not imposed on him. In dissent, Justice Antonin Scalia interpreted the majority opinion as an unjustified extension of Title VII intended to alter social standards. The case was the first to establish that voluntary affirmative action programs to overcome the effects of societal discrimination are permissible.

In *United States v. Paradise* (1987), the plurality opinion of the Court supported the promotion of one black state trooper for each white state trooper promoted. This course of action was allowed because of the narrowly defined nature of the preference and because of the egregious nature of past violations of equal rights. The Court noted that the plan was flexible and temporary and that it postponed rather than denied the promotion of white officers.

In *San Francisco Police Officers' Association v. City and County of San Francisco* (1987), a federal appeals court again applied the Weber test. The city used three criteria in promoting police officers: a written examination, a multiple choice test, and an oral examination. After administering the first two parts, the city found that the percentage of minorities who passed was lower than desired. The results were then rescored on a pass or fail basis, with the deciding factor for those who passed being the oral examination. The city had thus rescored promotional examinations to achieve racial and gender percentages. The court found that rescoring the examinations unnecessarily trammeled the interests of the nonminority police officers. Candidates for promotion, the court ruled, are denied equal opportunity if test results can be rescored. The practice was deceptive in that candidates had a right to know how the test results were to be weighed as they prepared for the test. In addition, other methods of correcting the racial imbalance were available that were less dramatic or less costly to others.

In 1989, the Supreme Court handed down five decisions, all with five-to-four majorities, that reversed many of the 1986 cases. Essentially, these decisions shifted the burden of proof to the employee to prove that practices by an employer were unrelated to the requirements of a job. Statistical data indicating small proportions of minority group members holding a job were no longer sufficient to claim discrimination. The Court limited the extent to which positions could be set aside by state and local governments, to be filled only by minority group members. The Court also allowed for an affirmative action program to be reexamined if, over the course of the program, employees claimed reverse discrimination.

The view of the courts with regard to quotas is far from unanimous and continues to evolve. Title VII explicitly states that discrimination based on race is prohibited. In this context, quotas that discriminate are prohibited. Difficulties arise in determining whether these prohibitions are universal. Quotas implemented to achieve racial balance even though discrimination has not been demonstrated would be deemed illegal. Uncertainty occurs when discrimination has been found to exist and either voluntary or court-mandated programs are prescribed to rectify the problem. Critics argue that setting numerical standards in effect discriminates against the majority. Choosing one person over another is discriminatory toward the person not chosen, and the person chosen has not necessarily been discriminated against in the past. Therefore, the person chosen is given a preference that is undue and at the expense of someone else who was not a party to discrimination. The advocates of affirmative action argue that in cases in which discrimination has been proven to exist, setting numerical standards may be the only viable way of correcting a demonstrated problem. The essence of affirmative action is not to compensate actual victims of discrimination but rather to provide opportunities to groups of people who historically have been discriminated against. Individuals are given preference not because of anything done to them but rather for something done to their group. Further, the people not chosen do not lose anything they previously had or anything to which they had a unilateral right. In cases in which there is a direct loss, as in layoffs, the courts have been less willing to support numerical quotas. Businesses thus have had to walk fine lines in trying to be fair to all employees while maintaining productive work forces.

Bibliography

Becker, Gary. *The Economics of Discrimination.* 2d ed. Chicago: University of Chicago Press, 1971. One of the first efforts to apply economic analysis to the issue of discrimination in the labor market.

Hall, Kermit L., ed. *The Oxford Guide to United States Supreme Court Decisions.* New York: Oxford University Press, 1999. Multiauthored collection of essays on more than four hundred significant Court decisions, with supporting glossary and other aids.

Ratner, Ronnie Steinberg, ed. *Equal Employment Policy for Women.* Philadelphia: Temple University Press, 1980. A collection of readings on policies intended to ensure equal rights in employment for women in the United States, Canada, and Western Europe.

Reich, Michael. *Racial Inequality.* Princeton, N.J.: Princeton University Press, 1981. Summarizes the extent of the racial inequality that was the backdrop for Court decisions in the 1980's. The emphasis is on the relationship between discrimination and social unrest. Attention is given to economic theories of discrimination.

Twomey, David P. *Equal Employment Opportunity Law.* 2d ed. Cincinnati, Ohio: South-Western, 1990. Summarizes the major legal decisions concerning the interpretation of the Civil Rights Act of 1964. Analyzes the evolution and extension of employment practices. Includes lengthy excerpts from legal opinions.

United States Reports. Washington, D.C.: U.S. Government Printing Office, 1801- . These annual reports present the opinions of the Court along with dissenting opinions. Reading the decisions allows a firmer grasp of the complexity of the issues involved.

John F. O'Connell

Cross-References

The Civil Rights Act Prohibits Discrimination in Employment (1964); The Supreme Court Orders the End of Discrimination in Hiring (1971); The Pregnancy Discrimination Act Extends Employment Rights (1978); The Supreme Court Rules on Affirmative Action Programs (1979); *Firefighters v. Stotts* Upholds Seniority Systems (1984).

INSIDER TRADING SCANDALS MAR THE EMERGING JUNK BOND MARKET

CATEGORIES OF EVENT: Finance and business practices
TIME: May 12, 1986
LOCALE: New York, New York

The rise of Drexel Burnham Lambert as a major trader in the new market for junk bonds provided opportunities for illegal insider trading, with which Dennis Levine was charged

Principal personages:
DENNIS LEVINE (1952-   ), a Drexel Burnham Lambert investment banker who provided evidence against the insiders
IVAN BOESKY (1937-   ), a New York arbitrage trader, the first of the insiders convicted on evidence supplied by Dennis Levine
MICHAEL MILKEN (1946-   ), the pioneer of junk bonds and the central figure in the government's prosecution of insider trading in the 1980's

Summary of Event

In the 1980's, the emergent market for junk bonds offered opportunities for violations of insider trading laws. Those laws had prohibited stock and bond traders from profiting from transactions about which they had privileged information. The nature of placing such issues with buyers, however, blurred the line between information that was privileged and that which was not. On May 12, 1986, Drexel Burnham Lambert investment banker Dennis Levine, who had represented Pantry Pride in its battle with Revlon, was accused of trading on nonpublic information. As part of the deal Levine worked out with prosecutors, he testified against other insiders, including Ivan Boesky. Eventually Boesky received a deal from prosecutors for agreeing, along with Levine, to provide testimony against Drexel Burnham Lambert banker Michael Milken. In March, 1989, the federal government indicted Milken.

Businesses traditionally have raised capital by selling either stocks or bonds. Stock prices reflect immediate changes in companies' assets, profitability, net worth, or future prospects. Bonds, however, as a loan from the buyer to the company, usually carry a specified return payable at a future date. To convince buyers that certain bonds are sound, large investment banking houses grade the bond issuers as to their quality (or, inversely, as to the risk of their bonds). A company carrying a "AAA" rating on its bonds is considered to be extremely creditworthy; a company with a "B" will have a more difficult time obtaining capital.

The rating system in the 1980's tended to favor older, established companies and heavy industries at the expense of newer, rapidly growing companies and growth industries such as telecommunications, computers, and biotechnology. Another problem with the rating system was that by the 1980's some eight hundred companies had bond ratings of "BBB" or better—considered the minimum investment grade—and yet were in poor financial shape. Penn Central Railroad qualified for a "BBB" rating two weeks before it went bankrupt, and foreign nations such as Argentina and Mexico also received high bond ratings on the eve of their defaults to U.S. creditors. Moreover, not one business owned by a woman or a minority qualified for an investment-grade rating. On the contrary, by 1989 more than twenty-one thousand companies, mostly smaller businesses, failed to qualify for a "BBB" rating or better. Obtaining capital proved difficult. To receive an investment-grade rating on its bonds, a company had to have a long history of growth, but it could not grow without capital. A number of profitable, well-known companies found themselves in that situation, including Holiday Inns, Safeway, the MGM/UA and Orion motion picture studios, and MCI Communications.

In 1973, none of the major investment houses had any interest in those companies. Morgan Guaranty Trust, Shearson Lehman Brothers, Merrill Lynch, and the other large investment bankers had a bias toward older industrial companies. Virtually the only banking house that saw any profit in trading in the newer companies was Drexel Burnham Lambert in New York City (commonly referred to as Drexel), a banking house descended from the partner of J. P. Morgan's father, Junius. Even within Drexel, only one banker, Michael Milken, saw the potential of bond issues by such businesses. Milken, impressed with a study showing that yields on a diversified portfolio of low-grade bonds exceeded those of a higher grade portfolio even after accounting for defaults, decided to specialize in low-grade issues. He researched companies relentlessly, simply outworking almost everyone else. Like Boesky, Milken had the exceptional ability to work on four hours of sleep a night, and both men were in their offices before 6 A.M. Milken developed high-yield/high-risk bonds for those companies that could not obtain investment ratings. These became known as junk bonds.

The rise of a junk bond market irritated the old-line investment houses, which suddenly found themselves losing their ability to dictate financial life and death through their ratings system. Drexel soon had more than a thousand clients wanting to issue junk bonds. Milken's financial democracy also undercut the established houses from below, opening up a new network of customers whom the traditional houses had scorned, such as Carl Lindner, Sol Steinberg, Meshulam Riklis, and David Solomon. These corporate "raiders" looked to acquire companies to sell rather than to run as efficient businesses. To reach retail buyers, Milken and Frederick Joseph (later the chief executive officer of Drexel) invented a class of high-yield bond funds that provided diversified portfolios accessible to customers who had smaller amounts of money to invest. The funds paid a yield on average that was 2.5 percent higher than the yield on U.S. Treasury bonds.

Drexel grew rapidly as a dealer in junk bonds. In 1978, the company issued $439 million in junk, accounting for 70 percent of the market. Certainly not all junk bond deals were profitable. American Communications Industries, for which Drexel issued $20 million in bonds, became the first company to default without making a single interest payment. Risks came with junk, but so did potentially high returns. Increasingly, Drexel issued new debt paper to replace old debt a company carried. That built in an immediate pressure to conclude deals, requiring Milken to develop a new unregistered type of security that did not have to languish in the offices of the Securities and Exchange Commission (SEC). Under Section 3(a)9 of the Securities Act of 1933, companies could offer new paper in exchange for old without registering, provided that the investment bankers did not accept a fee for promoting or soliciting the exchange. Instead, Drexel (and Milken) took some of the paper for itself.

In the early 1980's, over a five-year period, Drexel completed 175 3(a)9 exchange offers totaling more than $7 billion in junk bond debt. Drexel's default rate was an astoundingly low 2 percent, whereas other traditional houses generally had default rates as high as 17 percent on their standard exchanges. In an era during which critics complained of the recklessness and high risk associated with junk bonds, Drexel's issues were the safest of any except government bonds. Drexel spotted firms primed for fantastic growth, such as MCI Communications (in which Drexel itself held $250 million in bonds) and businesses no other house would touch, such as the Golden Nugget casino in Atlantic City, New Jersey. The firm's profits soared from $6 million in 1978 to $150 million in 1983.

Milken developed another device, called the "highly confident" letter, known to insiders as the Air Fund, because nothing was in it. Drexel could raise a billion-dollar line of credit by claiming it had an account to purchase securities itself. In fact, the "highly confident" letters represented self-fulfilling prophecies: The issue of such a letter convinced others that Drexel had capital, so others invested until Drexel ultimately did have capital. Using that strategy, Milken financed T. Boone Pickens' hostile takeover of Gulf Oil by Mesa Petroleum, Sol Steinberg's Reliance Corporation's attempted takeover of Disney, and Carl Icahn's bid for Phillips Petroleum. In each case, Drexel and Milken earned phenomenal amounts, up to $500,000 in advisory fees plus 3 to 5 percent of the deal. In the Triangle-National Can takeover, for example, Drexel netted $25 million plus 16 percent of Triangle's stock. Milken earned such fees because he could do the seemingly impossible. In one 1985 deal, for example, he raised $3 billion from 140 institutions in less than seven days.

The difficulties and potential illegalities in junk bonds involved the requirement to move the bonds from the first tier of investors to the second tier, who generally wanted to avoid junk bonds publicly. Bonds had to change hands rapidly, far more quickly than they could be registered with the SEC, and technically, if the first-tier buyers intended to resell their bonds all along, they violated the law by doing so. Proving intentions in such cases was impossible without the testimony of insiders. Thus, when federal authorities finally found Dennis Levine, upon whom they could hang enough charges to persuade him to turn state's evidence, jurors had to choose between Milken's description of his buyers' intentions and Levine's account of events. In March, 1989, after more than five years of SEC investigations, federal authorities charged Milken with 98 counts of securities fraud violations. On April 20, 1990, Michael Milken pleaded guilty to six counts, and in November, 1990, he received a sentence of ten years in federal prison. Observers immediately noted that ninety-two counts had vanished, including some of those thought to be the strongest insider trading counts. Milken started serving his sentence in March, 1991, and was eligible for parole in March, 1993. A reduction in his sentence allowed his release on January 2, 1993, to a halfway house and his full release on February 4, 1993.

Impact of Event

The indictments of Levine, Boesky, and Milken reaffirmed the power of the federal government and its intent to regulate the securities markets. Certainly by 1980 technological changes in the exchanges themselves and the evolution of new instruments of debt, such as the 3(a)9 and the "highly confident" letter, had far outpaced the capability of the government to regulate securities exchanges. Neither the 3(a)9 nor the "highly confident" letter was illegal, but the pace at which deals were negotiated encouraged blurring the lines between a statement of a company's financial status and an illegal prediction of performance. The government took the view that the notices of offerings constituted "tips."

No public presentation of evidence was ever held. Both Levine and Boesky had personal incentives to slant their testimony for the purposes of the government prosecutors, as they bargained with the government and offered evidence intended to implicate others. Milken originally pleaded not guilty and seemed prepared to fight, but the indictment of his brother Lowell in March, 1989, put more pressure on Milken. Most observers believed the prosecution of Lowell Milken to be little more than leverage to force Michael Milken to plea-bargain instead of going to trial. The government also made it clear that it intended to go after the sizable Milken family fortune, whereas in the case of Ivan Boesky, who paid a record fine of $100 million, the SEC allowed Boesky to keep his considerable fortune.

Those factors caused Milken to change his plea to guilty on six felony fraud charges in April, 1990. On November 21, 1990, Judge Kimba Wood sentenced Milken to ten years in prison. In addition, Milken had to settle a lawsuit by the Federal Deposit Insurance Corporation (FDIC), adding $500 million to the $600 million he already had paid. Milken's total restitution came to an estimated $1.3 billion.

In the Milken case, the government used the Racketeer Influenced and Corrupt Organizations (RICO) Act, aimed at violent mobsters, to seize Milken's assets before the trial actually started. The use of the RICO statute to convict Milken, hailed as a victory by the government, represented an attack on capital and a victory of traditional Wall Street firms and their lawyers over capital entrepreneurs. Even the public opinion that came to be associated with the term "junk bonds" reflected the extent of the victory by the established capitalists. Few people ever would guess that Safeway, MCI Communications, or dozens of other rising businesses had benefited from high-risk bonds. Critic Ben Stein repeatedly contended that junk bonds had plummeted in value, harming buyers, yet the government built its case on the proposition that Milken's own junk bond assets had risen in value.

Not everyone agreed that Milken was a greedy opportunist. Supporters claimed that he had offered hope to companies that other firms were unwilling to help. His bond deal with MCI Communications made it possible for the firm to challenge American Telephone and Telegraph in the long distance market, for example. Despite his guilty plea, serious questions remain as to whether Milken actually broke any laws or merely plea-bargained to save his family and fortune. His own guilty pleas, if essentially obtained under duress, are not the smoking gun that critics have tried to find.

Milken's activities raised the more difficult question of what constituted "insider" trading. Some economists contended that the very concept of "insider" information was problematic. In an industry in which information is worth money, such as the stock and bond markets, all data about any company potentially is privileged.

Of greater significance was the reputation junk bonds acquired. The collapse of the savings and loan (S&L) industry in the 1980's further tainted junk bonds, although critics note that the incentive to use junk bonds came from the deposit insurance offered by the federal government. Several studies found a high correlation between deposit insurance and high-risk activities by banks and S&Ls. When the S&Ls found themselves in trouble in the early 1980's, many sought the high returns available in junk bonds. Economists and most traders understood that high returns carried high risks. For many S&Ls, however, the choice was between risky high-yield bonds that might cause losses and bankruptcy or business as usual, which would lead to certain bankruptcy. Few studies have focused on the S&Ls that survived by investing in junk. Milken himself maintained that the S&L industry lost money because of investments in real estate, not because of high-yield bonds.

As long as Milken and Drexel had control of junk bond offerings, the ratio of winners to losers was high. Once other houses started to offer junk, quality depreciated to approximate its name as firms accepted clients with lower creditworthiness once the best prospects had been taken. That in no way diminished the role of low-grade bond instruments, which offered capital to new companies or to "outcasts." Drexel's success and low default rates on its issues showed that markets had overlooked some worthy companies. Drexel's success also led to high expectations of performance for other instruments of lesser quality. Junk bonds in that respect became victims of their own success.

The insider trading scandals prompted new efforts to tighten securities laws. At the same time, the scandals reinforced the notion that the United States had become a nation that merely moved paper and made money from money rather than from products. The success of Milken and others encouraged business students to concentrate on investment banking in their search for the most lucrative careers. Buying and selling companies was perceived as a quicker route to financial success than was developing a strong company with a good product.

Milken operated on the frontiers of securities innovation, and often no law regulated or guided what he did. Although he frequently may not have known if his activities were strictly legal, most of the time the authorities would not have been able to ascertain their legality either. Milken can be compared to a biogeneticist developing new life-forms long before the law considered the ramifications of creating artificial life. Milken has been compared to J. P. Morgan for his democratization of the capital markets. Milken and his junk bond raiders arguably made the management of American companies much more responsive to their stockholders, as inefficient managers could find themselves bought out of their jobs by raiders who thought they could manage better.

Bibliography

Bruck, Connie. *The Predators' Ball: The Inside Story of Drexel Burnham and the Rise of the Junk Bond Raiders.* Rev. ed. New York: Penguin Books, 1989. An earlier edition was the first book to deal with Drexel Burnham Lambert and the rise of junk bonds. Provides a reporter's analysis of Wall Street. Bruck, while never excusing Milken's excesses, nevertheless is more balanced than are others in assessing the value of junk bonds and the revolution Milken created in financing small, growing companies. Indispensable for research on this topic.

De Trolio, Peter. "Ivan F. Boesky." In *Banking and Finance, 1913-1989.* Volume in *The Encyclopedia of American Business History and Biography*, edited by Larry Schweikart. New York: Facts on File, 1990. A biographical essay on Boesky based on news sources. Useful as a quick reference.

Schweikart, Larry. "Michael R. Milken." In *Banking and Finance, 1913-1989.* Volume in *The Encyclopedia of American Business History and Biography*. New York: Facts on File, 1990. One of the few capsule biographies of Milken available, this essay finds Milken as less culpable of criminal behavior than other reports suggest and supports elimination of insider trading laws. Published before Milken's conviction and imprisonment. Includes perspectives on Milken from numerous editorials and writers.

Stein, Benjamin J. *A License to Steal.* New York: Simon & Schuster, 1992. A longtime critic of leveraged buyouts and financial innovations, Stein, a lawyer, takes a negative view of Milken and Drexel's activities. His disgust with virtually all the new financial mechanisms, such as leveraged buyouts and junk bonds, puts him at variance with most other conservative writers on the subject, such as Jude Wanniski and George Gilder.

Stewart, James B. *Den of Thieves*. New York: Simon & Schuster, 1991. As the title implies, this is a "detective story" approach to the scandals, with Milken, Boesky, and others as the villains and a courageous group of government detectives as the heroes. Stewart is as critical as Stein, though much more thorough in his research. Stewart's evidence comes from the public record and testimony by Boesky—which Stewart maintains is more consistent than that of Milken—and lacks any inside testimony by Milken.

Larry Schweikart

Cross-References

The Federal Reserve Act Creates a U.S. Central Bank (1913); The Banking Act of 1933 Reorganizes the American Banking System (1933); The Banking Act of 1935 Centralizes U.S. Monetary Control (1935); Congress Deregulates Banks and Savings and Loans (1980-1982); Drexel and Michael Milken Are Charged with Insider Trading (1988); Bush Responds to the Savings and Loan Crisis (1989).

THE IMMIGRATION REFORM AND CONTROL ACT IS SIGNED INTO LAW

CATEGORY OF EVENT: Labor
TIME: November 6, 1986
LOCALE: Washington, D.C.

The immigration reform bill enacted in 1986 granted amnesty to some aliens in the United States, prohibited the employment of illegal aliens, and sought to curtail illegal immigration

Principal personages:

JIMMY CARTER (1924-   ), the president of the United States, 1977-1981

PETER RODINO (1909-   ), the sponsor of immigration reform bills in 1982 and 1986

ROMANO MAZZOLI (1932-   ), the cosponsor of reform bills in 1982 and 1986

THEODORE HESBURGH (1917-   ), the chairman of a select committee on immigration reform

RONALD REAGAN (1911-   ), the president of the United States, 1981-1989

ALAN SIMPSON (1931-   ), a congressional proponent of immigration reform

EDWARD KENNEDY (1932-   ), an advocate of important reform amendments

CHARLES SCHUMER (1950-   ), the congressman who negotiated a compromise on temporary farm workers

ROBERT GARCIA (1933-   ), a congressional opponent of proposed reforms

776

Summary of Event

Immigration-related problems had captured national attention in the United States by the late 1970's, despite the reforms intended by sponsors of the Immigration Reform and Nationality Amendments of 1965. By the early 1980's, spokespersons for trade unions, the American Legion and other patriotic associations, churches, organizations of social workers, the media, civil rights groups, and institutions for the study of immigration evinced serious concerns about the economic, social, and political consequences of the growing flood of immigrants.

Several specific causes fed the nation's deepening anxieties about post-1965 immigrants, aside from issues arising from their growing number and their Third World origins. First, ample evidence indicated that beyond America's borders, the reservoir of potential immigrants was brimming over. This was in addition to the 60 percent increase that marked the legal influx after passage of the 1965 amendments. Immigration was therefore not an issue that would go away.

Second, despite the frenetic efforts of the Immigration and Naturalization Service (INS), millions of illegal immigrants had poured into the country across the Mexican border during the late 1960's and 1970's. Some estimates placed their numbers at between two and four million, though experts conceded that no one could be sure of any figure. This invasion appeared to have no end.

Third, the backup of foreign refugees had reached unprecedented dimensions by 1980. Experts described a "global refugee crisis" involving between twelve and thirteen million people. Many of them were eager to come to America for refuge, leading one congressman to remark that nearly everybody in the world would emigrate to America if free to do so. Certainly communication and transportation technologies had made America more accessible than ever. Before passage of the 1980 Refugee Act, the United States had already accepted 677,000 refugees, three times as many as any other country. Seventy thousand more refugees were allowed entrance each year after the Refugee Act went into effect.

During the early 1980's, public attention was captured by issues brought up by the so-called "Fourth Wave" of legal and illegal immigrants. Could they be and should they be assimilated, since most were Asians or Latin Americans drawn from cultures radically different from that of the United States? What impacts would they have on the work force and the national economy? Would the INS prove capable of controlling America's borders, of ferreting out illegal aliens, and of maintaining respect for civil liberties? Was it possible to minimize the corruption with which nearly all aspects of immigration were tainted?

Addressing these fears, Congressman Peter Rodino initiated and President Jimmy Carter supported a 1978 bill imposing sanctions against employers who hired illegal immigrants. The bill failed to satisfy either pro- or anti-immigration forces. President Carter then appointed a committee, composed of members of the House and the Senate as well as cabinet members, to study and make recommendations on immigration and refugee problems. Chaired by the president of the University of Notre Dame, the Reverend Theodore Hesburgh, the committee concluded its two-year study in January, 1981.

The committee's report gave priority to restraining illegal immigration while judiciously accepting slight increments to legal immigration aimed at family reunification. Recognizing humanitarian considerations, it nevertheless determined that the time for massive legal immigration had passed. Following the final report, in December, 1981, an immigration task force created by President Ronald Reagan made recommendations that were forwarded to Congress. There, two proponents of immigration reform, Rodino and Kentucky's Congressman Romano Mazzoli, presented the Immigration Reform and Control Bill of 1982, embodying most of the Reagan Administration's proposals. Although the bill failed, it was persistently reintroduced through 1984 as the Simpson-Mazzoli bill. The hotly debated measure became the core of the Immigration Reform and Control Act of 1986 (IRCA).

IRCA superseded previous law, which had allowed the hiring of illegal aliens. It imposed sanctions on employers who did so and required them to maintain records proving the citizenship of employees. Fines were to be invoked against employers who hired illegal aliens, with criminal penalties imposed on those with a pattern of illegal employment. The act further offered an amnesty period to illegal aliens who had been resident in the United States since 1982, allowing them to apply to legalize their status. About three million previously illegal aliens opted to change their status.

Essential to IRCA's passage were provisions for temporary foreign workers, who entered the United States seasonally to harvest perishable crops. Congressman Charles Schumer successfully pressed for a Special Agricultural Workers amnesty (SAW) allowing aliens who had worked in the United States for ninety days between 1985 and 1986—their number was estimated at 250,000—to become temporary aliens and then permanent resident aliens. By 1988, 1.3 million people had claimed SAW amnesty, most of them from Mexico.

Impact of Event

IRCA was a highly politicized piece of legislation representing years of congressional controversy. Black leader Jesse Jackson and his Rainbow

Coalition had opposed it, and so too had members of the Congressional Black Caucus. Earlier versions of its provisions relative to agricultural workers had drawn consistent fire from the Congressional Hispanic Caucus, which included New York's Robert Garcia and Matthew Martinez, as well as from farm workers' organizations and the growers who employed their members.

Proponents and opponents of the law were not divided neatly along liberal/conservative or party lines. At various stages of its genesis, guarded support had come from Massachusetts liberal Edward Kennedy, Wyoming's conservative Alan Simpson, New Jersey's moderate conservative Peter Rodino (who at first battled reform), and Kentucky's Romano Mazzoli. The opposition variously enjoyed support from Speaker of the House Thomas "Tip" O'Neill, liberal Walter Mondale, and conservative Democrat Lloyd Bentsen.

Polls indicated during the early 1980's that most Americans wanted immigration reform. Proponents included majorities of Hispanic Americans, African Americans, church leaders and leaders of patriotic orders, and spokespersons for organized agricultural labor interests. Each group, however, tended to perceive reform from different perspectives. Despite extensive public and private studies of immigration problems, hard evidence on the number of potential immigrants, the number of illegal immigrants, the number of prospective refugees, and the extent of corruption undermining extant laws was elusive.

Amid these complexities, the impact of IRCA was hard to predict. Some results were quickly apparent. The INS reported that the entry of illegal aliens into the United States apparently declined during 1987 and much of 1988. There had been 1.6 million apprehensions in 1986. This decline was attributed to IRCA's amnesty provisions. By 1989, however, the INS estimated that its monthly apprehension rate had increased. Scholars cautioned that IRCA had been in operation for too short a time to allow accurate assessments of its effectiveness.

Stringent enforcement of IRCA was contingent on documentary information supplied by employers. The INS and immigration scholars agreed that in this regard corruption continued to be rife. Fabrication of false documents reportedly was a brisk trade. Already feeling overburdened by governmental regulations and interference with their workers, most employers were hostile toward sanctions against hiring illegal aliens. Growers in particular feared shortages of workers and resented INS seizures of undocumented persons in their fields. Nevertheless, official reports indicated that IRCA's deterrent effects on employers were becoming apparent by 1988, by which time several high-visibility prosecutions were under way.

The INS called for more funds, more personnel, and more elaborate ditching and fencing along the Mexican border. In addition, INS supporters continued to propose—as they had done for decades—that the federal government devise more foolproof forms of identification than were provided by easily forged Social Security cards and green cards. Arguments were made in favor of a national identity card, of the kind familiar to many Europeans, for all Americans.

Millions of illegal crossings of the Mexican border were only one large part of a complex pattern of illegal immigration. Thousands of Irish people, plagued by a depressed economy during the early 1980's, also came to America illegally. Failing to qualify under the preference system or as refugees, they arrived as tourists and stayed in the United States when their visas expired. Rough calculations placed their number at about 100,000 in the late 1980's, most of them holding jobs in construction and child care in the Irish enclaves of Boston, Chicago, and New York City. Although they were unlikely to be apprehended, they were locked in low-paying jobs and were without health insurance.

Illegal status notwithstanding, these Irish emigrants soon formed the Irish Immigration Reform Movement (IIRM), urging Congress to legalize their status and demanding the admission of additional Irish immigrants. After IRCA's passage, Massachusetts Congressman Brian Donnelly contrived to have ten thousand visas placed in lottery for countries, like Ireland, that had been hurt by provisions of the Immigration Reform and Nationality Act of 1965. Forty percent of these visas went to Irish applicants. Desiring still more visas, IIRM subsequently became one of the lobby groups behind the Immigration Act of 1990.

Meanwhile, IRCA's operation appeared to help resolve a running debate over the economic impact of Third World immigrants who, since the 1960's, had been the predominant elements in what had become the most massive immigration in American history. Legal immigration between 1980 and 1986 averaged 570,000 per year, nearly half from Asian nations and another one-third from Latin America. Critics of more open immigration argued that immigration laws were out of phase with the needs and conditions of the American economy. They dismissed contentions that newcomers created jobs, pointing, among other things, to such practices as "networking," through which newly arrived immigrants tended to hire members of their own families or other new arrivals rather than jobless Americans who had been in the country longer.

By the late 1980's, most economic research, according to a 1989 Labor Department survey, showed that while not an unmixed blessing, immigration produced more benefits than liabilities. These benefits were generalized in the form of lower product prices and higher returns to capital. Immigration created jobs and stimulated demand, thus producing overall economic growth that in turn reduced unemployment. Economists and demographers agreed that a slowdown in American population growth and America's inability to produce sufficient numbers of workers to fill future jobs would result in labor shortages, a shortfall of perhaps 27 million workers by the year 2000. Both business leaders and legislators seemed convinced by these conclusions, setting the stage for the Immigration Act of 1990.

Bibliography

Borjas, George J. *Friends or Strangers*. New York: Basic Books, 1990. A decade of research on post-1965 immigration and its effects on transforming the American economy. Focuses on the types of immigrants the United States attracts, their impact on the economy, and whether the United States is competitive in the immigration market. Part 1 is an excellent overview. Part 2, concerning immigration's effects on the jobless, the poor, and minorities, is clearly written and informative. Recognizes the importance of human rights, liberty, and human values, aside from economic considerations.

Bouvier, Leon F. *Peaceful Invasions*. Lanham, Md.: University Press of America, 1992. Written by a professional demographer with lengthy public service. Emphasis is on changes wrought by post-1965 immigration. Claims a pro-immigrant position but discusses economic and social destabilization flowing from politically expedient policy making. Brief chapter notes, tables, select bibliography, and fine index.

Briggs, Vernon M., Jr. *Mass Immigration and the National Interest*. Armonk, N.Y.: M. E. Sharpe, 1992. The author is a Cornell labor economist and former member of the National Employment Council. He is critical of the thoughtlessness of post-1965 policy for failing to give proper regard to the kind of human capital allowed to enter the United States. Advocates immigration policy consistent with the needs of the rapidly changing labor market. Important for critical perspectives.

Crewdson, John. *The Tarnished Door*. New York: Times Books, 1983. The author is a Pulitzer Prize-winning expert on immigration. Scholarly in substance, but clearly written for nonspecialists. Filled with telling personal vignettes and freshened by talks with policymakers. Crewdson's opinion is too many alarms have been sounded about adverse effects of immigration and that the United States increasingly will need immigration. Many well-integrated quotations, but no notes or bibliography.

LeMay, Michael C. *From Open Door to Dutch Door.* New York: Praeger, 1987. A fine historical survey of immigration policies since 1820. Highly critical of employer sanctions. Does a good job of placing policy changes in the context of depressions, social unrest, civil rights campaigns, and national anxieties such as the Red Scare after World War I and the anti-Communism of the McCarthy era. Chapter 6 deals with IRCA, its background, and its early effects. Instructive tables, graphs, and appendix.

LeMay, Michael C., and Elliott Robert Barkan. *U.S. Immigration and Naturalization Laws and Issues: A Documentary History.* Westport, Conn.: Greenwood Press, 1999. Collection of primary documents on immigration history, with bibliographical references and index.

Reimers, David M. *Still the Golden Door.* 2d ed. New York: Columbia University Press, 1992. The author is a social historian who emphasizes the character and effects of Third World immigration on the United States after 1945. The background of and controversies over IRCA are discussed principally in chapter 7. Sees Third World immigrants as positive contributors to American life.

Simcox, David E. *Measuring the Fallout: The Cost of the IRCA Amnesty After Ten Years.* Washington, D.C.: Center for Immigration Studies, 1997.

Clifton K. Yearley

Cross-References

Congress Restricts Immigration with 1924 Legislation (1924); The United States Begins the Bracero Program (1942); The Civil Rights Act Prohibits Discrimination in Employment (1964); American and Mexican Companies Form *Maquiladoras* (1965); The Supreme Court Upholds Quotas as a Remedy for Discrimination (1986).

THE U.S. STOCK MARKET CRASHES ON 1987'S "BLACK MONDAY"

CATEGORY OF EVENT: Finance
TIME: October 19, 1987
LOCALE: New York, New York

After sliding downward for weeks, stock prices on the New York Stock Exchange collapsed on "Black Monday," causing fear of a repetition of the crash of 1929

Principal personages:
ALAN GREENSPAN (1926-   ), the chairman of the Federal Reserve Board, whose prompt action helped prevent a further deterioration of stock prices after the crash
JOHN PHELON (1931-   ), the chairman of the New York Stock Exchange, who rallied floor brokers during the crash
JAMES A. BAKER III (1930-   ), the secretary of the treasury
NICHOLAS BRADY (1930-   ), chair of an influential committee that studied causes of the crash

Summary of Event
   Throughout the late summer and early autumn of 1987, prices of stocks on the New York Stock Exchange (NYSE) fell irregularly. Some analysts thought a major "correction" was coming, believing that prices were higher than merited by the earnings and financial outlooks of companies. Other analysts were convinced that there would be a rise in prices. In retrospect, it is not difficult to isolate elements in the market structure that indicated a major collapse. At the time, however, a drop of several hundred points of the Dow Jones Industrial Average (DJIA) in a single session seemed farfetched.

On August 25, 1987, the Dow Jones Industrial Average, a weighted average of the prices of the stocks of thirty major companies, closed at 2,747, a new high. Stock prices had more than tripled in the past five years, and the market had advanced 43 percent since the beginning of the year. The market began to falter, perhaps in fear of a correction. Some analysts warned of a repetition of the 1929 crash. The stock market as a whole was quite different in 1987 from what it had been in 1929, making comparisons unproductive. For one thing, it now was global, with New York, Tokyo, and London inextricably tied together. New financial instruments and techniques had developed in the 1970's and 1980's, along with changes in the customer base.

One change came in 1973, when the Chicago Board of Trade created the Chicago Board Options Exchange. Options, which are contracts to purchase or sell a specified number of shares of a stock at a set price on or before a specified time, offered a new way to wager on the price of shares or to hedge a position, protecting against a movement in a stock's price. Other options markets followed, along with additional derivative instruments. There were options on stock indices, options on stock groups, and even options on options.

These options were used imaginatively by speculators sitting in front of computer consoles, using software that triggered sales and purchases. Arbitrageurs, who simultaneously bought and sold stocks or options to profit from disparities in the markets, would buy options on a stock index and sell the underlying shares, or do the reverse, when profits might be realized, leading to wide activity and swings in price. A trade triggered by one computer might be large enough to change prices enough to trigger other computers, making the process rapid, interactive, and volatile. On the day options expired—when the contracts to buy or sell had to be fulfilled or settled— trading activity could be wild and unpredictable.

Another new feature of the markets was portfolio insurance. A portfolio manager could sell index futures, with the cash from the sale used to offset price declines. As stock prices moved in one direction, the value of the futures changed to offset the gain or loss. Most investors did not know what portfolio insurance was, but there was between $60 billion and $90 billion of it in force that summer.

As a result of the trade deficit of the United States and the lure of American securities, a substantial amount of foreign money entered the U.S. stock market. Pension funds were big players, as were insurance companies and trust accounts. There had been an explosion in mutual funds as small investors pooled their money to invest in diversified portfolios. Together these institutions owned half the shares in American companies and accounted for around 70 percent of trading activity.

To this mix were added other major factors. One was the climax of takeover activity, as corporate raiders such as T. Boone Pickens, Carl Icahn, and Sir James Goldsmith went after large companies, causing their share prices to rise. Several Wall Street figures already had been caught in insider trading, or using nonpublic information to profit on stock transactions. The prospect of further investigation into insider trading unsettled the financial community. More important was a February meeting of world financial leaders in Paris. They had agreed to maintain the relative value of their currencies, and toward that end U.S. Secretary of the Treasury James A. Baker III had agreed to bring down the U.S. federal deficit. At the same time, the Japanese and the Germans would stimulate their countries' economies. The dollar started to decline in value anyway, causing consternation in the money markets.

On September 4, Federal Reserve Board Chairman Alan Greenspan announced a boost from 5½ to 6 percent in the discount rate, the interest rate that Federal Reserve banks charge for loans to other banks. This indicated that Greenspan meant to fight the inflation likely to come with the lower dollar. Greenspan also may have wanted to stifle the vigorous bull market. Bond prices collapsed at the prospect of higher interest rates. The DJIA responded by declining 37 points that day, 38 the following day, and 16 on September 9 before leveling at 2,545. The market rallied and closed the month at 2,596.

The market was skittish in early October, as meetings between President Ronald Reagan and German leaders collapsed, leading to suspicion that the accords reached in Paris would not be honored. The U.S. trade deficit was larger than expected, and there was talk of higher taxes to balance the budget. The DJIA fell 92 points on October 6, closing at 2,549, and continued to slide on the days following. Between then and October 15, there were only two days on which the DJIA rose. On Friday, October 16, the DJIA lost 108 points to close at 2,247.

Even before the market opened on the following Monday, it was apparent that trading would be unsettled. Portfolio insurance and arbitrage activities, in addition to developing panic, would pull the market down. Later it was learned that major mutual and pension funds had placed large sell orders before the opening. Arbitrageurs were in action, placing their sell orders. Later it would be learned that five money managers had placed sell orders on contracts worth $4 billion before the opening. Meanwhile, Wall Street learned of sharp declines on the Tokyo and London markets.

With these factors in place, it is not surprising that stocks opened at 2,047, 200 points lower than the Friday close, on heavy volume. The DJIA then rose 100 points in half an hour, on record volume. Panic selling developed around the world. Many would-be sellers could not get through to their brokers. NYSE specialists in certain stocks suspended trading because they were unable to find support levels, at which prices buyers would balance sellers. Market makers for the National Association of Securities Dealers Automated Quotations (NASDAQ) market, an over-the-counter trading exchange, also refused to deal in some shares. Even so, prices held remarkably steady throughout the morning and early afternoon. The DJIA was at 2,053 at 1:30, but it collapsed, closing at 1,739. In one day, more than a trillion dollars in stock values had been wiped out on the NYSE, on a volume of 604 million shares. The DJIA had fallen 508 points, more than one-fifth of its value.

Largely unnoticed in all of this was a sharp rise in the bond market, which received a good deal of the money that went out of stocks. This was significant, since the government bond market, by itself, was ten times larger than the stock market. Gains in bonds more than outweighed losses in stocks. That night analysts spoke ominously of the crash and what might follow. Given more attention was the announcement that the Federal Reserve banks would aggressively purchase government bonds, thus providing financial markets with needed liquidity.

Impact of Event

That night, the stock markets of other countries plunged. Tokyo's Nikkei index fell 15 percent, and the slump in London continued, with a 22 percent loss in two sessions. The same held true in secondary markets. Singapore's was down 21 percent, Australia's fell 25 percent, and those in Hong Kong and New Zealand simply shut down. If there was proof needed that the world's markets were connected, it was provided early that week.

The NYSE opened up 211 points the following day, Tuesday, October 20, and for a while it seemed that the hoped-for "bounceback" had taken place. The DJIA then fell almost 100 points in the first half hour, rallied, and then fell again. By 12:30, it was at 1,712 and falling. In retrospect, this was the key moment in the panic. Stocks held at this level, rose, fell again, and rallied in the last three hours to close at 1,841, up 103 points on the day, its first triple-digit gain.

The market rose 187 points on Wednesday, fell 78 points on Thursday, and rose by 1 point on Friday to close the week at 1,950. There was a 157-point loss the following Monday, but trading volume indicated that it was not caused by a panic. Rallies enabled the DJIA to end the month at 1,994. The index had lost more than 600 points in October.

During that month, scare headlines and dour predictions prompted thoughts that the crash would follow the pattern of 1929. *The New York Times* charted the 1987 market against that of 1929. The market's recovery and continued strength soon caused such fears to dissipate.

By mid-November, it appeared that all would indeed be well. The shakeup in the stock market apparently had not caused more widespread problems. Payrolls swelled in October in the best performance since September, 1983. During the first ten months of 1987, factory employment expanded by 26,700 jobs per month, compared with average monthly losses of 30,000 in 1985 and 13,500 in 1986. Department store sales increased on a year-to-year basis by 1.4 percent, while consumer spending rose by 0.5 percent. Christmas sales would reach a new record. The Commerce Department would reveal that the U.S. gross national product had advanced by an annualized rate of 4.1 percent during the third quarter of 1987.

Foreign central banks began reducing their key interest rates, led by the German Bundesbank, which reduced short-term rates from 3.5 percent to 3.25 percent. There was talk of a new international monetary conference. Lower interest rates may have invigorated spending in other countries, increasing U.S. exports and lessening pressure on the trade deficit.

By the year's end, several fact-finding commissions were at work investigating the crash. One, sponsored by the federal government, was headed by former New Jersey senator and future secretary of the treasury Nicholas Brady. The NYSE conducted its own investigation, chaired by former attorney general Nicholas Katzenbach. In addition, there were investigations by the Chicago Board of Trade, the Chicago Mercantile Exchange, and the General Accounting Office. As might have been expected, the Chicago Board of Trade report exonerated the options market from blame, and the NYSE report did the same for its specialists. The Brady group, the most impartial of the lot, placed most of the blame for the crash's severity on portfolio insurance and program traders, the traders who placed huge orders based on computer programs.

The Brady Commission put forth several recommendations. The first involved "circuit breakers" between the stock indexes and the market. When certain disparities developed, trading would be suspended temporarily. In addition, all trading would be halted when prices declined by a specified figure. The Brady group recommended greater regulatory oversight of index options markets and higher margins (percentages of the value of an option that a buyer had to put up front) to be employed in their use. It wanted a single agency to oversee the entire stock market. Some thought it should be the Securities and Exchange Commission, while others opted for the Federal Reserve Board. Brady also recommended greater cooperation between the exchanges and a greater amount of disclosure of information. All these recommendations were adopted, with the Federal Reserve Board being assigned the task of oversight.

Bargain hunters bought many of the stocks that had fallen in price, aiding recovery of the market. Overall, losses were largely erased within two years of the crash. A smaller crash occurred in 1989, but share prices recovered and the DJIA soon flirted with the 3,000 level.

Bibliography

Bose, Mihir. *The Crash: Fundamental Flaws Which Caused the 1987-8 World Stock Market Slump and What They Mean for Future Financial Stability*. London: Bloomsbury, 1988. Valuable for insights regarding the interrelations of world financial markets.

Hughes, Jonathan R. T. *American Economy History*. 5th ed. Reading, Mass.: Addison-Wesley, 1998.

Kamphuis, Robert W., et al., eds. *Black Monday and the Future of Financial Markets*. Homewood, Ill.: Dow Jones Irwin, 1989. A scholarly, technical account of the crash along with an analysis of how future shocks can be prevented.

Sobel, Robert. *Panic on Wall Street*. Rev. ed. New York: Dutton, 1988. A reissue of an earlier work on the history of financial panics, with a new chapter on the panic of 1987, stressing the differences between it and the 1929 crash.

U.S. Congress. House. Committee on Banking, Finance, and Urban Affairs. *Impact of the Stock Market Drop and Related Developments on Interest Rates, Banking, Monetary Policy, and Economic Stability*. 100th Congress, 2d session, 1988. Discussion and analysis of the Brady Report. By the time of the hearings it had become evident that there would be no long-lasting effects of the crash, but the legislators did think in terms of reform.

U.S. Congress. Senate. Committee on Banking, Housing, and Urban Affairs. *"Black Monday": The Stock Market Crash of October 19, 1987*. 100th Congress, 2d session, 1988. Congressional discussion and analysis of the Brady Report. Contains the text of the report.

Wood, Christopher. *Boom and Bust*. New York: Atheneum, 1989. A journalistic account of the crash, its causes, and its aftermath.

Robert Sobel

Cross-References

The Wall Street Journal Prints the Dow Jones Industrial Average (1897); The U.S. Stock Market Crashes on Black Tuesday (1929); The Securities Exchange Act Establishes the SEC (1934); Insider Trading Scandals Mar the Emerging Junk Bond Market (1986); Drexel and Michael Milken Are Charged with Insider Trading (1988).

DREXEL AND MICHAEL MILKEN ARE CHARGED WITH INSIDER TRADING

CATEGORIES OF EVENT: Finance and business practices
TIME: 1988
LOCALE: New York, New York

In 1988, Drexel Burnham Lambert was charged with insider trading, beginning a chain of events that included the firm's declaration of bankruptcy and incarceration of its star investment banker, Michael Milken

Principal personages:
MICHAEL MILKEN (1946-   ), the leading banker at Drexel Burnham Lambert, where he pioneered in the use of junk bonds to finance expansion of mid-sized companies.
FREDERICK JOSEPH (1937-   ), the chief executive officer of Drexel
RUDOLPH GIULIANI (1944-   ), the prosecutor most closely associated with insider trading cases
IVAN BOESKY (1937-   ), a financier charged with insider trading
DENNIS LEVINE (1952-   ), a Drexel banker who funneled inside information to Ivan Boesky

Summary of Event

During the 1970's, the United States experienced inflation and economic stagnation. The prices of common stocks gyrated wildly but on average wound up about where they were in the late 1960's. Meanwhile, earnings and dividends rose steadily. Because of inflation, the underlying values of many companies increased, but this was not reflected in the prices of their shares. Large firms often were worth less as ongoing businesses than their value if sold in pieces. This helped set the stage for hostile takeovers, in which Drexel Burnham Lambert became the leader. Drexel's leadership and innovation in financing business dealings ultimately led to charges of illegal activity in December, 1988.

Mid-sized companies whose bonds were not deemed of investment quality by rating services had difficulties raising money for expansion during the 1970's and early 1980's. Bank loans were difficult to obtain, and the companies had problems selling shares because many had not proved their performance and stockbrokers and analysts did not promote the companies' stocks.

Interest rates climbed, harming savings and loan companies (S&Ls), which were forbidden by law from paying rates for deposits that were high enough to be competitive. In the elevated rate environment, depositors withdrew money to invest at higher yields. By 1982, one out of every five S&Ls had failed. In response to problems in the industry, Congress passed the Deregulation Act of 1980 and the Garn-St. Germain Act of 1982, deregulating the S&Ls and permitting them to invest in commercial ventures that might be more profitable than mortgages, their traditional investment outlet. During the same period, insurance companies, attempting to win new customers, offered new products such as single-premium deferred insurance and guaranteed investment contracts that offered high, usually tax-deferred, returns.

The combination of these factors had two major consequences: Many companies sought financing, and raiders looked for undervalued companies, hoping to take them over and carve them up for profits. Large numbers of people looked for and expected high yields. This set the stage for the activities of Drexel Burnham Lambert (commonly referred to as Drexel) and Michael Milken.

Milken started as a bond salesman at Drexel in 1969, specializing in low-rated bonds. He was convinced that these bonds offered a tremendous opportunity. Many were "fallen angels," bonds that were of investment grade when issued but whose companies had experienced reversals that resulted in downgrading of their debt. These bonds offered high yields, often more than compensating for the risk of default on them. Milken found customers in mutual funds, pension funds, insurance companies, and S&Ls, all of which wanted high yields to fulfill promises to their own customers or simply to survive. Milken's assessment of these bonds was correct. The "fallen angel" junk bonds performed well as a group, and his department became the largest money-maker at Drexel.

In 1977, Drexel started underwriting new issues of junk bonds, or bonds that were not rated as investment grade, and by the early 1980's it was the

790

leader in this area. In 1974, Frederick Joseph arrived at Drexel from Shearson Hayden Stone. He became Drexel's chief executive officer (CEO) in 1985. Joseph had observed the rise of hostile takeovers through leveraged buyouts, or buyouts financed with debt, and realized that junk bonds might be used as means to take over large companies.

Large profits could be made by individuals who had inside information regarding these raids. Those who knew of takeovers in advance could buy stock to sell once the takeovers became public knowledge and stock prices rose. Such trading, however, is illegal. Throughout the late 1980's, when hostile takeovers and leveraged buyouts were fueling a major bull market, rumors circulated regarding them. At the same time, leaders of large corporations, realizing their security was threatened, lobbied in Congress for legislation to limit hostile takeovers and the issuance of junk bonds. Their most important organization in this effort was the Business Round-table, comprising the CEOs of some of America's largest companies. In 1986, it appeared that these activities would result in laws prohibiting or at least limiting the use of high-yield bonds in corporate takeovers. Had this been done, the hostile takeover movement would have ended.

On May 12, 1986, while Congress debated several antitakeover bills, Drexel banker Dennis Levine was arrested on charges of insider trading in fifty-four stocks. Gary Lynch, chief of enforcement at the Securities and Exchange Commission, and U.S. Attorney Rudolph Giuliani offered Levine a plea bargain on the condition that he name his accomplices. Levine accepted, and on February 20, 1987, he was sentenced to two years in prison and a fine of $362,000.

One of those implicated by Levine was Ivan Boesky. On November 14, 1986, Boesky pleaded guilty to securities fraud and agreed to assist in identifying and prosecuting other malefactors. On April 23, 1987, Boesky received a sentence of three years in prison.

Giuliani went after other bankers, hoping to catch the "big one." Given the nature of the market, that could be none other than Milken. In his operations, Giuliani utilized provisions of the Racketeer Influenced and Corrupt Organizations statute, known as RICO. This act, passed in 1970, was aimed at curbing activities of organized crime. Racketeering was defined as "fraud in the sale of securities, or the felonious manufacture, importation, receiving, concealment, buying, selling, or otherwise dealing in narcotic or other dangerous drugs, punishable under any law of the United States." The penalties were harsh. Even if a business were run legitimately, it could be confiscated if purchased with illegally obtained money. In civil cases, treble damages could be levied. Funds and property could be seized before trial of those accused of RICO violations, presumably to prevent those assets from being hidden and protected from later seizure as penalties or fines.

On August 4, 1988, RICO was used against Princeton/Newport Partners, one of whose bankers was named by Boesky. The bank collapsed in December, and all the defendants were convicted on August 2, 1989. The conviction was overturned the following June, and two years later the government dropped the case.

In 1988, Giuliani turned on Drexel. In mid-December, he told Joseph that he would indict the company on RICO charges unless it agreed to a settlement. The company had no choice but to bow, since seizure of its assets as allowed by RICO would have ruined it. On December 26, it agreed not to contest charges, to pay $650 million in fines and restitution, and to accept outside management. In addition, it would place Milken on leave of absence and withhold $200 million of his earnings. On February 13, 1989, after being denied assistance, Drexel filed for bankruptcy.

Milken had formed a new company, International Capital Access Group (ICAG), which was intended to finance minority-owned businesses, unions, and Third World countries. ICAG had many clients eager to utilize Milken's expertise and contacts. In one daring plan, Milken attempted to have Japanese firms pay the debt Mexico owed the United States, in return for which they would obtain a free trade zone in Mexico from which to export to the United States. This deal fell through.

After protracted negotiations, on April 20, 1990, Milken agreed to plead guilty to six felony charges, none of which involved insider trading, bribery, racketeering, or manipulating the prices of stocks, the key elements of Boesky's plea bargain. He also agreed that after sentencing he would cooperate with the Justice Department. The government would not file additional criminal charges, but Milken remained subject to civil actions and criminal charges from other jurisdictions.

Impact of Event

Milken's sentence included ten years in a federal penitentiary, eighteen hundred hours of community service a year for three years, and $200 million in fines. This was in addition to $400 million already extracted from him for a restitution fund. Later, there would be an additional $500 million fine to settle anticipated legal actions, which numbered more than 150.

By the end of 1989, it seemed that the junk bond market had ended, as a result of the decline of customers and clients. Congress passed the Financial Institutions Rescue, Recovery, and Enforcement Act (FIRREA) in August, 1989, requiring S&Ls to redo their financial statements to reflect the current market values of any junk bonds that they held, a process called "marking to market." Many S&Ls showed large accounting losses because of marking to market. In addition, S&Ls were required to sell their junk bond portfolios by August, 1994. S&Ls held about 6 percent of all junk bonds, so the forced sale was expected to lower prices substantially. The thrifts were prohibited from purchasing junk bonds as well, removing a major player in that market. Almost at once, the thrifts started liquidating their portfolios. The losses involved caused several to file for bankruptcy.

New York ruled that state pension funds no longer could invest in junk bonds, and California declared that its pension funds would sell off its junk holdings, with face value of $530 million, for $380 million. The Resolution Trust Corporation (RTC), a government agency created to deal with insolvent thrifts, had seized the assets of many of them and was selling junk bonds. It soon had dumped $5 billion in bonds on the market. The SEC ruled that as of May, 1991, no more than 5 percent of the assets of money market funds could be dedicated to unrated or low-rated commercial paper. Previously, the figure had been 25 percent. This did not result in panic selling, but it did dry up another market for junk bonds. Most seriously, insurance companies, a prime junk customer, were told by the National Association of Insurance Commissioners to limit junk holdings and were required to establish reserves against such investments. Thus many of the major buyers of junk bonds were removed from the market.

There were several failures of corporations which had large junk issues outstanding. This led to price declines for the bonds, reflected in the share prices of high-yield mutual funds. Declining share prices led to massive redemptions. The funds sold junk bonds to pay for redeemed shares, further depressing the market. The hostile takeover movement came to an end in the wake of the collapse of the junk bond market. Unable to obtain backing, the raiders disappeared.

The panic selling in the junk bond market turned out to be overdone. Bargain hunters appeared, and new high-yield mutual funds were organized to capitalize on the situation. Leon Black, one of Milken's chief aides, was one of the more sophisticated individuals in this market, picking up hastily sold portfolios and making more money at it in the 1990's than he had when dealing in junk bonds during the 1980's.

Merrill Lynch and Goldman Sachs led the way in the new creation of junk, most of which was used in restructurings or was issued for mid-sized companies. In 1986, a record $31.9 billion in junk had been sold before placements declined. In 1990, $1.4 billion was taken to market. In 1991, the price of junk rose sharply, and demand reappeared. More than $40 billion in junk was sold that year, and slightly less than $38 billion was sold in 1992. Junk was the best-performing financial asset in 1991 and close to the top in 1992. By then, some critics wondered whether any of Drexel's transgressions merited the destruction of a firm that had employed seven thousand workers.

Milken entered prison at Pleasanton, California, on March 4, 1991. On August 5, 1992, after Milken had served seventeen months, Judge Kimba Wood announced that she was reducing his sentence to thirty-three months. He was released on January 2, 1993, and so served twenty-two months. Initially he went to a halfway house and worked for his attorney, Richard Sandler. On February 4, he was permitted to return home. The reductions in his prison term were for cooperation with the government, but in fact Milken had not cooperated. The sharp reduction in prison time was taken by Milken's defenders as a tacit admission that the crimes to which he had pleaded guilty had not merited so harsh a sentence.

The government had gone after Milken in part to stop hostile takeovers, which endangered the security of leaders of large, mismanaged companies. With the end of hostile takeovers, such individuals felt more secure, but the security did not last. Large pension and trust funds introduced measures to limit salaries and bonuses, indicating displeasure with executives who appeared to place their own interests above those of the corporation. Even though takeovers were rare, the threat of them encouraged managements to be more responsive to shareholders. Managerial responsibility should be counted as one legacy of the junk bond revolution.

Bibliography

Bailey, Fenton. *Fall from Grace: The Untold Story of Michael Milken.* New York: Birch Lane Press, 1991. Generally sympathetic to Milken, written with his cooperation.

Bainbridge, Stephen M. *Securities Law: Insider Trading.* New York: Foundation Press, 1999.

Bruck, Connie. *The Predators' Ball: The Inside Story of Drexel Burnham and the Rise of the Junk Bond Raiders.* New York: Simon & Schuster, 1988. The first of the books on Drexel Burnham Lambert, one that the company attempted to suppress. Critical of the company.

Johnston, Moira. *Takeover: The New Wall Street Warriors, the Men, the Money, the Impact.* New York: Arbor House, 1986. The best book on the merger mania of the mid-1980's, but written before the biggest and most important deals were concluded.

Katz, Leo. *Ill-Gotten Gains: Evasion, Blackmail, Fraud, and Kindred Puzzles of the Law.* Chicago: University of Chicago Press, 1996.

Kornbluth, Jesse. *Highly Confident: The Crime and Punishment of Michael Milken.* New York: Morrow, 1992. A pro-Milken book, written with his cooperation. Strong on Milken's personality and the trial, weak on an understanding of how investment banking is conducted.

Levine, Dennis B. *Inside Out: An Insider's Account of Wall Street.* New York: G. P. Putnam's Sons, 1991. A self-serving work by the banker whose arrest set off the trail of indictments that led to the destruction of Drexel.

Madrick, Jeff. *Taking America: How We Got from the First Hostile Takeover to Megamergers, Corporate Raiding, and Scandal.* New York: Holt, Rinehart & Winston, 1987. A journalistic account of the merger movement, tending toward the sensational.

Smith, Roy C. *The Money Wars.* New York: Dutton, 1990. A clear and informed study of the takeover movement, with special attention to Drexel.

Sobel, Robert. *Dangerous Dreamers.* New York: Wiley, 1993. An attempt to place the merger movement in the perspective of post-World War II markets, concentrating on the merger movement and the sources of Milken's ideas and activities.

Stewart, James B. *Den of Thieves.* New York: Simon & Schuster, 1991. A contentious best-seller about the decline of Drexel and Milken, apparently based on leaks from the SEC and the U.S. attorney's office.

Yago, Glenn. *Junk Bonds: How High Yield Securities Restructured Corporate America.* New York: Oxford University Press, 1990. A scholarly defense of the use of junk bonds in corporate creation and takeovers, by one of the more prominent Milken defenders.

Robert Sobel

Cross-References

Congress Deregulates Banks and Savings and Loans (1980-1982); Insider Trading Scandals Mar the Emerging Junk Bond Market (1986); Bush Responds to the Savings and Loan Crisis (1989).

MEXICO RENEGOTIATES DEBT TO U.S. BANKS

CATEGORY OF EVENT: Finance
TIME: 1989
LOCALE: Washington, D.C.

Government pressure on U.S. banks to renegotiate Mexico's debt led to the Brady debt reduction plan

Principal personages:

NICHOLAS F. BRADY (1930-   ), the United States secretary of the treasury, 1988-1992

CARLOS SALINAS DE GOTARI (1948-   ), the president of Mexico beginning in 1988

JAMES BAKER III (1930-   ), the United States secretary of the treasury, 1985-1988

Summary of Event

Banks located in major financial centers of the world participated in an expansion of international lending in the 1970's. Loans to less developed countries (LDCs) were the fastest growing category of international bank loans. A combination of sharply increased bills for oil imports and a recession in the industrial countries that cut into the LDCs' export earnings, compounded by unrealistic exchange rate policies, sharply raised these countries' aggregate balance of payments deficits from an annual average of about $7 billion in the 1970-1973 period to $21 billion in 1974 and $31 billion in 1975. Banks were replete with funds and faced declining domestic loan demand. They were thus willing and able to provide financing in the form of direct government loans and development financing. Bank lending to LDCs continued to grow rapidly during the early 1980's. In the summer of 1982, however, international financial markets were shaken when a number of developing countries found themselves unable to meet payments to major banks around the world on debt amounting to several hundred billion dollars. With the onset of the debt crisis, lending to LDCs dried up rapidly.

Several developments set the stage. One of these was a growing trend in overseas lending to set interest rates on a floating basis, rather than fixing an interest rate for the life of the loan. Floating rate loans made borrowers vulnerable to increases in real interest rates as well as to increases in the real value of the dollar, because most of these loans were in dollars. A second development was the oil price increase implemented by the Organization of Petroleum Exporting Countries (OPEC) in 1979. In the absence of policies that promoted rapid adjustments to this new shock, the LDCs' balance of payments deficits soared to $62 billion in 1980 and $67 billion in 1981. The deficits increased the LDCs' need for external financing, and banks responded by increasing the flow of loans to the LDCs to $39 billion in 1980 and to $40 billion in 1981. Interest rates increased at the same time. The variable interest rates of the loans combined with increased indebtedness boosted the LDCs' net interest payments to banks from $11 billion in 1978 to $44 billion in 1982.

The final element setting the stage for the crisis was the onset of the recession in industrial countries. The recession reduced the demand for the LDCs' products and thus the export earnings needed to service their bank debt.

The first major blow to the international banking system came in August, 1982, when Mexico announced that it was unable to meet its regularly scheduled payments to international creditors. Shortly thereafter, Brazil and Argentina found themselves in a similar situation. By the spring of 1983, about twenty-five LDCs were unable to meet their debt payments as scheduled and had entered into loan rescheduling negotiations with creditor banks.

By late 1983, the intensity of the international debt crisis began to ease as the world's economic activity picked up, boosting the LDCs' export earnings. In October of 1985, United States Treasury Secretary James Baker III called on fifteen principal middle-income debtor LDCs to undertake growth-oriented structural reforms that would be supported by increased financing from the World Bank, continued modest lending from commercial banks, and a pledge by industrial nations to open their markets to LDC exports. By 1989, most of the fifteen nations were behind in delivering on promised policy changes and economic performance. Citicorp and other banks added to their reserves against losses from loans and put themselves in a stronger position to demand reforms in countries to which they had loaned money.

During the late 1980's, recognizing the deteriorating financial situation,

Mexico's President Carlos Salinas de Gotari undertook programs to turn the economy around. Mexico cut its budget deficit by 20 percent, to 13 percent of gross domestic product, between 1987 and 1988. The government also sold into private hands two-thirds of the twelve hundred businesses it owned and obtained concessions from labor and business to help control inflation. In 1989, the inflation rate was reduced to 20 percent, down from 160 percent in 1987. Mexico opened its doors to foreign competition through trade liberalization policies. These changes did not occur without costs. The Mexican infrastructure suffered. Cutbacks in investment in public services, roads, telecommunications, and electrical systems led to deterioration. Salinas needed both private and public sources to provide stable jobs to attack the poverty level and develop the infrastructure. Mexico could not pay its $10 billion a year in loan payments and also finance growth. Repayments of principal and interest added up to 6.5 percent of the country's gross domestic product. Something had to be done.

In 1989, Nicholas Brady, the treasury secretary, put forth a new plan to replace the Baker Plan. It emphasized debt relief through forgiveness instead of new lending. It would cover $54 billion of Mexico's $69 billion debt to foreign banks. On July 23, 1989, an agreement was reached by Mexico and the fifteen-bank committee representing the country's five hundred bank creditors. Under the terms of the agreement, banks could choose to swap old loans for thirty-year bonds at a 35 percent discount of face value. These bonds paid interest at the same rate as the old loans, $13/16$ of a percentage point over the London Interbank Offered Rate. Another option was to swap old loans for thirty-year bonds with the same face value. These bonds would pay a fixed interest rate of 6.25 percent, much lower than the prevailing rate. The last option was to lend new money or reinvest interest received from Mexico for four years in an amount equal to one-fourth of their current medium- and long-term exposure. The interest on the new bonds would be guaranteed for at least eighteen months. The bonds' principal would be secured by a zero-coupon Treasury bond financed by the International Monetary Fund, the World Bank, Mexico, and Japan. For the Brady Plan to work, commercial banks had to both make new loans and write off existing loans.

Impact of Event

Banks accounting for only 10 percent of Mexico's debt chose to make new loans, less than was predicted. The designers of the plan also thought that most banks would prefer to cut the face value of the loans rather than reduce interest rates, but this too did not come to pass. Instead, many banks used the Brady Plan as an opportunity to exit the LDC debt market. These outcomes led to a $300 million shortage and the need for Mexico to contribute an additional $100 million and renegotiate the loan terms. Originally, the banks required that cash be made available immediately to pay eighteen months worth of interest, but because of the shortfall, they agreed to take the money in eighteen months rather than immediately.

Although the plan did not completely resolve Mexico's debt problems, it was a step in the right direction. It allowed President Salinas to begin programs to rebuild Mexico's infrastructure and provided relief from interest payments that was necessary for the Mexican economy to stabilize and gain economic footing.

If any country had earned the reduction in debt, it was Mexico. Salinas was committed to free market policies and to opening the economy. Even while asking for help from abroad, Mexico was working to solve its own problems. The message to other countries facing similar debt servicing problems was to emulate Mexico by cutting government waste, liberalizing the economy, and joining the international trading system, and then ask about debt relief.

Mexico provides just one example of the extent of the debt problems experienced by Latin American countries in 1989. The hyperinflation existing in Argentina, Brazil, and Peru, and the political instability in Latin America in general, threatened already-fragile political and economic conditions. Many countries found themselves far behind on their debt payments. Debtor nations such as Argentina, Bolivia, Costa Rica, the Dominican Republic, Ecuador, Brazil, Venezuela, Honduras, and Peru needed economic breathing room to impose reforms. Mexican relief was only the tip of the iceberg.

Latin America continued to account for the world's biggest debt problems but showed several of the most promising turnarounds. The sixteen major borrowers there owed a total of $420 billion in 1991, slightly more than half of that to banks. Brazil, the largest borrower in the developing world, remained a problem. Its debt came to $122.6 billion in 1991, $80 billion of it owed to banks. It suspended all debt payments in 1989 and agreed reluctantly in March of 1991 to start paying back a portion of its $8 billion in arrears. In Peru, bankers virtually abandoned hope of getting back the $8.6 billion owed to them. In 1991, Peru's debt certificates sold at 4 percent of their face value.

The good news was that some countries, notably Colombia, never rescheduled their payments. Chile, through the use of a creditor swap, cut its bank debt by 40 percent. Argentina, a slow payer, began a debt-equity swap program to help cut the cost on its $34 billion debt.

The Brady Plan proved to be helpful to several countries, Mexico being the first. It ended the game in which banks kept lending new money that countries used to pay interest on old debts. "Brady Bonds" were thirty-year bonds guaranteed by a zero-coupon bond from the United States Treasury. The interest was backed by the World Bank. Brady Bonds helped Mexico, Costa Rica, and Venezuela reduce their debt and proved to be easier to sell than the original bank loans. Trading in loans to LDCs climbed from $200 million in 1982 to more than $100 billion in 1990, showing that the market for Third World sovereign debt was becoming more liquid.

After years of problems from Latin American government debtors, United States banks finally got some return. Sounder economic policies in Mexico, Argentina, Venezuela, and some other Latin American countries bolstered the value of their outstanding debt, easing the pressure on banks holding loans. The market for LDC debt remained fragile, with buyers continuing to demand steep discounts from face value. The market could not absorb all the loans that banks wanted to sell, but the debt crisis of the 1970's and 1980's appeared to have lessened.

During the early 1980's, a widespread fear was that countries that had piled up substantial international debt, such as those in Latin America, would find their economies crushed by the pressure of loan payments. Defaults on loans would bring down big banks and cause a financial crisis in lender nations. One by one, however, the Latin American countries negotiated agreements under which their creditors agreed to accept smaller repayments; the countries in return enacted economic reforms. Steps to control inflation and open up foreign investments were taken. In July of 1992, Brazil, the biggest Third World debtor and a holdout on renegotiating, worked out an arrangement with nineteen banks representing private creditors. The Brady Plan and Mexico's debt restructuring provided a beginning. Cooperation between banks and governments softened the debt crisis.

Bibliography

Chambliss, Lauren, and James Srodes. "Mexico: How to Break the Mexican Debt Impasse Before It's Too Late." *Financial World* 158 (July 25, 1989): 18-21. This article gives an excellent review of the changes that took place under President Salinas in Mexico. It discusses the various economic and political changes that led to the improved Mexican economy and finally to the willingness of banks to renegotiate the terms of Mexican debt.

Finn, Edwin A., Jr. "Giving a Little to Save a Lot." *Forbes* 143 (March 6, 1989): 38-39. Discusses the plan proposed by Secretary of the Treasury James Baker III. Salinas' efforts to work on the debt relief proposal are also included. A good article to set the stage for the Brady Plan.

Hughes, Jonathan R. T. *American Economy History.* 5th ed. Reading, Mass.: Addison-Wesley, 1998.

Main, Jeremy. "A Latin Debt Plan That Might Work." *Fortune* 119 (April 24, 1989): 205-212. Sets out the details of the Brady Plan, the history behind its development, and the reactions it caused from the bankers involved and Mexico's president.

O'Reilly, Brian. "Cooling Down the World Debt Bomb." *Fortune* 123 (May 20, 1991): 122-124. An excellent article to put the Latin American debt crisis in perspective. It was written long enough after Mexico's debt restructuring that the results and impact of the Brady Plan can be assessed.

Sachs, Jeffrey. "Robbin' Hoods." *The New Republic* 200 (March 13, 1989): 16. Discusses the various ways that banks have in the past approached the idea of restructuring debt. Offers insights into how the Brady Plan differed from previous attempts at debt relief.

Patricia C. Matthews

Cross-References

Congress Deregulates Banks and Savings and Loans (1980-1982); The Immigration Reform and Control Act Is Signed into Law (1986); Bush Responds to the Savings and Loan Crisis (1989); The North American Free Trade Agreement Goes into Effect (1994).

BUSH RESPONDS TO THE SAVINGS AND LOAN CRISIS

CATEGORIES OF EVENT: Government and business; finance
TIME: August 9, 1989
LOCALE: Washington, D.C.

The Financial Institutions Rescue, Recovery, and Enforcement Act of 1989 was passed to bail out the savings and loan industry and to strengthen its regulatory standards

Principal personages:
GEORGE BUSH (1924-   ), the president of the United States, 1989-1993
RICHARD C. BREEDEN (1949-   ), the executive director of the White House Regulatory Task Force, 1989
L. WILLIAM SEIDMAN (1921-   ), the chairman of the Federal Deposit Insurance Corporation, 1985-1991
DANNY M. WALL (1939-   ), the chairman of the Federal Home Loan Bank Board, 1987-1989, and the director of the Office of Thrift Supervision, 1989-1990

Summary of Event

On August 9, 1989, President George Bush signed into law the long-awaited legislation designed to stem the stream of losses in the savings and loan industry. The Financial Institutions Rescue, Recovery, and Enforcement Act (FIRREA) had four explicit goals. The first was to improve the ability of regulators to supervise savings institutions by strengthening industry capital and accounting standards. The second was to return the federal deposit insurance fund to a sound financial base. The third was to provide funds to deal with the disposal of failed institutions. The fourth was to strengthen the enforcement ability of regulators through reconfigured powers and a new organizational structure. An unstated goal of FIRREA was to return the emphasis of the business to its roots of home mortgage lending.

Savings institutions had enjoyed more than fifty years of economic success. By the end of the 1970's, however, industry prosperity was threatened by unprecedented high inflation and interest rates. The financial structure of the typical thrift was at the core of the problem. Most institutions borrowed for short terms, in the form of depositors' savings accounts, but lent for long

President George Bush. (Library of Congress)

terms through fixed-rate home mortgages. While interest rates remained stable, thrifts could earn acceptable profits. When market forces caused rates to soar, the delicate balance was threatened, as payments to depositors rose without a corresponding increase in receipts from mortgages. In 1978, regulators allowed thrifts to pay higher interest rates on certificates of deposit. This checked disintermediation (savers going to other institutions), but the cost of funds rose. Profits, therefore, shrank or turned into losses.

Thrift executives knew that erosion of net worth jeopardized the industry's health. They sought relief from long-term, fixed-rate loans that tied them to low returns. The U.S. Congress was not prepared to back an industrywide bailout. As a compromise, it passed the Depository Institutions Deregulation and Monetary Control Act (DIDMCA) in 1980, granting additional lending powers to thrifts. Most promising was the ability to originate short-term consumer loans and high-yield commercial real estate loans. Despite DIDMCA, about 36 percent of all thrifts were losing money by the end of 1980. Even worse, in 1981 about 80 percent of the industry lost money. Congress reacted with additional deregulation in 1982. It passed the Garn-St. Germain Act, giving thrifts even broader investment powers.

The government also allowed thrifts favorable reporting treatment. Purchasers of failing institutions were given special accounting privileges. In addition, thrifts were authorized by the Federal Home Loan Bank Board

(FHLBB) to utilize lenient Regulatory Accounting Principles (RAP). Moreover, the FHLBB allowed thrifts to reduce their capital requirements from 5 percent to 3 percent between 1980 and 1982. This leniency was allowed to keep troubled thrifts from being taken over by regulators.

After deregulation, and with interest rates subsiding in 1983, the industry appeared to be heading toward prosperity. Thrifts attempted to grow out of their problems by generating more high-yield investments. The real estate market was booming, so thrift managers were tempted to invest in risky commercial ventures. They often disregarded such factors as lack of expertise, unfamiliar geographic territories, and questionable appraisals and underwriting. Loan brokers and junk bond brokers also found an eager market in the thrift industry.

Depositors continued to patronize savings institutions despite growing losses and failures. DIDMCA had increased deposit insurance coverage to $100,000. With this level of insurance, depositors had little fear of losing their savings at faltering institutions. Indeed, the failing institutions often offered the highest rates.

In 1986, the Tax Reform Act was passed. This repealed liberal depreciation and personal deduction provisions. Many commercial real estate deals were structured around such tax shelters. Without them, the enormous market for real estate syndicates dried up. At the same time, worldwide oil prices dropped. This negatively affected the economic health of states that relied on the oil industry. The real estate market in the Southwest went sour almost overnight, affecting real estate values throughout the country. The booming real estate market of 1983-1986 was transformed into an overbuilt market by 1987.

The FHLBB committed nearly $40 billion in 1988 to take over failing institutions, merge them into marketable packages, and sell them to investors. This program almost bankrupted the Federal Savings and Loan Insurance Corporation (FSLIC). FHLBB Chairman Danny C. Wall either concealed the depths of the FSLIC insolvency or did not recognize the extent of the problem. Matters were made worse by errors in judgment on the part of thrift managers, the greed of investors, weak examination and supervision practices by regulators, and numerous alleged cases of fraud and misconduct on the part of thrift insiders, regulators, investors, and members of Congress.

In this environment, George Bush took over the presidency in 1989. He was extremely concerned about the unstable condition of the FSLIC and the accumulated losses at hundreds of thrifts. A draft of a new law came out of the White House in February, 1989. Three people were primarily responsible for this proposal. Richard C. Breeden took the lead in Bush's efforts on the thrift crisis as executive director of the White House Regulatory Task Force. Breeden was assisted by Robert R. Glauber, an undersecretary in the Treasury Department. The senior member of this effort was L. William Seidman, chairman of the Federal Deposit Insurance Corporation (FDIC), which insured the commercial banking industry. In August, 1989, the act was approved by Congress. President Bush signed FIRREA into law a few days later.

FIRREA featured several key provisions. It dissolved both the FSLIC and the FHLBB. The responsibility of insuring the thrift industry's deposits reverted to the FDIC. The duty of supervising the Federal Home Loan Bank (FHLB) system and individual thrifts was passed to a new organization, the Office of Thrift Supervision (OTS). Danny Wall was appointed director of the OTS. Two new additional organizations were created. The Resolution Trust Corporation (RTC) was formed to dispose of the assets of failed thrifts. Seidman, as FDIC chairman, became chairman of the RTC. The Resolution Funding Corporation (RFC) was created as the fund-raiser for the RTC. The RFC was initially authorized to borrow up to $50 billion, through bonds, to fund RTC activities.

Numerous thrift powers were restructured. FIRREA banned investment in junk bonds, limited investment in nonresidential loans, set loan-to-one-borrower limits to national bank levels, and placed strict limitations on loans to affiliated parties. Most important, it mandated that thrifts hold at least 70 percent of their assets in mortgage-related investments. Penalties for failure to comply were tough at both the corporate and the individual levels.

FIRREA directed the OTS to set capital requirements for thrifts at levels no less stringent than those of national banks. Core capital requirements were set at 3 percent of total assets, and tangible capital was set at 1.5 percent of total assets. Thus, the definition of capital itself was altered. The previous reliance on RAP standards of accounting was abolished.

President Bush's stated intention was to fix the thrift industry permanently by closing down or selling hundreds of thrifts. His method of ensuring that old problems would not resurface was to subject surviving thrifts to the capital and accounting rules applied to national banks.

Impact of Event

FIRREA was a sharp response to the thrift crisis. Opinions differed as to whether this harshness was required to return the industry's profitability or whether it was punitive action for perceived transgressions. Considerable controversy arose in the business community, especially among the thrifts that were directly affected.

Some analysts believed that the capital requirements would bankrupt more institutions than necessary. There was a large group of thrifts working slowly to recover from their problems. They were not grossly insolvent but would not be able to meet new capital requirements for years. Continued weaknesses within the real estate markets did not help. Imposing stringent standards on a weakened industry pushed hundreds of these thrifts over the brink. This presented the RTC with a larger, more expensive task than the government had expected.

The short-run impact of FIRREA on the business community extended further than the thrift industry. FIRREA caused all lending institutions to tighten credit practices, so businesses had to postpone or cancel worthy projects. Tight credit contributed to a recessionary economic climate. Banking regulators tightened oversight and enforcement in their industry. Although inflation and interest rates were in check, banking became more conservative. Many banks were satisfied to watch profit margins improve through lower costs of funds. The resulting "credit crunch" contributed to job losses throughout the economy. Closings and mergers within the thrift industry meant an additional dramatic drop in jobs.

By the end of September, 1991, the OTS estimated that 464 thrifts (21 percent of the industry) were on the brink of takeover. These institutions had not been seized because there was no money available to do so. The OTS intended to take over all failing institutions and have the RTC either sell them intact or liquidate them piecemeal. To dispose of a thrift intact, the RTC had to make up any negative net worth. The goal was to entice investors, especially commercial banks, to purchase failing thrifts through the financial backing of bonds issued by the RTC/RFC. Unfortunately, FIRREA stripped thrifts of many powers that had made them attractive investments. Unless a thrift could open new depository markets for a bank, it did not offer much advantage to the prospective purchaser.

FIRREA's objective of making depository insurance financially sound also failed to be met. FIRREA did not correct the problems that existed in the FSLIC; it merely pushed the problems onto the FDIC, jeopardizing its solvency. Because the $100,000 insurance coverage was not changed, depositors and institutions remained susceptible to risk-taking. Since fixed insurance premiums were not changed, risky institutions were afforded the same degree of protection at the same cost as safe institutions.

Resolving the thrift crisis involved huge federal payments to honor commitments made by the FSLIC and new ones resulting from FIRREA. A substantial amount of the borrowing was to be repaid from the sale of assets of failed thrifts. Unfortunately, asset sales could not cover the large borrowings. This shortfall became the responsibility of taxpayers. Like the national debt, the FIRREA debt will likely fall on future generations of taxpayers. Several lessons emerged from FIRREA and the events that led to its passage. First, deregulation in the early 1980's seemed to hamper thrift industry efforts to reverse losses. More lenient rules and broadened powers were not accompanied by stricter supervision. Second, the deposit insurance system encouraged carelessness on the part of depositors and depository institutions. Fixed-price premiums ignored risk and transgressed the cardinal rules of insurance. Third, FIRREA may have been based on sound intentions, but the effect was similar to that of overmedication of a sickly patient. Good principles applied abruptly may have led the industry toward extinction. Fourth, an improperly funded program cannot expect success. FIRREA was more ambitious than its budget would allow. The final costs may not be known for generations.

Bibliography

Calavita, Kitty, Henry N. Pontell, and Robert H. Tillman. *Big Money Crime: Fraud and Politics in the Savings and Loan Crisis.* Berkeley: University of California Press, 1997.

Bush, Vanessa, and Katherine Morrall. "The Business Reviews a New Script." *Savings Institutions* 110 (October, 1989): 30-35. Presents a thorough yet concise overview of the specific provisions of FIRREA. Summarizes in chart form the restructured powers, regulatory reorganization, and objectives of the legislation. Highly recommended.

Lowy, Martin E. *High Rollers: Inside the Savings and Loan Debacle.* New York: Praeger, 1991. Highly recommended reading for a detailed understanding of the factors that caused the thrift crisis. Despite the title, commentary is not excessive; a balanced approach is used. Offers suggestions for improvement of the industry's health.

Mayer, Martin. *The Greatest-Ever Bank Robbery: The Collapse of the Savings and Loan Industry.* New York: Charles Scribner's Sons, 1990. A thorough review of causal factors in the savings and loan crisis. Emphasizes the role of key persons involved, placing blame and making accusations of wrongdoing. Interesting and informative to the reader who recognizes the point of view of the text.

Pilzer, Paul Z., and Robert Deitz. *Other People's Money: The Inside Story of the S and L Mess.* New York: Simon & Schuster, 1989. Emphasizes the effects of greed, mismanagement, and illegal practices on the thrift problem. Examines the growth of problems in the Southwest and the effects on the industry overall. Offers suggested solutions.

United States. Congressional Budget Office. *The Economic Effects of the Savings and Loan Crisis.* Washington, D.C.: Author, 1992. A Congressional Budget Office study that focuses on the role of the deposit insurance system in the savings and loan crisis. Explores how the problem originated but stresses the ramifications of thrift losses. Examines the future effects on the economy and fiscal policy.

Victor J. LaPorte, Jr.

Cross-References

The Kennedy-Johnson Tax Cuts Stimulate the U.S. Economy (1964); Congress Deregulates Banks and Savings and Loans (1980-1982); Federal Regulators Authorize Adjustable-Rate Mortgages (1981).

SONY PURCHASES COLUMBIA PICTURES

CATEGORY OF EVENT: Mergers and acquisitions
TIME: September, 1989
LOCALE: New York, New York

The purchase of a major film studio by a Japanese corporation accentuated fears of a Japanese takeover of American business

Principal personages:

AKIO MORITA (1921-1999), a Japanese physicist and engineer who cofounded the Sony electronics company and became its chief executive

MICHAEL SCHULHOF (1942-   ), an American physicist and businessman who became vice chairman of Sony USA and who engineered the purchase of Columbia Pictures

NORIO OHGA (1930-   ), a Japanese musician and businessman who became chairman of Sony USA and second in command of Sony Corporation

JON PETERS (1947-   ), a film producer who took charge of Columbia Pictures after the acquisition by Sony

PETER GUBER (1942-   ), a film producer who became chairman and chief executive officer of Sony Pictures Entertainment

Summary of Event

The purchase of Columbia Pictures in September, 1989, was one part of a business strategy intended to make Sony Corporation of Japan a multimedia entertainment empire. Sony had purchased CBS Records in 1988 and went on to acquire several software publishing companies in 1990 and 1991. The Sony Software Corporation was created in 1991 to oversee the record business (renamed Sony Music Entertainment), Columbia Pictures,

Digital Audio Disc Corporation (a manufacturer of compact discs), Sony Electronic Publishing, and the SVS video distribution operation. The other branch of Sony USA was the Sony Corporation of America, a producer of electronic equipment, videotape, audiotape, semiconductors, and in-flight entertainment.

Sony Corporation began life as the Tokyo Telecommunications Company in post-World War II Japan. It made electrical and electronic equipment for industrial, business, and home use. Its first great successes were in the field of home entertainment. Its transistor radios and magnetic tape recorders quickly established a reputation as affordable yet high-quality equipment incorporating the latest technology. In 1957, the company changed its name to Sony to reflect the importance of its Soni brand of audiotape to the company.

The American market became enormously profitable for Sony, and the company's audio equipment, radios, and televisions quickly established dominant positions in the home entertainment field. Sony remained committed to producing hardware, leaving the software—records, prerecorded tapes, and television shows—to other entities. A damaging and humiliating defeat over the format for videocassette recorders changed this strategy. Sony developed its U-matic magnetic video recorder in the 1960's and sold it to institutional and business users in the early 1970's. It followed this innovation with a videocassette player for home use, called the Betamax, which was introduced in 1976. Sony's great rival in Japan, the Matsushita company, introduced a competing videocassette system called VHS.

Although Sony had taken the lead in magnetic video recording technology and considered its Betamax technology superior to VHS, Matsushita convinced more manufacturers to adopt the VHS format. By the 1980's, many film producers were releasing their products on VHS cassettes only. VHS beat Betamax in the marketplace because the majority of software producers released their programs in this format. Sony finally had to retreat from the Betamax format at great cost, but in the process the company learned a valuable lesson in the home entertainment field. Superior hardware alone is not sufficient to succeed in this market: It needs to be supported by software. One of the indications that the Sony Corporation was planning to expand in this direction was the appointment of Norio Ohga as president and chief executive. Ohga was neither a factory manager nor an engineer, but instead was a musician and conductor of international repute. In a company founded by two engineers, Akio Morita (the chairman of Sony Corporation) and Masaru Ibuka, and dominated by scientists, the choice of Ohga marked a significant break with past corporate culture.

In the early 1980's, Sony introduced a major innovation in audio technology, the compact disc, which brought about a revolution in sound recording. In 1967, Sony had entered into a joint venture with CBS Records, one of the major record companies in the United States, to produce records. In 1988, Sony purchased CBS Records for $2 billion in the largest Japanese acquisition of an American company up to that time. As a leading producer of compact discs, Sony now had the manufacturing and artistic resources to provide music for its digital recordings. Sony was also a major producer of television sets and had invested heavily in new video technologies such as high definition television (HDTV) and 8 millimeter video recording. It soon began to look for a film and television studio to complement its well-established position in video technology.

The vice chairman of Sony USA, Michael Schulhof, led the search. He had begun his business career at CBS Records, then moved to Sony and served on the CBS/Sony board. Schulhof had played the leading role in Sony's acquisition of CBS Records. In his search for a film and television complement to acquire for Sony, he first courted MCA, an entertainment conglomerate that included Universal Pictures, the highly successful Universal Television, and record, music, and home video operations. Rebuffed by MCA's chairman, Lew R. Wasserman, Sony next turned to Columbia.

Columbia Pictures was created in the image of Harry Cohn, who co-founded the organization in 1920 and perfectly fitted the image of the mogul of the Golden Age of Hollywood in the 1930's and 1940's. By the 1980's, Columbia Pictures had important production units in film and television. In 1982, the Coca-Cola Corporation bought Columbia Pictures for $750 million, beginning an uneasy union that ended in 1987 when Coca-Cola retreated from film production and Columbia Pictures Entertainment (CPE) was born. CPE had two major film studios (Columbia and Tri-Star), the Loew's theater chain, a library of three thousand films, and some very successful television programs, including *The Young and the Restless*, *Designing Women*, and *Married . . . With Children*. This made it an attractive target for Sony, which offered to purchase the company for $3.4 billion in September, 1989.

Impact of Event
The news that Sony had bought a large film studio with a long history and strong image brought an immediate outcry in the American press. The American public interpreted the event not as a logical business strategy but as a glaring reminder of the power and ambition of Japanese companies. A survey carried out by *Newsweek* magazine and published in October, 1989, found that 43 percent of those surveyed believed that the acquisition was "a bad thing" for the United States. This was not the first Japanese incursion

into American business; Sony and numerous other Japanese companies had been purchasing American companies for decades. Several Japanese electrical manufacturers had set up their own plants in the United States in the 1970's and 1980's. Some of the leading Japanese car manufacturers, such as Honda, had bought out American suppliers and built factories in the United States. None of these moves, however, generated the publicity and the criticism that followed Sony's purchase of Columbia.

Unlike an automobile factory or a software publishing company, a film studio has a highly visible public profile and a strong association with an industry that could be considered to be the quintessential American business. By buying Columbia Pictures, the Japanese were buying a piece of an industry founded on American technology, nurtured by American business, and part of the American Dream. Columbia, standing with the torch of liberty in her hand, was the corporate symbol of Columbia Pictures Entertainment and had meaning as a symbol of the United States itself. Many newspaper articles posed the question of Japanese censorship of films dealing with sensitive issues such as the attack on Pearl Harbor and Japanese war crimes. Several American films had been censored or banned in Japan because they dealt with these issues. Discussions of the acquisition in the United States Congress revealed that if Sony had been an American company there might have been an antitrust suit challenging the takeover.

Sony Corporation not only bought CPE in this transaction but also hired two well-known film producers to run the organization. Peter Guber and Jon Peters had achieved great successes with films such as *Batman* (1989) and *Rain Man* (1988) and were considered to be the leading film producers in Hollywood at this time. Warner Communications had Guber and Peters under contract, and an acrimonious law suit followed their departure to Columbia. Sony paid a cash settlement to end the suit.

The furor over the sale of Columbia had hardly settled down before Sony's greatest rival made its move. Matsushita paid $6.6 billion for MCA in 1990 in a much bigger takeover than Sony's buyout of CPE. Matsushita acquired Universal Pictures, Universal Television, MCA Home Video, MCA Records, a large number of film theaters, and numerous other holdings to make it the largest entertainment conglomerate in the world. Another public outcry followed this purchase. Matsushita diplomatically agreed that some parts of MCA, especially the food and lodging concessions at Yosemite National Park, should be sold to American buyers.

The business and entertainment press maintained continuous scrutiny of the affairs of Columbia and MCA after the acquisitions to determine if Sony and Matsushita were keeping their promise not to impose a Japanese management style and Japanese decisions on the creative process of making films and television programs. Many analysts of the entertainment business believed that the Japanese companies had paid too high a price for their film studios and for the services of film producers and leading entertainers. Both Sony and Matsushita followed the policy of engaging well-known (and highly paid) talent for their entertainment divisions, banking on established stars of screen and recording rather than taking a chance on new talent.

The short-term financial results of the acquisitions were very poor and gave substance to the viewpoint that the Japanese companies had made expensive forays into businesses in which they were unprepared to compete. Several Columbia films that were put into production at the time of the takeover were expensive failures, despite the big names associated with them. These included the 1991 releases of *Hook*, directed by Steven Spielberg and starring Robin Williams; *Hudson Hawk*, starring Bruce Willis; and *Bugsy*, starring Warren Beatty. On the other hand, Sony Music Entertainment scored some hits with artists such as Mariah Carey, New Kids on the Block, and Michael Bolton.

The losses from film production, combined with poor sales of consumer electronics products, depressed Sony's economic position in the first half of 1992. The company had incurred $1.2 billion in debt to buy Columbia and experienced difficulties generating enough revenue to maintain operations. The departure of Jon Peters in 1991 was another blow to the company. Guber remained to direct the renamed Sony Pictures Entertainment operation. By the end of 1992, the entertainment part of Sony USA returned a profit, and the entire company's sales and profits posted an increase over the figures for 1991.

Although the wisdom of the Japanese incursion into American show business remained in doubt, Sony and Matsushita maintained their strategy of acquiring software companies. Both moved into video production and computer software. Sony acquired the Carolco Pictures independent studios and a large interest in RCA-Columbia Pictures Home Video in 1991. It continued to make long-term contracts with high-profile media stars such as Michael Jackson.

Sony had always been innovative in terms of developing new technology for its hardware, but in the software area it tended to be conservative and averse to risk. It introduced many dramatic new technologies in video and audio but did not produce innovative new music, films, or television shows in the first few years following the Columbia acquisition. In an industry in which financial success is usually the result of a small number of "blockbuster" films or record albums, creative decisions count for a great deal. Sony Software Corporation had yet to demonstrate that it was capable of identifying and exploiting new trends.

Several large Japanese and European electronics manufacturers realized the benefits of creating fully integrated media empires and continued to acquire American companies involved in entertainment. The Dutch Phillips company, the French Pathe organization, and the Australian News Corporation all acquired significant holdings in the American entertainment and communications businesses.

Bibliography

Dick, Bernard F., ed. *Columbia Pictures: Portrait of a Studio*. Lexington: University Press of Kentucky, 1992. A collection of scholarly papers about the workings of this film studio. Assesses some of its famous motion pictures. The editor provides a concise business history of the company from its founding to 1991.

Klein, Edward. "A Yen for Hollywood." *Vanity Fair* 54 (September, 1991): 200-209. An account of Sony's purchase of Columbia Pictures that incorporates it into Akio Morita's management strategy. Highly critical of Sony's strategy; gleefully relates the financial difficulties following the takeover.

Mahar, Maggie. "Adventures in Wonderland." *Barron's* 71 (October, 1991): 8-12. Describes the management style of Michael Schulhof and the purchase of Columbia. Discusses the operation of the film studio under Sony management and analyzes the financial returns.

Morita, Akio, with Edwin Reingold and Mitsuko Shimomura. *Made in Japan: Akio Morita and Sony*. New York: E. P. Dutton, 1986. A personal account of the rise of Sony from the 1940's to the 1980's. Although it does not contain information on the purchase of Columbia Pictures, it does outline Morita's philosophy of business and gives insights into Sony's overall strategy. As a personal account of one of the creators of Sony, this book often sinks into promotion of the company and Japanese culture.

Nathan, John. *Sony: The Private Life*. Boston: Houghton Mifflin, 1999. Study of the inner workings of the giant corporation.

Rothman, Andrea, and Ronald Grover. "Media Colossus." *Business Week*, March 25, 1991, 64-68. An overview of Sony's entertainment acquisitions in the United States, with a profile of Michael Schulhof. Concise description of Sony's American operations, including a useful diagram of its corporate structure.

Schlender, Brenton R. "How Sony Keeps the Magic Going." *Fortune* 125 (February 24, 1992): 76-82. An up-to-date profile of Sony that describes its product line and operations. Contains the latest figures on revenue and profits.

Andre Millard

Cross-References

The 1939 World's Fair Introduces Regular U.S. Television Service (1939); Cable Television Rises to Challenge Network Television (mid-1990's); Awarding of an NFL Franchise to Houston Raises the Ante in Professional Sports (1999).

BUSH SIGNS THE AMERICANS WITH DISABILITIES ACT OF 1990

CATEGORY OF EVENT: Government and business
TIME: July 26, 1990
LOCALE: Washington, D.C.

President George Bush signed into law the Americans with Disabilities Act, the world's first comprehensive civil rights law for people with disabilities

Principal personages:
GEORGE BUSH (1924-   ), the president of the United States, 1989-1993
TOM HARKIN (1939-   ), a U.S. congressman from Iowa, 1974-1991
TONY COELHO (1942-   ), a U.S. congressman from California, 1979-1989

Summary of Event

On July 26, 1990, President George Bush signed into law the Americans with Disabilities Act (ADA), the world's first comprehensive civil rights law directly aimed at protecting people with disabilities. The legislation was introduced in 1989 by Senator Tom Harkin (D-Iowa) and Congressman Tony Coelho (D-California). The primary purpose of the legislation was to ensure that disabled Americans, estimated to be up to forty-three million in number, would not be subjected to discrimination in employment, transportation, communications, public access, and other spheres of life. The law reinforces the fact that disabled Americans are full-fledged citizens and, as such, are entitled to legal protections that ensure them equal opportunity and access to the mainstream of American life. Section 106 of the ADA required that the Equal Employment Opportunity Commission (EEOC) issue substantive regulations implementing Title I of the act, regarding employment, within one year of enactment. The Department of Justice had responsibility for providing technical assistance for Title II, pertaining to nondiscrimination on the basis of disability in state and local government services, and substantive regulations for Title III, relating to nondiscrimination on the basis of disability by public accommodations and in commercial facilities.

President Bush signs the Americans with Disabilities Act on July 26, 1990, as representatives of the National Council on Disability and government agencies look on. (Joyce C. Naltchayan/The White House)

The employment provisions of Title I of the ADA apply to private employers, state and local governments, employment agencies, and labor unions. Employers with twenty-five or more employees were covered starting July 26, 1992, with employers with fifteen or more employees covered beginning July 26, 1994. The ADA prohibits discrimination in all employment practices, including job application procedures, hiring, firing, advancement, compensation, training, and other terms, conditions, and privileges of employment. Employment discrimination is prohibited against "qualified individuals with disabilities." The ADA defines an "individual with a disability" as a person who has a physical or mental impairment that substantially limits one or more major life activities, has a record of such an impairment, or is regarded as having such an impairment. Impairments that limit major life activities include those that affect seeing, hearing, speaking, walking, breathing, performing manual tasks, learning, caring for oneself, and working. As such, individuals with epilepsy, paralysis, substantial hearing or visual impairment, mental retardation, or a learning disability are covered by the ADA. People with acquired immune deficiency syndrome (AIDS) and infected with human immunodeficiency virus (HIV) are also covered under the ADA. Individuals with minor, nonchronic conditions of short duration such as sprains, infections, or broken limbs are not covered. Users of illegal drugs also are not covered by the ADA.

The ADA defines a "qualified individual with a disability" as a person who meets legitimate skill, experience, education, or other requirements of an employment position that he or she holds or seeks, and who can perform the "essential functions" of the position with or without reasonable accommodation. The ADA defines "reasonable accommodation" as a modification or an adjustment to a job or the work environment that will enable a qualified applicant or employee with a disability to perform essential job functions. Because the ADA specifically covers "qualified individuals with disabilities," a job applicant may be subjected to inquiries, tests, or other selection devices, provided that the evaluations are job related, all applicants are subjected to the same evaluations, and an applicant's disability does not prevent obtaining an accurate measure of qualifications. To ensure fair and accurate evaluation, the employer must identify and document the position requirements (skills, experience, and education) and essential functions of the job prior to recruiting applicants. These job descriptions must distinguish between essential and marginal job functions. Essential job functions are fundamental to successful performance of the job, as opposed to marginal job functions, which may be performed by particular incumbents at particular times but are incidental to the main purpose of the job.

The ADA specifies consideration of several questions in determining whether each of the described job functions is essential. Specifically, does the position exist to perform the function? Would the removal of the function fundamentally alter the position? What is the degree of expertise or skill required to perform the function? How much of the employee's time is spent performing the function? What are the consequences of failing to perform the function? How many other employees are available among whom the function can be distributed?

If an applicant is qualified in terms of the position requirements but unable to perform one of the essential job functions because of a disability, the ADA requires that the employer make a "reasonable accommodation" unless it would result in "undue hardship." "Undue hardship" means "significant difficulty or expense in, or resulting from, the provision of the accommodation." This refers to "any accommodation that would be unduly costly, expensive, substantial, or disruptive, or that would fundamentally alter the nature or operation of the business." According to the law, determining reasonable accommodation is an informal, interactive problem-solving process involving both the employer and the qualified individual with the disability.

Examples of reasonable accommodation include making existing facilities used by employees readily accessible to and usable by an individual with a disability, restructuring a job, modifying work schedules, acquiring or modifying equipment, providing qualified readers or interpreters, or appropriately modifying examinations, training, or other programs. Employers, however, are not required to lower quality or quantity standards, nor are they obligated to provide items of personal use such as eyeglasses or hearing aids.

The ADA allows a job offer to be conditioned on the results of a medical examination, provided that the examination is required for all entering

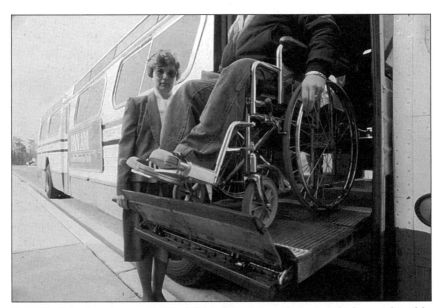

Title III of the Americans with Disabilities Act requires that new vehicles purchased by public transportation systems be accessible to persons with disabilities. (?)

employees in the same job category regardless of disability and that the information obtained is handled according to confidentiality requirements specified in the act. The ADA does allow testing for use of illegal drugs, in that a test for illegal drugs is not considered a medical examination.

Title II of the ADA stipulates that a public entity may not deny the benefits of its programs, activities, and services to individuals with disabilities because its facilities are inaccessible. A public entity does not, however, have to take any action that it can demonstrate would result in a fundamental alteration in the nature of its program or activity or cause undue financial and administrative burdens. Public entities were to achieve program accessibility by January 26, 1992. If structural changes were needed to achieve program accessibility, they were to be made as quickly as possible, but in no event later than January 26, 1995. Title II of the ADA also requires that all facilities designed, constructed, or altered by, on behalf of, or for the use of a public entity must be readily accessible by individuals with disabilities, if the construction or alteration was begun after January 26, 1992.

A public entity must ensure that its communications with individuals with disabilities are as effective as communications with others. A public accommodation is required to make available appropriate auxiliary aids and services where necessary to ensure effective communications. These accommodations include provision of qualified interpreters, note takers, telephone handset amplifiers, telecommunications devices for deaf persons, audio recordings, and brailled materials.

Title III of the ADA requires removal of physical barriers to the entrance and use of existing facilities. In addition, regulations require that new vehicles bought by public transit authorities be accessible to people with disabilities. The requirements include that all new fixed-route, public transit buses be accessible and that supplementary paratransit services be provided for those individuals with disabilities who cannot use fixed-route bus service.

Impact of Event

The Americans with Disabilities Act (ADA), signed into law by President George Bush on July 26, 1990, is a federal antidiscrimination statute designed to remove barriers that would prevent qualified individuals with disabilities from enjoying the same employment and accessibility opportunities available to persons without disabilities. The legislation affects not only state and local government but also places of public accommodation including more than five million private establishments such as restaurants, hotels, theaters, convention centers, retail stores, shopping centers, dry cleaners, laundromats, pharmacies, doctors' offices, hospitals, museums, libraries, parks, zoos, amusement parks, private schools, day care centers, health spas, and sporting centers.

The employment provisions of the ADA substantially increased regulation of employment practices, terms, and conditions affecting privileges of both state and local governments as well as millions of private enterprises. The ADA legislation covered employment applications, testing, hiring, assignments, evaluations, disciplinary actions, training, promotions, medical examinations, compensation, leave, benefits, layoffs, recalls, and termination practices.

One consideration that the ADA failed to address was that of health insurance issues. Employers were left in a difficult situation in that the ADA does not provide relief for health care insurance costs for disabled Americans. Health insurance for the disabled is complicated by two issues. There are problems related both to the preexisting-condition clauses in group insurance programs and to who provides health care coverage for the disabled. Individuals who are congenitally disabled (from birth or from an early age, so that the individual has never worked) typically receive care through Social Security Insurance (SSI). People who have acquired a disability after working normally receive coverage through Social Security Disability Insurance (SSDI). Disabled persons covered by SSI who begin work may continue to receive services through SSI. These services typically are inferior to those received by other employees in the organization. Individuals covered by SSDI are entitled to benefits only during a nineteen-month employment trial period. Once the trial period is over, the individual must either subscribe to the organization's group health policy or assume the cost of the SSDI benefits, which cost approximately $200 per month in 1990.

Another problem related to health care insurance is that people who have chronic illnesses or disabilities are vulnerable to clauses regarding preexisting conditions found in insurance policies. Such conditions often are not covered. Employers first have to investigate the benefits offered through SSI and SSDI and determine the length of coverage for disabled workers. Next, employers have to consult with their insurers and determine policies regarding preexisting-condition clauses as well as costs for potential additional required coverage for newly employed disabled workers.

Another consideration raised by the ADA is the cost of providing reasonable accommodations. These costs are determined on a case-by-case basis, depending upon the needs of the employees and the conditions of the work environment. For private enterprises, the Internal Revenue Code allowed a deduction of up to $15,000 per year for expenses associated with removal of qualified architectural and transportation barriers. A 1990 amendment also permitted eligible small businesses to receive a tax credit for certain costs of compliance with the ADA. An eligible small business was defined as having gross receipts of less than $1 million or with a work force of no more than thirty full-time employees. Qualifying businesses could claim a credit of up to 50 percent of eligible access expenditures that exceed $250 but do not exceed $10,250.

Given the newness and significance of the ADA, questions remained unanswered. Employers must be cognizant of the current requirements and carefully monitor legal developments applied through the courts. Given the significant regulations related to the ADA issued by the Equal Employment Opportunity Commission and the Department of Justice, employers should ensure that they create and validate job descriptions, train managers and supervisors how to act appropriately with respect to individuals who have any disability, determine essential and nonessential functions of any job, and be able to defend any employment decision regarding disabled applicants.

Bibliography

Barlow, Wayne E. "Accommodate the Disabled." *Personnel Journal* 70 (November, 1991): 119-124. Barlow summarizes the key EEOC regulations related to the ADA. He carefully explains the differences between essential and nonessential job functions as well as three categories of reasonable accommodation to enable an individual who has a disability to perform a job.

Barlow, Wayne E., and Edward Z. Hane. "A Practical Guide to the Americans with Disabilities Act." *Personnel Journal* 71 (June, 1992): 53-60. The authors provide an excellent guide for employers to ensure compliance with the provisions of the ADA in addition to recommendations to limit the associated costs to employers for potential claims of discrimination.

Hunsicker, J. Freedley, Jr., "Ready or Not: The ADA." *Personnel Journal* 69 (August, 1990): 81-86. Hunsicker describes the key legislative provisions of the ADA and what impact such regulation will have on governmental and corporate human resource policies and procedures.

Koen, Clifford M., Jr., Sandra J. Hartman, and Stephen M. Crow. "Health Insurance: The ADA's Missing Link." *Personnel Journal* 70 (November, 1991): 82-87. The article discusses the issue of health insurance and its significant omission from the ADA. Specifically, the authors discuss the options available to employers and disabled workers.

Lord, Mary. "Away with Barriers." *U.S. News and World Report* 113 (July 20, 1992): 60-63. Lord discusses compliance with the provisions of the

ADA and the economic impact some of the changes may have on employers and their places of business. She provides some common-sense examples as to what can be done at low cost as well as some examples of corporate innovations and imagination.

McKee, Bradford. "A Troubling Bill for Business." *Nation's Business* 78 (May, 1990): 58-59. Bradford discusses some of the concerns that owners of small businesses have voiced regarding the sweeping requirements of the ADA. Issues of possible litigation and questions of cost compliance are also discussed.

Mudrick, Nancy. "An Underdeveloped Role for Occupational Social Work: Facilitating the Employment of People with Disabilities." *Social Work* 36 (November, 1991): 490-495. Mudrick presents an extensive analysis of the issues confronting workers with disabilities and their employers. Provides information about disabilities and workplace disability policy important to the practice of occupational social work.

U.S. Equal Employment Opportunity Commission and the U.S. Department of Justice. *Americans with Disabilities Act Handbook*. Washington, D.C.: U.S. Government Printing Office, 1991. Excellent handbook containing regulations and interpretations of all three titles of the ADA.

John L. Farbo

Cross-References

Congress Passes the Equal Pay Act (1963); The Civil Rights Act Prohibits Discrimination in Employment (1964); The Pregnancy Discrimination Act Extends Employment Rights (1978); The Supreme Court Rules on Affirmative Action Programs (1979); The Supreme Court Upholds Quotas as a Remedy for Discrimination (1986).

BUSH SIGNS THE CLEAN AIR ACT OF 1990

CATEGORIES OF EVENT: Consumer affairs and transportation
TIME: November 15, 1990
LOCALE: Washington, D.C.

The Clean Air Act of 1990 established new standards for tailpipe emissions, mandated special devices to reduce fumes in selected areas, and required automakers to produce cars by 1995 that run on alternative fuels

Principal personages:
GEORGE BUSH (1924-   ), the forty-first president of the United States
WILLIAM REILLY (1940-   ), the administrator of the Environmental Protection Agency
JOHN D. DINGELL (1926-   ), the chairman of the House Energy Committee
HENRY A. WAXMAN (1939-   ), the leading pollution fighter in the House
ROBERT C. BYRD (1918-   ), a Democratic U.S. senator
GEORGE MITCHELL (1933-   ), the Senate Majority Leader
RICHARD AYRES (?-1992), the chairman of the National Clean Air Coalition, an environmentalist group
JOHN H. CHAFEE (1922-1999), a Republican U.S. senator
MAX BAUCUS (1941-   ), the Democratic floor manager of the clean air debate

Summary of Event

The Clean Air Act of 1990 (S. 1630) passed after nearly two years of deliberations in Congress and marked a significant departure by President George Herbert Walker Bush from the policies of his predecessor, Ronald

Reagan, who had resisted legislative initiatives in the area. The law amended the Clear Air Act of 1970 and yielded comprehensive air pollution legislation. It addressed air-quality standards to combat smog in polluted cities, proposed tougher standards and alternative fuels to mitigate ozone-related problems stemming from automobile tailpipe emissions, enunciated tough rules for toxic emissions from industrial plants, and mandated controls on emissions of sulfur dioxide and nitrogen oxides that contribute to acid rain.

Enacted in 1970, the Clean Air Act (CAA) was first amended in 1977. Although the CAA authorized the Environmental Protection Agency (EPA) to impose sanctions in order to attain federal air-quality standards related to ozone and carbon monoxide, they were rarely used. The blame for ineffective administrative enforcement has been traced by some analysts to frequent and inappropriate intervention from the courts. The EPA's distaste for judicial intervention may have created policies more preoccupied with surviving eventual judicial scrutiny than with effectively tackling air pollution. Regardless of whether ineffective enforcement stemmed from the administrative process in the EPA or from the judicial system, prolonged laxity on federal standards had seriously undermined air quality in several urban areas. Deteriorating air quality posed a rapidly growing public health hazard.

Despite the clear need to revise and strengthen the CAA to empower strict enforcement of tough air-quality standards, there was significant resistance within Congress to such action. Several members of Congress feared that stronger legislative initiatives on clean air would impose unreasonable social burdens, such as significant numbers of lost jobs and dramatically increased costs to industries and eventually to consumers. These fears found eloquent expression through John D. Dingell, who used his stewardship of the House Energy Committee to thwart any attempt to impose tough clean-air standards on his constituents, which included the automakers in Detroit. Similarly, Senator Robert C. Byrd of West Virginia vigorously opposed clean-air proposals aimed at industrial emissions of sulfur dioxide as a means of attacking the acid rain problem because such proposals, if enacted, would adversely affect demand for the high-sulfur coal mined in his home state. Congressional members from the Midwest were apprehensive that acid rain proposals would impose unreasonable additional costs on utilities in their states that traditionally burned high-sulfur coal, as a result of measures such as mandatory installation of scrubber devices.

These considerations often engendered intransigence and heated exchanges in congressional debates and eventually led to closed-door negotiations in which the set of 1990 CAA amendments was finalized. Senator George Mitchell and Representative Henry A. Waxman played vital roles in pushing the legislation though Congress. Senators John H. Chafee and Max Baucus and EPA administrator William Reilly also provided instrumental support for passage of the bill. Various interest groups including the National Clean Air Coalition, an environmentalists' group led by Richard Ayres, and the Clean Air Working Group, a business-sponsored lobby, critically analyzed the proceedings from their idiosyncratic perspectives. The final version of the amendments as signed into law on November 15, 1990, had far-reaching implications for businesses and consumers. It included elements pertaining to ambient air quality (smog), motor vehicles, air toxins, acid rain, stratospheric ozone, and enforcement.

The smog provisions required monitoring the attainment of National Ambient Air Quality Standards (NAAQS) in all areas. Five classes of air pollution problems were defined to assess the extent of such attainment: marginal, moderate, serious, severe, and extreme. Depending on the degree of severity of air pollution as reflected in this classification, different deadlines were imposed for each area to attain the NAAQS levels. Moreover, the amendments lowered the definition of a major smog source to any industrial unit that produced fifty tons of volatile organic compounds (VOCs) per year in areas classified under the "serious" ozone category, twenty-five tons for "severe" areas, and ten tons for "extreme" ozone areas. Many regions had not attained the NAAQS levels by 1992. The law requires states to develop implementation plans to reach these standards. In cases of failure of areas to attain standards, the EPA is required to bump up each such area into the next higher category; the law also empowers states to voluntarily bump up any area. Taken together, these key provisions empower state regulatory bodies and even enforcement agencies at the local level to monitor and control all pollution sources, ranging from huge utilities and oil refineries to the relatively small sources, such as local dry cleaners and paint contractors, that previously attracted little regulatory attention.

With regard to motor vehicles, the amendments delineated tailpipe emissions standards for harmful pollutants such as hydrocarbons (mandated to be cut by 35 percent by 1994) and nitrogen oxide (mandated to be cut by 60 percent by 1994). The longevity of emission control equipment in automobiles was also a subject of concern. The act stipulated that by the year 1998, such equipment should last for ten years or 100,000 miles. The law also empowered the EPA administrator to phase in by 1995 the use of reformulated gasoline, gasoline with chemical composition changed to achieve more favorable emission characteristics, in the nine most polluted cities in the nation. In addition, the law mandated a pilot program to sell 150,000 "clean fuel" automobiles (those using alternative fuels) by 1996 in California.

The law specified a list of 189 hazardous air pollutants and established procedures for evolving, reviewing, and enforcing standards designed to restrict these pollutants. From an operational standpoint, sources of such pollutants were required to achieve the maximum achievable control technology (MACT) standards. In other works the source should derive the maximum benefit from all available technological approaches in order to meet the standards prescribed. Provisions also identified sulfur dioxide and nitrogen oxide generated by the combustion of fossil fuels such as coal as the primary sources of acid rain. Specific deadlines for reducing such emissions were prescribed.

With regard to stratospheric ozone, the law promulgated steps to monitor, report, and control chlorofluorocarbons (CFCs). The EPA administrator was required to set standards for recycling and disposal of CFCs and to develop regulations concerning the servicing of refrigerant and air conditioning appliances. A timetable for phasing out the production of CFCs also was prescribed. Finally, the law devised a tough enforcement framework composed of judicial procedures and civil and criminal penalties.

Impact of Event

Because the CCA amendments of 1990 are broad and far-reaching in scope, their impact is likely to be felt in several facets of business activities. The following discussion critically assesses the likely costs and benefits of the amendments.

Available estimates suggest that the annual cost of achieving the CAA goals will amount to $25 billion by 2005, by which time all the time-bound programs are expected to be phased in. From a business perspective, however, this law's most important cost impact centers on economic implications for firms and industries that fail to meet the prescribed clean-air standards. If the law is enforced strictly, such entities may have to install costly devices to reduce harmful emissions to levels acceptable under the law or stop production entirely. Firms in the U.S. steel industry exemplify this dilemma. Rigid enforcement of the prescribed emission standards would force them to stop using coal for producing coke, a necessary input for manufacturing steel. Because there is no short-term solution that would allow production of coke without violating the new emission standards, these firms eventually will have to choose between importing coke from elsewhere or going out of business. Either option portends loss of jobs. Although the law has modest provisions for job-loss benefits, including needs-related payments and allowances for job search and relocation, it is unlikely to eliminate the hardships of unemployment caused indirectly by the law.

The law does provide for an elaborate market system of emission credits or "allowances" that firms are eligible to receive if they meet certain requirements in complying with emission standards. In the case of sulfur dioxide emissions, these allowances can be "traded" between firms. The law mandates that utility firms decrease sulfur dioxide emissions to one-half of the emission levels produced ten years ago. A firm that successfully reduces emissions more than is required will be given "credits" that either can be held as a "buffer" to accommodate increased emissions from future production expansion or can be sold to other firms that were unsuccessful in meeting emission standards. This provision could become an incentive to motivate industries to overperform in the clean-air context, to exceed minimum standards for compliance stipulated in the law. This incentive approach, taken together with the provisions for civil and criminal penalties in case of noncompliance with federal air-quality standards, lends balance and strength to the enforcement process by integrating both positive rewards and negative punishments into the regulatory system. This duality could enhance compliance with CAA provisions. Compliance levels of the 1980's left much to be desired.

The Clear Air Act of 1990 was designed to achieve the following key benefits: reduced levels of acid rain (through reduction in annual emissions of ten million tons of sulfur dioxide and two million tons of nitrogen oxide) and consequent protection of lakes, streams, national monuments, and public health; new health standards that were to be met by most cities by the year 2000; phasing out of CFCs and other harmful products that damage the protective ozone layer; and a reduction of 2.7 billion pounds in the amount of toxins put into the air each year. Other benefits include the encouragement of industries that produce alternative fuels that are less damaging to the environment. The law mandates a phased introduction of reformulated gasoline but is essentially silent on several other substitutes for conventional gasoline that decrease the level of ozone-forming hydrocarbons. These include methanol, ethanol, compressed natural gas, propane, butane, hydrogen, and electricity. Although reformulated gasoline is relatively less effective in reducing harmful tailpipe emissions than are other alternative fuel options, it nevertheless commands a big advantage: unlike other alternative fuels, it can be distributed through the same system used for conventional gasoline. Stated differently, other alternative fuels could entail additional costs for refitting automobiles currently refueled by conventional gasoline as well as for building or refitting distribution centers for fuel.

A less tangible benefit of CAA is the law's framework for building a meaningful dialogue among government, industry, and environmental groups. Various interested parties including the American Petroleum Institute, the Motor Vehicles Manufacturers Association, the Natural Resources Defense Council, the Sierra Club, and the methanol and ethanol industries reached an agreement on reformulated gasoline and oxygenated fuels (gasoline with oxygen added to diminish the severity of automobile emissions) through a unique regulatory negotiation process. The purpose of this joint exercise was to help the EPA refine the details of rules that promote cleaner air while providing industry with a greater degree of flexibility. Rules developed through negotiation will save an estimated six billion gallons of gasoline per year.

Other evidence indicates a healthy convergence of viewpoints among businesses and consumers. Several consumer surveys suggest that Americans consider environmental protection to be an important issue. Examples abound of practices in American firms aimed at decreasing all forms of environmental pollution. The Clean Air Act of 1990 formalizes this general business sensitivity and focuses attention on one aspect of the environment, clean air.

Bibliography

Bryner, Gary C. *Blue Skies, Green Politics: The Clean Air Act of 1990 and Its Implementation.* Washington, D.C.: Congressional Quarterly Press, 1995.

"The Clean Air Act Amendments of 1990." *Journal of Property Management* 56 (January/February, 1991): 6. Assesses implications of the law for property values in specifically targeted cities.

"Clean Air Act Rewritten, Tightened." In *Congressional Quarterly Almanac 1990*, edited by Neil Skene. Washington, D.C.: Congressional Quarterly, 1991. Provides a comprehensive overview of the Clean Air Act of 1990, including earlier legislation and how the 1990 law evolved. Discusses provisions of the law in depth.

Melnick, R. Shep. *Regulation and the Courts: The Case of the Clean Air Act.* Washington, D.C.: Brookings Institution, 1983. A well-researched study of the impact of the judicial process on the effectiveness of enforcing provisions of the early versions of the Clean Air Act. Reviews several cases and evidence suggesting how the judicial process may have adversely affected the administration of the Clean Air Act.

Rosenberg, William G. "The New Clean Air Act of 1990: Winds of Environmental Change." *Business Horizons* 35 (March/April, 1992): 34-36. An informative, albeit favorably biased, account of the Clean Air Act of

1990, its implications, and its consequences. Rosenberg was an official of the Environmental Protection Agency at the time the article was written. Provides several examples of corporate efforts to help the environment.

Zimmerman, Fred. "A Small Business Environmental Primer." *The National Public Accountant* 37 (June, 1992): 18-24. Discusses specific elements of the Clean Air Act of 1990. Reviews implications of selected aspects of the Clean Water Act of 1987, the Oil Pollution Act of 1990, the Resource Conservation and Recovery Act of 1976 as amended by the Solid Waste Disposal Act of 1984, and the Comprehensive Environmental Response, Compensation, and Liability Act of 1980 as amended by the Superfund Amendments Reauthorization Act of 1986. Useful source for businesses for basic information on environmental regulations.

Siva Balasubramanian

Cross-References

Congress Passes the Motor Vehicle Air Pollution Control Act (1965); The Environmental Protection Agency Is Created (1970); The United States Plans to Cut Dependence on Foreign Oil (1974); The Alaskan Oil Pipeline Opens (1977).

THE NORTH AMERICAN FREE TRADE AGREEMENT GOES INTO EFFECT

CATEGORY OF EVENT: International business and commerce
TIME: January 1, 1994
LOCALE: Washington, D.C.

The North American Free Trade Agreement promised to eliminate tariffs and other trade barriers among the United States, Canada, and Mexico, creating the world's largest and richest trading bloc

Principal personages:
GEORGE BUSH (1924-   ), the president of the United States, 1989-1993
BILL CLINTON (1946-   ), the president of the United States, 1993-
CARLOS SALINAS DE GORTARI (1948-   ), the president of Mexico
JEAN CHRÉTIEN (1934-   ), the prime minister of Canada

Summary of Event

The North American Free Trade Agreement (NAFTA), initialed by President George Bush in 1992 and signed by President Bill Clinton in 1993, brought Mexico into a free trade area with the United States and Canada. As of 1993, Mexican tariffs against American products averaged about 13 percent but were complemented by a host of nontariff restrictions on everything from blue jeans to frozen orange juice concentrate. NAFTA would eliminate these tariffs and restrictions over the next fifteen years. Not all barriers were to fall on January 1, 1994, the effective date of the free trade agreement. Some of the most sensitive—for example, Mexico's restrictions on imported auto parts—would allow breathing spells for industries expected to be devastated by foreign competition. According to the

Clinton Administration, however, half of all American exports would have open access to Mexico at the beginning of 1994.

Tariffs on all farm products would be phased out, but producers would be given fifteen years to adjust to a duty-free status on sensitive products. These included corn and dry beans for Mexico and orange juice concentrate, melons, sugar, and asparagus for U.S. farmers. Mexican import licenses, which covered about one-fourth of U.S. exports, would be dropped immediately.

In the areas of trucking and automobile manufacturing, qualification for duty-free treatment would require the North American content of cars to be at least half, rising to 62.5 percent in eight years. Mexico would also allow foreigners to invest in its trucking firms. Mexican, Canadian, and American trucking companies would be allowed to do business on cross-border routes. That commerce previously was prohibited.

Mexico would allow U.S. and Canadian banks, brokerage firms, and insurance companies free access after a six-year transition period during which bans on foreign ownership would be phased out. U.S. companies would be allowed to compete for contracts from Mexico's public telephone system, and investment restrictions would be eliminated by July, 1995.

For clothing made from yarns and fabrics from North America, Mexico would be able to escape high duties on textile shipments to the United States and Canada. In addition, NAFTA established a trinational commission to oversee environmental and labor laws. Sanctions—punitive trade tariffs in the case of the United States and Mexico, fines in the case of Canada—would be levied for failure of a country to enforce its own laws.

Passage of NAFTA required political maneuvering in attempts to placate various constituencies. Investors nervously shuffled in preparation to jump out of markets—particularly in Mexico—should NAFTA fail. Most U.S. executives doing business with

President Bill Clinton signed the NAFTA agreement that had been initialed by his predecessor, George Bush. (Library of Congress)

Mexico or Canada planned to stick with their optimistic investing and exporting strategies even if Congress rejected the trade pact.

The rapidly modernizing Mexican economy was a big importer of machines and commodities, which the United States excelled in producing. Because Mexico already was relatively open to these goods, the agreement itself was expected to have a modest impact on American sales. Locking into place President Carlos Salinas de Gortari's commitment to free markets, however, would boost American industries ranging from aircraft to grain to telephone equipment. By keeping Mexico's growth on track, NAFTA would serve many other American industries satisfying the Mexican consumer's thirst for material goods.

The pact was striking for its marriage of economies with vastly different levels of wages and productivity. Jobs and profits would undoubtedly be lost in labor-intensive, low-wage American industries including apparel, shoes, and household glassware. Proponents of NAFTA argued that relatively few U.S. jobs would go south because the Mexican economy was tiny compared to that of the United States. Even the most optimistic scenarios for Mexican growth showed it remaining a minor player in most American markets for decades. In any case, Mexican industry already had relatively easy access to American consumers, as did producers in low-wage countries from Thailand to Turkey. So, for that matter, did illegal Mexican immigrants, who arguably constituted greater competition for low-wage American jobs than did legal Mexican imports.

NAFTA proponents predicted that job growth in American high-wage industries would initially exceed job losses in the low-wage industries because exports to Mexico would grow rapidly. If the past is a good indication, the net impact on U.S. jobs would be small, since redundant workers would be redeployed quickly to more competitive American industries.

Environmentalists worried that Mexican industrial pollution would poison the American side of the border as well as fouling Mexico's air and water. American unions jumped on the regulatory bandwagon, pointing to Mexico's malign neglect of working conditions. It was not clear, however, why the accord would undermine the environment or labor standards. Trade and investment liberalization would probably reduce cross-border pollution, as it would end the artificial concentration of industries in the free-trade border zones. The Clinton Administration worked to defuse the issues by writing a side agreement providing for a watchdog group to monitor compliance.

Another challenge came from economists troubled by the rise of regional trade blocs. They feared that an open border with Mexico would divert cost-reducing trade with Asia and Eastern Europe. They also wondered whether the North American economic alliance would spur Japan to form a competing bloc on the other side of the Pacific. Objections to NAFTA appeared to be strongest in the United States. The legislatures of Canada and Mexico approved the agreement before it passed the U.S. Congress. President Bill Clinton signed the agreement on December 8, 1993, less than a month before it took effect.

Impact of Event

NAFTA was one of the most emotionally charged economic issues in the United States during the early 1990's. The agreement provoked enthusiasm from many business leaders and academic free traders but passionate opposition from many workers and businesspeople fearing competition. Organized labor and its allies in Congress opposed NAFTA, as did a coalition of interest groups with preoccupations ranging from the environment to child abuse.

To its opponents, NAFTA represented everything wrong with the U.S. economy. With unemployment concerns at the top of the nation's agenda, the idea of free trade seemed shocking. How could free trade with low-wage Mexico mean anything but a massive loss of jobs? Competition from Canada prompted almost no debate.

A rational examination of facts calmed some of the hysteria concerning potential job loss. The $5 trillion gross domestic product (GDP) of the United States dwarfed Mexico's $300 billion GDP. The Mexico economy simply did not have the capacity to absorb U.S. jobs; if job transfer occurred, it would be gradual. NAFTA merely applied the final touches to opening trade between the United States and Mexico. Trade was already basically open; NAFTA liberalized trade in the least competitive areas. It also allowed for a transition period to soften the blow.

NAFTA foes emphasized the experience of the maquila industry, which had a special customs regime. In this rapidly growing sector, U.S. companies had labor-intensive assembly work performed by low-wage Mexican workers. What happened was what NAFTA opponents claimed would become a pattern. NAFTA proponents suggested that if assembly work were not done in Mexico, it was plausible that U.S. jobs would disappear because entire production processes would move offshore.

Opponents of NAFTA believed there would be dramatic U.S. job losses and lowered wages as Mexico benefited from exports to the United States, plant relocations, and massive investment across the border by U.S. companies. Experience following the opening of the Mexican economy and a semblance of prosperity there suggests a different picture. From 1985 to 1993, the U.S. trade balance with Mexico improved by approximately $10 billion, turning from deficit to a surplus of about $5 billion. The improved balance of trade implied a net gain of about 350,000 U.S. jobs. Under NAFTA, Mexican demand for U.S. goods was likely to expand at a healthy rate as Mexicans increasingly took advantage of access to U.S. goods.

Some American environmentalists worried that the weaker environmental and labor market regulations in Mexico would give an unfair advantage to producers there. The United States had legitimate concerns about pollution spilling over the border. NAFTA therefore contained numerous environmental provisions. A glaring example of transnational effects is the extensive pollution from maquiladora factories in Mexico that were permitted to export freely to the United States. One advantage of NAFTA is that it would lessen border pollution because some maquiladora plants would move to Mexico's interior, since they would no longer have to be located along the border.

NAFTA proponents argued its benefits to U.S. labor and business as well as its foreign policy aspects. Prosperity in Mexico would help ensure that modernization and increased political access would take place. Moreover, a prosperous Mexico would help stem migration and spread some growth to Central America. Opposition to NAFTA led to fears abroad about a protectionist drift in U.S. policy, prompting speculation on how the United States would behave in negotiations on the General Agreement on Tariffs and Trade. Japan also questioned the U.S. position on a variety of market-opening measures under discussion.

In domestic terms, NAFTA was a test of U.S. confidence. It measured whether Americans believed in their ability to compete in open markets and in the face of a changing global economy. In foreign policy terms, NAFTA presented the opportunity to test America's willingness to cooperate across a diverse range of issues with Mexico. Given the clear choice, the American people chose to compete in an international economy, not cower in fear of it. Undoubtedly, NAFTA would harm certain sectors of the U.S. economy. The challenge for all three signatory countries was to exploit the opportunities offered by free trade while minimizing the harms resulting from adjustment.

Bibliography
Bentsen, Lloyd. "NAFTA: A Vehicle for Economic Growth." *U.S. Department of State Dispatch* 4 (May 10, 1993): 335-336. Deals with the position of the secretary of the treasury on NAFTA. Contains a variety of statistics intended to dispel opposition. Issues covered include growth, trade impact, and jobs.
Carey, Patricia. "NAFTA or Not, Here We Come." *International Business*, October, 1993, 46-52. An article dealing with debate on NAFTA. Con-

cludes that U.S. international business leaders have no plans to alter their aggressive investing and exporting strategies for Mexico and Canada. They are convinced that economic integration of North America is inevitable.

_____. "Trade War." *International Business*, November, 1993, 62-68. Focuses on debates by Ross Perot and Bill Clinton concerning NAFTA. Concludes that free trade and the U.S. economy's future are the primary issues. Suggests that Perot diverted attention from the real issues.

Cremeans, John E., ed. *Handbook of North American Industry: NAFTA and the Economies of Its Member Nations.* Lanham, Md.: Bernan Press, 1998.

Hage, David. "Free Trade: Fear, Frenzy, and Facts." *U.S. News and World Report* 115 (September 13, 1993): 65-66. Draws an interesting parallel between the European free trade zone and the NAFTA agreement.

Harbrecht, Douglas. "NAFTA: Let's Make a Deal." *Business Week*, November 8, 1993, 32-34. Describes the chain of events that led to the NAFTA debate. Also discusses the compromises between Congress and the president necessary to pass NAFTA.

Mayer, Frederick. *Interpreting NAFTA: The Science and Art of Political Analysis.* New York: Columbia University Press, 1998.

Nano, John B. "Neighbors, Yes—But Partners?" *Financial Executive* 9 (March 1, 1993): 16. Six financial executives share their hopes for and worries about NAFTA. Provides unique perspectives on controversial issues.

Salinas, Carlos. "NAFTA Is a Building Block, Not a Trade Bloc." *New Perspectives Quarterly* 10 (Spring, 1993): 14-18. An interview with Salinas concerning the impact of NAFTA on the U.S. and Mexican economies. Salinas states that the whole point of NAFTA for Mexico is to be able to export goods and not people. That means creating jobs in Mexico. Salinas addresses major points of opposition from Mexican perspectives.

Smith, Geri. "Gearing Up for a 'No.'" *Business Week*, November 1, 1993, 50-51. Outlines the plans of Mexico's President Salinas if NAFTA fails. Stresses the importance of the trade agreement to Mexican economic and political growth and stability.

Patricia C. Matthews

Cross-References

The General Agreement on Tariffs and Trade Is Signed (1947); American and Mexican Companies form *Maquiladoras* (1965); The United States Suffers Its First Trade Deficit Since 1888 (1971); Mexico Renegotiates Debt to U.S. Banks (1989).

CABLE TELEVISION RISES TO CHALLENGE NETWORK TELEVISION

CATEGORY OF EVENT: New products
TIME: The mid-1990's
LOCALE: The United States

During the 1990's the cable television industry dramatically increased its market share of television viewers and brought about a revolution in program options

Principal personages:
JEFFREY L. BEWKES, president, chairman, and chief executive officer of Home Box Office (HBO)
GEORGE BODENHEIMER, president of Entertainment and Sports Programming Network (ESPN)
DAVID CHASE, creator of HBO's critically acclaimed series *The Sopranos*
JOSEPH COLLINS, chairman of Time Warner Cable
ROBERT EDWARD "TED" TURNER III (1938-   ), founder of the Turner Broadcasting System

Summary of Event

While cable television was first offered during the late 1940's in order to provide television signals to people who lived in remote areas where regular television broadcasts were difficult or impossible, the growth of the cable industry during the 1990's went far beyond anything that could have been imagined. By 1999 almost 75 million American households subscribed to cable television. With more than 99 million American households owning television sets, the percentage of households that had decided to pay for cable service had reached 75. The cable television industry had first shown signs of growth during the 1950's and 1960's. At that time, cable service was offered to many small cities and towns across the country. Subscribers paid for the signals of television network affiliates, educational television, and possibly a number of independent stations. Compared to what became available to cable subscribers during the 1990's, these early offerings were modest.

By the early 1960's, there were only 850,000 cable subscribers in the United States. During this period, local television stations began to think of cable television as a competitor that was to be feared. The Federal Communications Commission (FCC) stepped in and placed restrictions on the cable industry. It was not until the early 1970's when any federal deregulation took place that made it easier for the cable industry to grow. The first pay-television network, Home Box Office (HBO), was started by Charles Dolan and Gerald Levin of Sterling Manhattan Cable in 1972. Out of this venture, a national satellite distribution system was created.

This new satellite system paved the way for an increase in cable program networks. Ted Turner, the owner of a local Atlanta, Georgia, television station, also changed his station over to satellite distribution and in so doing created the first "superstation." By the year 2000, Turner's WTBS "superstation" was available to almost every cable subscriber throughout the country. In 1980, the number of cable subscribers had grown to 15 million households. With the passage of the federal Cable Act of 1984, the cable television industry became almost entirely deregulated. Because of deregulation, the cable industry boldly invested vast sums of money to wire the country and to develop new programming. More than 15 billion dollars was spent by the cable industry on wiring alone. By 1998, there were more than 10,000 cable systems, 174 national cable networks, and more than 127,000 cable employees in the United States. In 1992, the number of national cable networks was 82. In a span of six years, the number of national cable networks had increased by 100 percent.

In August, 1998, the Cablevision Bureau (CAB) gathered data that confirmed that "basic cable attracted a larger monthly viewing audience than the combined broadcast networks." This was the first time in the history of television that cable television had accomplished this. During the 1997-1998 television season, basic cable programming was watched by an average of 21.9 million households (a 38.5 share of the total audience). This constituted a 2.6 million household increase and a 4.2 share increase over the previous television season. During this same period, the broadcast networks lost 1.4 million viewing households and a 3.2 share of the audience.

In 1999, cable television continued to gain viewers. During the second week of the new television season (September 27-October 3, 1999), basic cable rose 7.6 percent in average prime time ratings according to CAB's analysis of Nielsen ratings data. For this time period, some of the basic cable programming that did extremely well included ESPN's coverage of professional football, USA's World Wrestling Federation (WWF) *Monday Night Raw*, and original films on Turner Network Television (TNT). By the late 1990's, the average cable subscriber could choose from a wide selection of programming options. More than half of all cable subscribers could choose from among at least fifty-four channels in 1998. In 1996, the number of channels available had been forty-seven. As the cable television industry grew, the public demanded more diverse and quality programming.

The first major new federal communications law since 1934 was enacted in 1996. The Telecommunications Reform Act of 1996 spurred the cable industry to expand since the new law offered regulatory relief and flexibility. While the growth experienced by the cable industry during the early 1990's was tied more to the wiring of unserved or underserved areas, it appeared likely that growth in the twenty-first century would be tied more closely to new housing starts.

American cable subscribers were able to watch a number of quality cable programs during the 1990's. The premium cable network HBO produced the critically acclaimed and popular programs *The Sopranos*, *Sex and the City*, and *Oz*. In 1999, *The Sopranos* was nominated for sixteen Emmy Awards. The series also won a number of Golden Globe and Screen Actors Guild Awards in early 2000.

Impact of Event

With the growth of cable television and public clamor for ever greater variety and quality programming, it seemed almost inevitable that change and innovation would become buzzwords during the twenty-first century. In addition to cable's ever-increasing role in television, the cable industry also hoped to be a major force in offering online services, data delivery, and high-speed access to the Internet. Through the use of fiber optics and coaxial cable, cable systems were able to offer Internet access that was hundreds of times faster than that provided over telephone lines. Cable networks were already putting Web sites on the Internet. Some of the sites include ESPN Sports Zone, Cable News Network (CNN) Interactive, and Discovery Online. One of the most promising growth areas for the cable industry was digital-package sales. Cable companies batched together special packages for customers that were hard to resist. Whether they offered digital packages, premium-channel packages, or pay-per-view packages, cable companies looked to hook new subscribers with innovative and attractive sales offers.

By the year 2000, network stations in the top thirty American markets reached more than 60 percent of households with televisions through the use of a digital signal. Meanwhile, however, the industry began facing strong competition from direct broadcast satellite (DBS) technology. By the end of 1998, more than 12 million customers were getting their programming from noncable multichannel video providers. The Department of Justice stated that "while programming services are delivered via different technologies, consumers view the (DBS and cable) services as similar and to a large degree substitutable." During the 1990's, the top ten cable multiple systems operators (MSOs) grew extremely large. In 2000, 75 percent of the nation's cable subscribers looked to the top ten MSOs for their programming. With more than 16 million subscribers, the largest MSO in the country was AT&T Broadband. Time Warner Cable ranked second with roughly 13 million subscribers. None of the other top ten MSOs had more than six million subscribers.

It was predicted that the number of cable channels that could be offered to subscribers would reach five hundred sometime in the twenty-first century. During the 1990's, cable services were divided into basic and premium. Basic cable service packages usually offered subscribers set numbers of channels for flat monthly rates. Subscribers wishing to add premium channels, such as HBO, Showtime, The Movie Channel, Playboy, Disney, or Cinemax, had to pay additional fees. The MSOs put together package deals on a regular basis in order to make the premium channels look more attractive to subscribers.

Cable television has altered the way the American public watches television. Viewers can watch the 24-hour all-news network CNN, old films on specialty film channels, Spanish-language programming on Galavision, women's programming on Lifetime, religious programming on the Family Channel, or music videos on Music Television (MTV) or Video Hits One (VH1). They can also shop on the Home Shopping Network or QVC and see premium sporting events on ESPN, or children's programming on Nickelodeon. These were but a few of the viewing choices available to cable subscribers by the year 2000.

It has been argued that with all the choices available to it, the public audience has become more fragmented. While in decades past the majority of viewers typically tuned in to the same popular programs, viewers of the 1990's tended to tune in to increasingly different programs. Throughout the 1990's, the old network television networks were unable to curtail the erosion of their market share. They had to work harder to maintain viewership.

It was estimated that of the thirty-eight new shows of the 1999-2000 season offered by the networks, half would make it through the season. In previous seasons, the number of new shows that were canceled was more than half. The number of game shows and investigative-reporting programs on the networks increased during the late 1990's. Cheaper to produce than original programming, these shows are popular with a large segment of the viewing public that still watches regular network television. It can be argued that more quality original programming is being produced on both basic cable channels and premium cable channels.

While basic cable channels still have to worry about censorship issues with their programming, premium cable channels do not have such worries. Original series, such as *The Sopranos* or *Sex and the City*, can include graphic violence, nudity, and coarse language, just as theatrical films can. Moreover, cable series episodes are repeated many times, allowing subscribers to watch them at their own convenience.

Critics of cable television have charged that the industry is driven principally by the high-profile programs, such as recent films, miniseries, wrestling, and premium sporting events, and that until the quantity and quality of regular cable series improves, the industry will not attract loyal viewers. However, because cable does not have the same restrictions that network television does, it can run counter to what is found on network television, taking chances that network television shuns. When the networks show reruns during summer months, cable television is free to win over new viewers with original programming.

Deregulation has encouraged cable companies to venture into telephony and made it possible for telephone companies to distribute cable television programming. Cable providers also have felt emboldened to try their hand at video compression, digital transmission, and high-definition television (HDTV). Some cable operators also have experimented with two-way channel capability. This process allows subscribers to interact with the programming facilities or the system's information headquarters. Home viewers can reply to public-opinion polls or have access to written or graphic materials.

While the variety of cable television's programming has been criticized as being nothing more than "a map of our most noble and base instincts," the cable television industry rightly can point to how far it has come in such a relatively short period of time. American viewers have shown that they are willing to pay for the expanded choices offered to them by cable operators. Time will tell whether the public is merely paying for just another "vice," or if the historical promise that was dreamed for television during the first decades of the twentieth century finally will come to fruition through the bold steps taken by the cable industry and the other new viewing options that will take hold in the twenty-first century.

Bibliography

Aufderheide, Patricia. "Cable Television and the Public Interest." *Journal of Communication* 42 (Winter, 1992): 52-65. Solid overview of how the public interest can best be served by the growth of cable television.

Baldwin, Thomas F., and D. Stevens McVoy. *Cable Communication.* 2d ed. Englewood Cliffs, N.J.: Prentice-Hall, 1988. Detailed look at every aspect of the cable industry, from the technical to public policy. Although somewhat dated, it remains essential reading for those interested in how the cable industry has evolved.

Blanchard, Margaret A., ed. *History of the Mass Media in the United States.* Chicago: Fitzroy Dearborn, 1998. The entries "Cable Networks," "Cable News," and "Cable Television" are all insightful overviews. Both the "Cable Networks" and "Cable Television" entries include useful bibliographies.

Brenner, Daniel L., and Monroe E. Price. *Cable Television and Other Nonbroadcast Video: Law and Policy.* New York: Clark Boardman, 1986. Discusses the various rulings, judicial decisions, and the Cable Communications Act of 1984 and how each has affected the cable industry.

Ciciora, Walter S., James Farmer, and David Large. *Modern Cable Television Technology: Video, Voice, and Data Communications.* San Francisco: Morgan Kaufmann Publishers, 1999.

Hodes, Daniel, Kiran Duwadi, and Andrew Wise. "Cable's Expanding Role in Telecommunications." *Business Economics* 34 (April, 1999): 46-51. Points out that as the cable industry takes on a larger role in the "telecommunications arena" it should make sure that it reduces its debt and improves its customer service in order to hold on to the subscribers that it already has.

Sheffield, Rob. "The Cable Universe: Scratching the Niche." *Rolling Stone* (September 17, 1998): 61-65. Survey of what cable television has to offer, from the noble to the raunchy.

Stevens, Tracy, ed. *International Television and Video Almanac.* 45th ed. La Jolla, Calif.: Quigley, 2000. In addition to providing a detailed overview of 1998-1999 in television, it also lists the cable networks and cable systems operators.

Jeffry Jensen

Cross-References

Station KDKA Introduces Commercial Radio Broadcasting (1920); The 1939 World's Fair Introduces Regular U.S. Television Service (1939); The Cable News Network Debuts (1980); Home Shopping Service Is Offered on Cable Television (1985); *Time* magazine Makes an E-commerce Pioneer Its Person of the Year (1999).

TIME MAGAZINE MAKES AN E-COMMERCE PIONEER ITS PERSON OF THE YEAR

CATEGORY OF EVENT: Marketing
TIME: December 27, 1999
LOCALE: New York

By bestowing its person-of-the-year honor on Amazon.com founder Jeffrey P. Bezos, Time *magazine paid tribute to electronic commerce as a dynamic new marketplace, thereby highlighting the influence of the Internet and World Wide Web on American business*

Principal personage:
JEFFREY PRESTON BEZOS (1965-   ), founder and chief executive officer of Amazon.com, an Internet retailer of books and other goods that began in 1995

Summary of Event
At the age of thirty-four in 1999, Jeffrey P. Bezos became the fourth-youngest person to appear on the cover of *Time* magazine as its person of the year. However, it was not Bezos's age that made his selection a surprise to most readers. *Time* magazine usually reserves the distinction for news-makers and celebrities, and although known as the king of cyberbusiness, Bezos was not a national figure. However, his creation, Amazon.com, had become a household name—credited, in fact, with starting and defining the rapidly expanding field of electronic commerce (e-commerce) via the Internet and the World Wide Web. Through the honor to Bezos, therefore, *Time* also recognized a novel, powerful cultural force. Though only four years old, the new form of marketplace not only transformed how companies sell products and services to each other and to consumers but also affected social behavior and politics as well.

Bezos founded Amazon in 1995 to sell books to consumers over the Internet. Many business commentators predicted failure. Instead, the company's sales skyrocketed. In 1998, its book sales grew 275 percent, followed by another 82 percent the following year, and by then books accounted for only about one-half of its total sales. Amazon had expanded to offer so many other retail goods that its Web site amounted to an online mall. Investors, initially skeptical, took note. When Amazon began trading its stock publicly in 1997, shares sold for $1.50 each; at the end of 1999, a share cost $80. In part its success came from being the first company of its kind in cyberspace, but it also placed great emphasis upon customer service to ensure speed of delivery and customer satisfaction and provided browsers with handy consumer information, such as reviews, product ratings, and technical data.

Other innovators soon capitalized on the Internet too, some enjoying success that was nearly as spectacular. For instance, the first business to offer online auctions to general customers—Ebay, started in late 1995— had more than four million listings in 4,320 categories by early 2000. Beginning in 1997, Handiman Online offered to match homeowners with craftsmen and contractors in their locale for construction projects. In 1998, HomeGrocer began delivering groceries, ordered from its Web site, to residences on the West Coast, and the same year Ticketmaster began selling tickets online for events nationwide.

A host of other electronic retailers (e-tailers) joined Amazon, many of them startup companies that copied its sales and customer service methods. The number of small American and Canadian businesses operating via the Internet increased 40 percent between 1996 and 1998. By 2000 more than half were online. At first large corporations, such as Sears and Whirlpool, shied away from Internet business, worried that it was just a fad. By 2000, so many had joined the trend and opened Web sites that "dot-com" (".com") was firmly embedded in world business culture and Americans' vocabulary. Even advertisements in other media included firms' e-mail addresses and Web sites as a matter of course. During the 2000 Super Bowl more than a dozen "dot-com" companies bought television advertising spots. Meanwhile, other strictly Internet companies, such as Yahoo and Excite, opened virtual malls of their own in direct competition with Amazon.

Goods offered on the Internet spanned nearly the entire range of the traditional "bricks-and-mortar" retail business stock: books, prescription drugs, toys, electronic equipment and computers, airline tickets, tools and instruments, clothes, and even cars. The convenience, speed, and wealth of information directly accessible online appealed to technologically sophisticated consumers—so much so that e-commerce firms stole away customers from other venues. Bookstores claimed that they were being driven out of business by Amazon and Barnes and Noble, which also opened its own Web site. Car dealers began to worry as well when it was found that 5 percent of car purchases in the United States were being conducted over the Internet. Travel agents lost much of their reservation-making business to online self-enrollment reservations services, such as Netscape's Travelocity, and to Web sites maintained by individual airlines, hotels, and car rental agencies.

Companies also sold services online. Infoseek and AltaVista, for example, conducted information searches, while other Web sites offered professional consultations in such fields as law and insurance, arranged contacts among single men and women, or posted advertisements for job seekers. Banks administered accounts via the Internet, and investment firms sold stocks and bonds. Charles Schwab, in fact, conducted two-thirds of its business on the Web. Auction Web sites became popular almost overnight because they appealed to the American craving for bargains and antiques. Through Ebay and others, private owners could sell new and used items to the highest bidders—from books and clothes to automobiles and speedboats.

Even though companies specializing in dealing directly with customers earned $14.9 million in 1999, nearly double the amount of 1998, theirs was the smallest portion of e-commerce profits. Businesses selling to other businesses earned $109 billion during the same period. In fact, business-to-business e-commerce grew so important that it spurred a revolution in American supply and manufacturing procedures. Online catalogs allowed large manufacturers to order parts from suppliers more quickly, and the records of online sales let companies respond to demand more efficiently, saving time and reducing errors. The reduction in overhead expenses, estimated at between 10 and 50 percent, and the reduced waste increased profits. Governments also realized the benefits of e-commerce, distributing benefits and information and allowing citizens and businesses to file taxes electronically.

Fundamental problems with e-commerce emerged during its dramatic success, however. Security systems had to be installed to protect Web sites from the vandalism of hackers, and new laws were passed to punish offenders. More important, because credit cards were the usual means of payment for consumer orders, encryption systems had to be devised to ensure thieves could not intercept credit card numbers. Some companies found that their supply and shipping systems could not keep up with the rapidly accumulating orders posted on their Web sites. In order to support its expansion, Amazon itself had to borrow $1.25 billion in bonds to pay for new warehouses, a distribution system, acquisition costs, and operating expenses in 1999, which gave it a $611 million net loss; nevertheless, Bezos believed the company would soon become profitable again. Most inhibiting of all, however, was the scarcity of workers with the technical skills for e-commerce. An estimated 360,000 jobs were waiting to be filled in the United States and Canada alone in the year 2000.

Impact of Event

Bezos's recognition by *Time* magazine symbolized e-commerce's sudden emergence as a significant part of American life. With approximately 2.2 million Web sites available to the public, and 300 million pages of information, the Internet presented a vast commercial potential. Increasing numbers of Americans took advantage of it through the late 1990's, and industry experts confidently expected large upswings in holiday sales in 1999. They were not disappointed. Between Thanksgiving and New Year's Day, 26.4 million shoppers spent more than $5 billion online, a threefold increase from 1998.

The successes of 1999 attracted ever more firms to e-commerce, especially after studies found that online small businesses brought in an average of nearly one-third more revenue than traditional companies. Moreover, companies often modified their corporate structure to accommodate the new type of market. Many found that they had to expand customer service departments because customers contacted retailers directly more frequently by phone or e-mail to ask questions or arrange for replacements or refunds. Companies doing substantial business online could eliminate "middleman" distributors and offered differential pricing for small items as well as for such big items as cars. Even small businesses found that they suddenly could sell products worldwide. At the same time, e-companies saw some expenses rise, especially in training to keep workers abreast of evolving Internet capabilities and in purchases of sophisticated hardware and software. Meanwhile, e-commerce became deeply involved in other sectors of the economy. For example, the increase in direct shipping of goods to customers multiplied the demand on commercial shippers, such as the U.S. Postal Service, United Parcel Service, and Federal Express.

The implications of e-commerce for society, first studied in the late 1990's, promised to be profound. Stanford University researchers found that Internet use in general tended to isolate people, even from other family members, an antisocial trend abetted by e-commerce: Most online shoppers said that they resorted to the Web to avoid crowded shopping malls and traffic. There was also concern that the ease of purchase online would tempt people to overspend, which could lead to a risky general increase in personal debt and bankruptcies.

A clear relation existed in 2000 between income and online shopping. The likelihood of a household having a computer that was connected to the Internet rose with its income level. Because the level of education also rose with income, the wealthy and well educated were the people who used the Internet most often. The Internet threatened to intensify divisions between rich and poor and create a class-dominated marketplace through e-commerce. Accordingly, social observers called for more public-financed Internet facilities at such places a libraries and schools. Public schools were urged to increase instruction devoted to computers and information technology.

Similar concern arose over issues of nationalism. The Internet could internationalize commerce in a way difficult to control by local governments, opening traditionally closed markets to global products and affecting both a nation's economy and autonomy. Countries with extensive technological infrastructure and research and development would certainly dominate developing countries online, increasing global economic stratification. Moreover, global connectiveness via the Internet created an autonomous behavioral milieu, which could erode cultural differences—a possibility as disturbing to nationalists as it was pleasing to e-commerce companies.

Proponents and critics alike predicted that e-commerce could to some degree reconstruct society in the twenty-first century. Accordingly, politicians anticipated that local and federal government policies would require reshaping as well, but exactly how remained controversial as the century began. Taxation was such a divisive issue that Congress imposed a three-year moratorium on new federal, state, and local taxes on e-commerce in 1998. In fact, business leaders resisted regulation of any sort, fearing it would cripple e-commerce, and wanted governmental support only in developing new technology. Starting in 2000, the U.S. Census Bureau began collecting data on e-commerce to help the nation settle such policy issues.

Bibliography

Burnham, Bill. *How to Invest in E-commerce Stocks.* New York: McGraw-Hill, 1999. Concise introduction to e-commerce precedes a practical guide to the advantages and dangers of investing via the Internet.

Fellenstein, Craig, and Ron Wood. *Exploring E-commerce, Global E-business, and E-society.* Englewood Cliffs, N.J.: Prentice-Hall, 2000. Explains e-commerce for business owners and considers its future influence on government, medicine, and education.

Ramo, Joshua Cooper. "Why the Founder of Amazon.com Is Our Choice for 1999." *Time* 154 (December 27, 1999): 50-51. The article announcing the choice of Bezos as person of the year, with accompanying articles about e-retailing and prominent cybermerchants.

Schiller, Dan. *Digital Capitalism: Networking the Global Marketing System.* Cambridge, Mass.: MIT Press, 1999. Analyzes market-driven policies, economic potentiality, and influence on educational and social policy of cyberspace, warning powerful corporations could misuse it.

Tiernan, Bernadette. *E-Tailing.* Chicago: Dearborn, 2000. Guide to the basics of e-commerce structure and procedures, Internet psychology, on-line merchants, and likely products and technology of the future.

Roger Smith

Cross-References

The A. C. Nielsen Company Pioneers in Marketing and Media Research (1923); Jobs and Wozniak Found Apple Computer (1976); IBM Introduces Its Personal Computer (1981); Home Shopping Service Is Offered on Cable Television (1985); Dow Jones Adds Microsoft and Intel (1999).

DOW JONES ADDS MICROSOFT AND INTEL

CATEGORY OF EVENT: Finance
TIME: November 1, 1999
LOCALE: New York, New York

Dow Jones and Company added two technology stocks, Microsoft and Intel, to its Dow Jones Industrial Index

Principal personages:
CHARLES HENRY DOW (1851-1902), financial analyst and reporter
PAUL E. STEIGER, managing editor of *The Wall Street Journal*

Summary of Event

The Dow Jones Industrial Average (DJIA) was created by Charles H. Dow, cofounder of Dow Jones and Company. A financial analyst, Dow believed that a summary measure of the prices on the New York Stock Exchange (NYSE) would be useful to members of the financial community and help them follow business trends. He developed a composite list of major stocks and an index of their prices, the DJIA. When the DJIA was first published on May 26, 1896, it consisted of the stocks of twelve companies. These stocks included Distilling and Cattle Feeding, American Sugar, and American Cotton Oil—major companies now forgotten by most modern investors—and General Electric, the only original stock that remained on the list in the year 2000. On October 1, 1928, the average was expanded to encompass thirty stocks and closed at 240.01, marking the first day that the average was comparable to the thirty-stock DJIA of the present.

The stocks in the DJIA are selected by the editors of *The Wall Street Journal*, a financial and business newspaper that is the main publication of Dow Jones and Company. The editors select stocks of major companies that represent the broad market and U.S. industry and are widely held by individual and institutional investors. Often referred to as "blue-chip" industrials, DJIA stocks are rarely changed in order to maintain continuity and to ensure that past, present, and future averages are comparable. Many of the substitutions made over the years have been the result of mergers or dissolutions, but changes have also been made to alter the representation of industry within the stocks. For example, in 1924, a nonindustrial stock, that of the retailer Woolworth, was added. Since 1976, about two-thirds of the DJIA stocks have been substituted, largely to reflect the shift away from heavy industry and toward service industries that developed rapidly during the 1960's.

In the 1990's, DJIA stocks were changed three times. The first change occurred on May 6, 1991, when Caterpillar, the Disney Company, and J. P. Morgan were added. Navistar, U.S. Steel (USX), and Primerica were dropped. Interestingly, Primerica was returned to the average six years later after it became Citigroup. On March 17, 1997, Citigroup, Hewlett-Packard, Johnson & Johnson, and Wal-Mart Stores were added. Westinghouse Electric, Texaco, Bethlehem Steel, and Woolworth were dropped.

On October 26, 1999, *The Wall Street Journal* announced four new changes to the DJIA. The additions included two technology stocks, Microsoft, Inc., and Intel Corporation, as well as former Baby Bell SBC Communications and retailer Home Depot. These four stocks replaced retailer Sears Roebuck and the so-called "smokestack" stocks Chevron, Goodyear Tire and Rubber, and Union Carbide—all of which had been in the list since at least 1930. The additions and deletions were the result of a Dow Jones review conducted over several months, partly in response to the planned takeover of Union Carbide by the Dow Chemical Corporation. The technology stocks Microsoft and Intel are traded on the electronic Nasdaq (National Association of Securities Dealers Automated Quotations) Stock Market and are the first DJIA stocks not to be on the New York Stock Exchange. The Nasdaq Stock Market lists nearly 5,000 companies, and a far larger number of technology stocks are traded on Nasdaq than on the NYSE.

As of November 1, 1999, the thirty stocks of the DJIA were Allied Signal, Aluminum Company of America, American Express Company, AT&T Corporation, Boeing Company, Caterpillar, Citigroup, Coca-Cola Company, DuPont Company, Eastman Kodak Company, Exxon Corporation, General Electric Company, General Motors Corporation, Hewlett-Packard Company, Home Depot, Intel Corporation, International Business Machines Corporation (IBM), International Paper Company, J. P. Morgan and Company, Johnson and Johnson, McDonald's Corporation, Merck and Company, Microsoft Corporation, Minnesota Mining and Manufacturing

Company (3M), Philip Morris Companies, Procter and Gamble Company, SBC Communications, United Technologies Corporation, Wal-Mart Stores, and Walt Disney Company.

Market analysts regarded the change in the DJIA as an acknowledgment of the growing importance of technology in U.S. industry and in the stock market. The addition of Microsoft was probably also motivated by the top software maker's market dominance and its high stock market value. The substitution of Home Depot for Sears was evidently made to reflect consumer preference for discounters over traditional department stores.

Impact of Event

Before its latest changes, some analysts had criticized the DJIA as being stodgy and no longer representative of the economy in the United States; they charged that the DJIA's usefulness was reduced in comparison to the Standard & Poor's 500-stock index. The S&P index, whose list is 25 percent technology, is a broader index. Many professional investors favor the broader S&P, although to many individual investors and much of the general public, the DJIA is virtually synonymous with the stock market. Only about $165 million is invested in mutual funds designed to copy the performance of the DJIA, but about $700 billion is invested in funds that track the S&P. Nevertheless, moves in the DJIA can have a major impact on investor psychology and can increase or decrease confidence in the stock market.

The addition of Microsoft and Intel to the DJIA brought the number of technology stocks in the average to four. The editors of *The Wall Street Journal* added IBM in 1979, after dropping the stock in 1939, causing the index to ignore the company's dramatic performance on the stock market during those forty years. The second technology stock on the average was Hewlett-Packard Company, added in 1997. With the 1999 additions, technology stocks reached 16 percent of the average's weight. After November 1, 1999, nineteen out of thirty of the DJIA stocks were service industries, including technology, consumer products, and financial services. This proportion roughly reflects the share of service industries in the U.S. economy.

The DJIA, which closed at 240.01 on October 1, 1928, fell to a low of 41.22 on July 8, 1932. It did not close above 1,000 until November 14, 1972, more than forty years later. On January 8, 1987, the Dow closed above 2,000 for the first time in history. In the 1990's, however, the Dow would hit new records with increasing frequency. It climbed above 3,000 on April 17, 1991, above 4,000 on February 23, 1995, above 5,000 on November 21, 1995, and above 6,000 on October 14, 1996. In 1997, it rose

Most Active Stocks

AP Abbrev	Tick	Last	Chg.	Dlv. % Chg.	YTD % Chg.	PE/ PPE
Microsft	MSFT	104.06	−7.63	−6.8	−10.9	64/56
Cisco s	CSCO	80.06	+0.69	+0.9	+49.3	cc/na
DellCptr	DELL	57.88	+1.44	+2.5	+13.5	95/61
MCI Wld s	WCOM	43.00	+0.33	+0.8	−19.0	32/21
AmOnlne s	AOL	74.38	+3.50	+4.9	−2.0	cc/na
AT&T	T	60.31	+1.56	+2.7	+18.7	35/26
Qualcom s	QCOM	148.94	+2.94	+2.0	−15.4	cc/na
Intel s	INTC	142.69	+3.63	+2.6	+73.3	68/47
Compaq	CPQ	29.31	+0.75	+2.6	+8.3	86/25

After being added to the Dow Jones index, Microsoft and Intel continued to rank among the most active stocks traded on the New York Stock Exchange.

above 7,000 on February 13 and above 8,000 on July 16. April 6, 1998, saw the Dow climb above 9,000. In 1999, the Dow surpassed 10,000 on March 29 and 11,000 on May 3. On January 14, 2000, the Dow cleared 11,700. Many analysts believed that the Dow's rise would have been faster if more technology stocks had been included earlier, given these stocks' high growth rates, and argued that these changes should have taken place earlier. For example, Microsoft's price gains for a ten-year period were 7,395 percent, versus the Dow's 275-percent rise. Intel's price gain for the same period was 3,346 percent.

Although most market analysts praised the changes in the DJIA as making the average a better representation of the state of the market, some analysts feared that the addition of inherently volatile technology stocks might make the average too volatile. Some noted that the technology stocks, particularly Microsoft and Intel, are at their peaks, making their inclusion a somewhat risky and destabilizing proposition. Paul E. Steiger, managing editor of *The Wall Street Journal*, defended the decision to include the two technology stocks in an interview conducted shortly before the changes took place. He argued that some increase in volatility was an acceptable consequence of making the DJIA more representative. Both technology companies, he stated, were massive companies that play an important role in the U.S. economy.

Some analysts argue that although the addition of Microsoft and Intel, which both have high price-earnings ratios (as is typical of technology stocks) and low dividends, increases the overall value of the stocks, it is unlikely to result in a more volatile index. They reason that in the Dow, because of the way the average is computed, stocks with the highest prices have the greatest impact. Microsoft is not among the highest priced DJIA stocks; Intel is much closer to the top, but it falls behind stocks such as American Express and General Electric. The DJIA, calculated almost continuously by computer, totals the prices of the component stocks and divides by a regularly adjusted divisor. This divisor, published every business day in *The Wall Street Journal*, is recalculated to allow for stock splits, spinoffs, and changes in the component stocks, and is designed to ensure comparability of past, present, and future averages.

In the first five months after the change in the DJIA stocks, the average did not show markedly increased volatility. Although it experienced some of its biggest one-day net gains and losses in terms of index points in March, 2000, these changes were minimal when measured in percentage change. For example, on March 16, 2000, the DJIA rose 499.19 points, the largest one-day gain ever, but in terms of percentage change, the average rose only 4.93 percent. Historically, the largest one-day gain occurred on October 6, 1931, a rise of 14.87 percent—which accounted for only 12.86 points.

In the early months of 2000, technology stocks continued their rapid growth as investors were drawn to their ever-increasing growth rates. Investors seemed to shy away from stocks of companies such as banks and consumer product manufacturers, which were unable to produce continued, large growth rates like those of the technology companies. What this trend means for the DJIA is not clear. On any given day, the DJIA, because of its emphasis on blue-chip industrials, sometimes moves in a different direction from other indexes such as the Nasdaq Composite Index. However, historically, over long periods of time, the DJIA and other major, popular indexes tend to trend in the same direction. The phenomenal growth in technology stocks is reflected in another area, the different percentage increases in the indexes over time. Although all the major indexes experienced an increase over a ten-year period ended December 31, 1999, the Nasdaq Composite grew 794.71 percent, while the S&P 500 grew 315.75 percent and the DJIA grew 317.59 percent. Given this trend, the addition of Microsoft and Intel to the DJIA should translate to a higher percentage increase in the index. However, five months after the change, the long-term effects of the inclusion of additional technology stocks in the DJIA was still unclear.

Bibliography

Glassman, James K., and Kevin A. Hassett. *Dow 36,000: The New Strategy for Profiting from the Coming Rise in the Stock Market*. New York: Times Business, 1999. Provides an investment strategy based on the predicted rise in the Dow Jones Industrial Average to 36,000.

Hamilton, William Peter. *The Stock Market Barometer*. 1922. Harper & Row Bros. Reprint. New York: John Wiley & Sons, 1998. Hamilton, an editor of *The Wall Street Journal* who worked with Charles H. Dow, the paper's founder and publisher, wrote a series of editorials on business and finance for the paper. Most of these editorials describe the workings of the Dow theory.

Presto, John, ed. *Markets Measure: An Illustrated History of America Told Through the Dow Jones Industrial Average*. New York: Dow Jones, 1998. Presents a historical perspective in pictures and text of the Dow Jones average over the years in the United States.

Stillman, Richard Joseph. *Dow Jones Industrial Average: History and Role in an Investment Strategy*. Homewood, Ill.: Dow-Jones-Irwin, 1986. Examines the history of the Dow Jones Industrial Average and describes how the average is computed as well as its use as an investment tool.

Rowena Wildin

Cross-References

The Wall Street Journal Prints the Dow Jones Industrial Average (1897); The U.S. Stock Market Crashes on Black Tuesday (1929); Jobs and Wozniak Found Apple Computer (1976); IBM Introduces Its Personal Computer (1981); The U.S. Stock Market Crashes on 1987's "Black Monday" (1987); Federal Court Rules That Microsoft Should Be Split into Two Companies (2000).

AWARDING OF AN NFL FRANCHISE TO HOUSTON RAISES THE ANTE IN PROFESSIONAL SPORTS

CATEGORY OF EVENT: Business practices
TIME: October 6, 1999
LOCALE: The United States

The amounts of money needed to support professional sports franchises jumped to a new level when investors in the city of Houston paid $700 million to the National Football League (NFL) merely for the privilege of fielding a team—which still required an additional substantial investment to create

Principal personages:
LEE BROWN, mayor of Houston, Texas
ROBERT "BOB" MCNAIR, billionaire who paid $700 million for the Houston franchise
PAUL TAGLIABUE (1940-), commissioner of the NFL
RICHARD RIORDAN (1930-), mayor of Los Angeles
MICHAEL OVITZ (1946-), head of a Los Angeles group working to bring a new NFL franchise to Los Angeles
ED ROSKI, head of a rival group seeking to bring the NFL back to Los Angeles
ELI BROAD (1933-), a prominent member of the Roski group
AL DAVIS (1929-), owner of the NFL's Raiders team, which left Los Angeles in 1995, who claimed to own the Los Angeles franchise rights
GEORGE STEINBRENNER (1930-), majority owner of the New York Yankees baseball team

Summary of Event

In 1995, the Los Angeles area lost both of its National Football League (NFL) teams. The Raiders returned to their original home, Oakland, California, and the Rams moved to St. Louis, Missouri—for whom they would win a Super Bowl in 2000. In 1997, the Oilers moved from Houston to Nashville, Tennessee. These were merely the latest moves in a trend of professional teams moving from one city to another when the price was right. In early 1999, three groups—two from Los Angeles and one from Houston—presented their cases to the NFL's expansion and stadium committees. The NFL then had 31 teams and wished to add another to begin playing in the 2002 season. Each of the groups was given thirty minutes for its presentation. It was estimated that the new franchise to be awarded would cost between 700 million and 1 billion dollars. In commenting on the choices faced by the committee, McNair said he thought that "the NFL wants to be back in Houston and wants to be in Los Angeles and is trying to figure out how to do that."

During his presentation to the committee, McNair showed the league's team owners a model of the proposed new stadium that would be built for the new Houston franchise: a retractable-roof stadium that would cost roughly $310 million. The model alone cost $85,000 to be built—a third the cost of the original Rose Bowl. It took McNair and his advisers more than two years to put on the table a convincing package for the NFL.

In March, 1999, the NFL owners voted to award the league's thirty- second franchise to Los Angeles. The league seemed to regret that the second-largest American city had lost its two teams in 1995. However, the league attached some strings to finalization of the deal. Los Angeles was given six months to decide where the stadium would be and draw up plans for its construction. The league also was concerned about how a new stadium or a refurbished existing stadium would be financed and how the franchise fee would be paid. The mayor of Los Angeles, Richard Riordan, supported the idea of bringing a professional football team back to the city. With investors such as Eli Broad and Michael Ovitz willing to raise the franchise fee, it seemed that a deal could be worked out that met all the NFL stipulations by the September 15, 1999, deadline. However, while Riordan strongly supported the local business leaders who were negotiating with the NFL for a new franchise, he was still willing to work out a deal that would have brought the Raiders back to Los Angeles. For the Raiders to return, someone would have had to persuade Raider owner Al Davis that it was in his best interest to return. It is a high-wire act that the mayor was walking, since he wanted to avoid facing a backlash from city taxpayers who might end up paying most of the tab for bringing professional football back.

In the end, there were too many obstacles for Los Angeles to succeed in putting together a package by September 15. A crucial issue that made it difficult for Los Angeles to succeed was its refusal to use public financing to build a new stadium. The $310 million stadium that Houston was proposing was to require raising $195 million from public financing. A number of studies showed that relying on public financing to build stadiums is usually not a good investment for cities. It is, however, an extremely good deal for NFL owners. Of the $700 million Houston had to pay to get a franchise, each existing NFL owner was to receive $22 million. The new influx of money into the league also would add value to the other teams as well. The mere fact that investors are willing to pay $700 million to own a team makes all other teams more valuable. At the October 6, 1999, NFL meeting, the owners voted 29 to 0 for the new franchise to go to Houston. Both the St. Louis Rams (whose 1995 move to St. Louis had left much ill-feeling in Los Angeles) and the Arizona Cardinals (who had moved to Phoenix from St. Louis in 1988) abstained from voting.

As the owner of the new Houston franchise, Bob McNair projected that it would take between fifteen and twenty years to recoup his $700 million investment. He stated that he believed in the old expression "Long-term gain and short-term pain." Some of this short-term pain, though, would be relieved by the $195 million that would come from the public funding used to build a new state-of-the-art stadium. Since football has been described as a "religion" in Texas, the citizens of Houston looked forward to having an NFL team once again. However, they were also a little leery of what might happen because of their experience with the recent move to Tennessee of the Oilers—who were to face the St. Louis Rams in the 2000 Super Bowl.

Impact of Event

While a great deal of press coverage is regularly given to the multi-million-dollar signings of professional athletes, comparatively little attention is paid to how much money flows into the pockets of the team owners. It is, however, not surprising that some of the richest persons in the world own professional sports franchises. There are more than one hundred major-league-level teams in the United States, including baseball, basketball, football, and hockey. During the late 1990's, the revenue generated per year by these four sports alone reached more than five billion dollars. In addition to the money coming in through gate receipts, the team owners earned money from media arrangements and from the buying and selling of franchises

In earlier decades, most sports franchises remained in their home cities for long periods of time. It became common during the 1990's for "bidding wars" to break out among cities and states contesting for new teams. Hundreds of millions of dollars would be promised by a locale in order to guarantee that a franchise would be coming to the area. While winning cities might cheer their good fortune, others bemoaned the loss of their teams, as well as lost revenue and jobs. Communities losing teams were also often stuck with unpaid bonds on stadiums that had been built for their lost teams.

Professional sports plays such a large emotional and cultural role in American society that it has been difficult for elected city leaders to say no to owners who demand improved stadiums, while threatening to look for new homes. Experts have pointed out that major sports leagues have long used their cartel status to obtain subsidies and make profits. Since the 1950's, critics have argued against financing stadiums with public funds. In 1999, George Steinbrenner threatened to move his legendary New York Yankees baseball team to New Jersey if he did not get a new stadium for his team in New York City—even though the Yankees had been one of baseball's most successful and valuable franchises. In the late 1990's, the team had agreed to a $496 million cable television deal, and yet the owner still felt it necessary to pressure the city for a new stadium.

Since major professional sports leagues have monopoly status in the United States, each league has the right to negotiate television contracts that will benefit all its teams. In 1961, the federal Sports Broadcast Act made it possible for the leagues to work as a group in the selling of their television rights without worrying about American antitrust laws. The Fox Television network alone paid more than $17 billion in 1997 to secure non-exclusive television broadcast rights to NFL games through the year 2005. With this one contract, each NFL team received approximately $75 million per season. In 1998, *Forbes* magazine estimated that the average major professional sports team was worth almost $200 million.

In addition to McNair's paying $700 million for the new Houston franchise in 1999, another group paid $800 million to purchase the Washington Redskins football team and stadium, and Alfred Lerner paid $530 million to buy the Cleveland Browns football team. During the 1990's, there were many new arenas and stadiums built. About $9 billion was spent during the decade for new sports facilities. More than 80 percent of this money was raised with state and community funding.

The majority of professional sports teams played in privately owned facilities in 1950. By the 1990's, more than 75 percent of the teams were playing in publicly owned facilities. With the average net worth of professional sports teams owners hovering at around $400 million, it seemed less likely that in the future the public would automatically vote for bonds to finance new sports facilities, so long as owners had other avenues in which to put together funding for their projects. On March 26, 2000, however, Seattle's Kingdome stadium was imploded in order to make room for a new multipurpose stadium in the same location.

Bibliography

Cagan, Joanna. *Field of Schemes: How the Great Stadium Swindle Turns Public Money into Private Profit.* Monroe, Me.: Common Courage Press, 1998. Argues that communities should be wary of owners who insist that the public pay for teams' new stadiums.

Colangelo, Jerry, with Len Sherman. *How You Play the Game: Lessons for Life from the Billion-Dollar Business of Sports.* New York: Amacom, 1999. Inside story on professional sports ownership from the owner of the Phoenix Suns basketball and Arizona Diamondbacks baseball teams.

Eitzen, D. Stanley. "Public Teams, Private Profits." *Dollars & Sense* 228 (March/April, 2000): 21-23. While fans may concern themselves with wins and loses, the owners are busy making a huge profit on both the fans and taxpayers.

Fisher, Daniel, and Michael K. Ozanian. "Cowboy Capitalism." *Forbes* 164 (September 20, 1999): 170-177. Examines the creative ways the new breed of NFL owners uses to make profits.

Noll, Roger, and Andrew Zimbalist, eds. *Sports, Jobs, and Taxes: The Economic Impact of Sports Teams and Stadiums.* Washington, D.C.: Brookings Institution Press, 1997. Collection of essays that take a close look at the economic impact of new stadiums and if a sports franchise really does add revenue to its local community.

Quirk, James, and Rodney D. Fort. *Pay Dirt: The Business of Professional Team Sports.* Rev. ed. Princeton, N.J.: Princeton University Press, 1997. Thorough and balanced guide to such matters as "The Market for Sports Franchises," "The Reserve Clause and Anti-Trust Laws," "Why Do Pro Athletes Make so Much Money?," and "Competitive Balance in Sports Leagues."

Rosentraub, Mark S. *Major League Losers: The Real Cost of Sports and Who's Paying for It.* New York: BasicBooks, 1997. Detailed account of how professional sports has become a massive recipient of corporate welfare. While team owners are pampered, the public pays millions in taxes to subsidize new sports facilities.

Scully, Gerald W. *The Market Structure of Sports.* Chicago: University of Chicago Press, 1995. Detailed examination of the business of professional sports, including a close look at management practices, players' salaries, and the monetary value of teams. Scully points out how the recent economic growth of sports has been primarily the result of the sale of television rights.

Shropshire, Kenneth L. *The Sports Franchise Game: Cities in Pursuit of Sports Franchises, Events, Stadiums, and Arenas.* Philadelphia: University of Pennsylvania Press, 1995. In-depth analysis of how the owners go about manipulating the system in order to almost guarantee themselves huge profits.

Jeffry Jensen

Cross-References

Station KDKA Introduces Commercial Radio Broadcasting (1920); The 1939 World's Fair Introduces Regular U.S. Television Service (1939); Cable Television Rises to Challenge Network Television (mid-1990's).

THE Y2K CRISIS FINALLY ARRIVES

CATEGORY OF EVENT: Government and business
TIME: January 1, 2000
LOCALE: Worldwide

Despite predictions of disaster to businesses, governments, and public services due to expected computer malfunctions when computers confronted January 1, 2000, on their internal calendars, the world-wide transition to the year 2000 caused few problems, thanks to extensive preparations

Principal personages:
ROBERT BEMER (1921-   ), codeveloper of COBOL who was the first to publish warnings about the date problem hidden in most computer software
PETER DE JAGER (1955-   ), Canadian computer consultant who was an early, influential advocate of preparing for the Y2K transition
GRACE MURRAY HOPPER (1906-1992), inventor of the English-based computer language Flow-matic, which evolved into COBOL
JOHN A. KOSKINEN (1939-   ), chair of the President's Council on Year 2000 Conversion, which oversaw efforts to prepare for Y2K
DANIEL PATRICK MOYNIHAN (1927-   ), chair of the U.S. Senate committee that persuaded the federal government to prepare for Y2K

Summary of Event
Across North America and around the world, people waited nervously as midnight, December 31, 1999, approached. Many wondered whether predictions of doom about the year 2000 computer transition, popularly called the Y2K (for "year 2000," with *k* representing the Greek *kilo* for "thousand") or millennium bug, would prove correct: Would power and

water supplies fail, food distribution be disrupted, the economy begin to disintegrate, nuclear missiles launch accidentally, and widescale civil disturbances begin as computers and computer networks failed everywhere? No one was completely sure how to answer these questions, even though a massive effort to fix the problem occupied governments and businesses throughout the late 1990's.

A definitive answer came within days after January 1, 2000, came and went: There were no disasters. Some computer problems did occur on New Year's Day and afterward; however, they were so few, so inconsequential, and so easily corrected that even the most optimistic experts were surprised.

The story of the Y2K transition problem began with the development of commercial computing. In 1957, Rear Admiral Grace Murray Hopper invented a programming language called Flow-matic, the first to be based on English in order to make computers easier for businesses to use. Flow-matic formed the basis for COBOL, for "common business-oriented language." The principal data storage device of the times was the eighty-column punch card. To conserve space, COBOL used only six digits to represent any given calendar date—two each for the day, the month, and the year, as in "04/15/53" for April 15, 1953. The shortcut dating method saved as much as twenty dollars in production of a date-sensitive record, an important way of economizing as businesses grew dependent upon computers.

Computer scientists, lead by Robert Bemer, one of COBOL's developers, warned that using only two digits for each year designation would later cause problems and argued for a four-digit style. However, the desire of businesses to minimize their immediate expenses overwhelmed such objections. When International Business Machines (IBM) designed its System/360 mainframe computer (marketed in 1964), it incorporated the COBOL two-digit year format. That computer, and its dating style, became the industry standard. Bemer again published warnings about the dating problem in 1971 and 1979 but stirred little interest and no change. To most businesses and government agencies the heart of the danger—the arrival of the year 2000—seemed too far away to worry about at the time.

In 1993 Peter de Jager, a Canadian computer engineer, published an article with the alarming title "Doomsday 2000" in *Computerworld*. In that article and subsequent lectures de Jager argued that the Y2K bug could initiate massive disruptions and plunge the economy into a recession. Computers, he pointed out, would read a date such as "01/01/00" as "January 1, 1900" or "January 1, 1980," depending on their default settings, because there was no provision for numbers 2000 and higher in their software, and computer-processed date-sensitive information was fundamental to national infrastructures. There were already signs that he was right: That same year, a U.S. missile warning system malfunctioned when its computer clocks were experimentally turned forward to January 1, 2000.

During the next seven years, other glitches turned up sporadically during testing. At the same time, with gathering momentum, attempts were underway to remedy the date problem. In 1996, Senator Daniel Patrick Moynihan of New York held committee hearings on the Y2K bug and directed the Congressional Research Service to study it. Its report helped persuade President Bill Clinton to establish the President's Council on Year 2000 Conversion, directed by John A. Koskinen, in 1998. Koskinen oversaw programs to adjust software used by government agencies. The federal government also ordered many organizations essential to the economy, such as stock brokerages, to fix the problem—that is, "become Y2K compliant"—by August 31, 1999.

Despite initial skepticism about the true seriousness of Y2K, big companies soon undertook remediation efforts of their own. Most employed one or more of three basic methods. *Windowing*, the most common, entailed teaching computers to read 00 as 2000 and place other two-digit year dates in their appropriate century. *Time shifting* programmed computers to recalculate dates automatically following a formula. *Encapsulation*, a refinement of time shifting, added 28 to two-digit years to synchronize computers with the cycles of days of the week and of leap years. January 1, 2000, for instance, does not fall on the same day of the week as January 1, 2005, and so adjustments were necessary to accommodate such discrepancies. All three techniques required exhaustive searches and reprogramming of mainframes and personal computers that processed time-sensitive information, such as pay schedules and product expiration dates.

Computer chips embedded in equipment posed a further difficulty. After their introduction in the early 1970's, microprocessors were included in appliances, tools, automobiles, and machinery of all kinds: They eventually controlled the operations of nuclear power plants, utilities, hospital technology, weaponry, climate control systems in buildings, and even such mundane devices as home microwave ovens. With between thirty-two billion and forty billion chips in use by 2000, their potential for causing trouble was enormous, even if only a fraction of them controlled time-sensitive operations, and often the chips were difficult to extract and replace.

As Y2K approached, the frenzy of preparation increased, and predictions of disaster grew more ominous. Some consumers stockpiled generators, money, food, and fuel in case utility and supply systems became disrupted on January 1, 2000. Some government agencies failed to meet their August 31 deadline for Y2K compliance. Large corporations worried that their preparations were insufficient, while about a third of small American businesses had made no preparations whatsoever.

When the moment of truth came and passed on New Year's Day 2000, no system failures occurred, and essential services were uninterrupted even in countries, such as Russia, that were both sophisticated and largely unprepared for the date turnover. There were problems, however. Some were comical, as when a 105-year-old man was directed to attend kindergarten, some newborn children were registered as born in 1900, and the Web site of the U.S. Naval Observatory, the government's official timekeeper, proclaimed the date as "January 1, *19100.*" Most problems were simply annoyances. Some records were accidentally deleted, software used to service credit cards double-charged some users, renters returning one-day overdue videos were billed for thousands of dollars in late charges, and cell phone messages were lost. Most such problems were easily corrected. Others problems were potentially more serious. For example, one Wall Street computer inflated a few stock values, and a small number of company security systems failed. Some satellites, including one U.S. spy satellite, lost contact with their controllers. Software modifications, or simple common sense, rectified the errors.

The Y2K problem did not end with the New Year's date turnover, however. One expert calculated that only about 10 percent of the problems would turn up immediately. For instance, the leap year day, February 29, 2000, caused at least 250 glitches in seventy-five countries, although none was major.

Impact of Event

Even though the Year 2000 turnover passed without disaster, the event itself and the preparations for it revealed how thoroughly modern society had come to rely upon a sophisticated technological infrastructure. Controlling and coordinating that technology are computers and, increasingly since about 1990, computer networks, especially the Internet. The Y2K threat to information technology (IT) elicited one of the largest, most effective joint responses among businesses and government agencies in U.S. history, as well as extensive international cooperation. Programmers successfully corrected well over 95 percent of Y2K-related problems. The nation did learn about its dependence upon computers, but it also learned that computers were not beyond its control.

Because of its very success, the remediation effort had its critics, some of them bitterly vocal. In part critics wondered how so little could go wrong if the Y2K bug was really as big a threat as IT experts had insisted. Editorials and letters in business periodicals accused the large coterie of

Y2K experts of exaggerating the danger in order to scare businesses into spending money unnecessarily on remediation. They denounced the media hoopla and claimed the predictions of doom had been psychologically harmful. Critics were also outraged by the price of remediation. In 1993, de Jager estimated it would require between $50 billion and $75 billion worldwide. He was far too conservative. The United States alone spent $100 billion, including $8.5 billion by the federal government alone, according to the U.S. Department of Commerce. The worldwide bill is estimated at between $500 billion and $600 billion. De Jager and his colleagues admitted that costs may have been unnecessarily high but that nevertheless the money was well spent because without remediation wide-scale systems malfunctions would have occurred, costing much more money and causing civil disorder. The controversy created a measure of ill-will between businesses and IT specialists.

In addition to avoiding disaster, Y2K remediation had some immediate tangible benefits. The rush to stockpile food and equipment before the New Year brought record profits to some manufacturers and retailers. Computer programmers were in high demand, and consultants earned money with books, articles, lectures, and Web sites offering advice. Companies were launched specifically to solve Y2K problems for businesses; many of them afterward diversified to serve the general needs of electronic commerce. The close scrutiny of programmers benefited companies' overhead expenses as well. They removed the clutter of computer code that had accumulated during decades of reprogramming and computer upgrades and uncovered applications that could be eliminated, streamlining business computer systems. Many companies learned how to conduct contingency planning for IT malfunctions. Others, especially small businesses, learned how to use computers effectively for the first time.

Less tangible, but at least as important, were two general lessons. First, businesses and governments were forced to reevaluate their dependence upon technology, its complexity, and the danger to it from an unforeseen condition, such as the Y2K date problem. Second, they learned dramatically that forty years of development and use had built a computer infrastructure with serious inconsistencies and imperfections. Accordingly, commentators suggested that IT specialists, especially those developing large projects, undergo certification to ensure coherent planning.

The President's Council on Year 2000 Conversion was demobilized after February 29, but the Y2K bug continued to have direct and indirect effects on business. Many organizations had deferred computer data entry and innovations in order to devote employees to Y2K remediation. For example, the stock exchange delayed its planned conversion of stock quotes from fractions to dollars and cents. Following the New Year businesses had to clear up the work backlog. Moreover, according to de Jager and other analysts, the programming techniques used to remedy Y2K dating problems were stopgaps, often not coordinated between computer systems and potentially only temporarily effective. Windowing and time shifting could insinuate subtle changes into computer codes, changes that might not cause problems for decades.

Bibliography

De Jager, Peter. "Y2K: So Many Bugs . . . So Little Time." *Scientific American* (January, 1999): 88-93. Although de Jager's forecast about Y2K was far too pessimistic, his technical explanation of the computer problems is thorough and geared toward business computing and record keeping.

JD Consulting. *Y2K Procrastinator's Guide*. Rockland, Mass.: Charles River Media, 2000. The introduction of this book lucidly explains the source and nature of the date problem in business computers and embedded computer chips.

Kuo, L. Jay, and Edward M. Dua. *Crisis Investing for the Year 2000: How to Profit from the Coming Y2K Computer Crash*. Secaucus, N.J.: Birch Lane Press, 1999. After offering a balanced summary of the computer problem for business people, the authors discuss potential economic developments in detail.

McGuigan, Dermot, and Beverly Jacobson. *Y2K and Y-O-U: A Sane Person's Home-Preparation Guide*. White River Junction, Vt.: Chelsea Green Publishing, 1999. An example, sensible and practical, of the better-safe-than-sorry advice to people worried about the millennium transition.

Yourdon, Edward, and Jennifer Yourdon. *Time Bomb 2000*. 2d ed. Upper Saddle River, N.J.: Prentice Hall PTR, 1999. An example of a gloomy assessment of Y2K risks to most segments of society.

Roger Smith

Cross-References

Jobs and Wozniak Found Apple Computer (1976); IBM Introduces Its Personal Computer (1981); Dow Jones Adds Microsoft and Intel (1999).

FEDERAL COURT RULES THAT MICROSOFT SHOULD BE SPLIT INTO TWO COMPANIES

CATEGORY OF EVENT: Monopolies and cartels
TIME: June 7, 2000
LOCALE: Washington, D.C.

A federal court ruled that Microsoft had used predatory practices unfairly to monopolize the web browser market and ordered its breakup.

Principal personages:
BILL GATES (1955-   ), founder of Microsoft Corporation
THOMAS PENFIELD JACKSON (1937-   ), federal district court judge
JANET RENO (1938-   ), U.S. attorney general
JOEL KLEIN (1946-   ), assistant U.S. attorney general
WILLIAM NEUKOM (1941-   ), senior vice president of law and corporate affairs at Microsoft
JAMES BARKSDALE (1943-   ), founder of Netscape Communications

Summary of Event

The federal court ruling against Microsoft on June 7, 2000, was the apparent culmination of a legal battle going back to 1991, when the Federal Trade Commission (FTC) began investigating whether Microsoft was monopolizing the personal computer (PC) operating systems market. The commission closed its investigation in 1993 after its members deadlocked on votes formally to file a complaint against Microsoft. During that same year, the Justice Department and European Commission began their own independent antitrust investigations. These probes ended in July, 1994, when Microsoft agreed to alter its restrictive contracts with PC manufacturers and remove other restrictions that had been imposed on software companies.

The 1994 consent decree came back to haunt Microsoft in 1997. In October that year, the Justice Department sued the company for forcing computer makers to include Internet Explorer, its web browser software, on new PCs using its Windows operating software. The Justice Department contended that Microsoft had bundled Internet Explorer with Windows 95 in order to capture market share from Netscape Communications Corporation. On December 11, 1997, federal court judge Thomas Jackson issued a preliminary injunction to stop Microsoft from requiring PC makers to install Internet Explorer with Windows 95.

Seven weeks later, the Justice Department and Microsoft reached a partial agreement that would allow PC makers to hide or remove Internet Explorer from computers with the new version of Windows 95. In March, 1998, Microsoft chairman Bill Gates and other leading technology company executives testified before the Senate Judiciary Committee. Gates's testimony portrayed Microsoft as an innovator and denied that his company was a predatory monopoly. In a bold and defiant move, Microsoft announced a month later that Windows 98 and Internet Explorer would be integrated. This angered the Justice Department and a number of state attorneys general. In mid-May Microsoft began negotiating with the federal government and twenty states in order to quell an antitrust lawsuit. After negotiations broke down, the Justice Department and twenty state attorneys general sued Microsoft.

The new antitrust trial began on October 19, 1998. During the trial, Judge Jackson heard testimony from twenty-six witnesses and considered a mountain of physical evidence, including videotapes, e-mail, and other documents. In early November, 1999, Jackson issued his preliminary findings, which found Microsoft to be a monopoly.

Between November 19, 1999, and April 1, 2000, federal appeals judge Richard Posner attempted to mediate a settlement. After mediation failed, Jackson ruled that Microsoft had broken antitrust law. Jackson stated that Microsoft had abused its power as a monopoly through its unfair PC operating systems policies. The final blow came on June 7, 2000, when Jackson ordered Microsoft to be split into two smaller companies. He called Microsoft "untrustworthy" and believed that breaking it up would prevent it from again violating federal and state antitrust laws. Under Jackson's ruling, one of the new companies would run Microsoft's PC operating systems and the other would run the rest of Microsoft's business.

Impact of Event

Since passage of the 1890 Sherman Antitrust Act, several major U.S. antitrust cases have been decided by federal courts. In 1911, for example, the U.S. Supreme Court ruled in favor of the federal government's argument that John D. Rockefeller's company Standard Oil had behaved as an predatory monopoly. The ruling led to the breakup of Standard Oil. Ironically, however, the new companies created from the breakup increased the value of stock owned by Rockefeller, making him even richer. A similar outcome might follow the breakup of Microsoft.

The Microsoft case has been compared to the long legal struggle waged between the Justice Department and International Business Machines (IBM). Beginning in 1969, the federal government argued that IBM had bundled software and hardware together, along with other anticompetitive practices in order to keep a large market share. In 1982, the case was dismissed since the long delay was reasoned to have made the whole issue irrelevant to where the computer market had evolved. It remained possible that lengthy appeals might render the Microsoft case meaningless.

After Judge Jackson's Microsoft ruling, many people debated whether antitrust actions might be brought against other high-technology companies. Some computer business experts feared that the federal government might be meddling in technological areas that it cannot comprehend. The Federal Trade Commission investigated both Intel and Cisco for potentially being monopolies. In late July, 2000, Microsoft asked the U.S. Supreme Court not to take its case directly and allow the full appeals process to go forward.

Bibliography

Cusumano, Michael A., and David B. Yoffie. *Competing on Internet Time: Lessons from Netscape and Its Battle with Microsoft.* New York: Simon & Schuster, 2000. Definitive examination of the Netscape-Microsoft battle for web browser supremacy.

Liebowitz, Stan J., and Stephen E. Margolis. *Winners, Losers, and Microsoft: Competition and Antitrust in High Technology.* Oakland, Calif.: Independent Institute, 2000. Updated edition covers the Microsoft antitrust case.

McKenzie, Richard B. *Trust on Trial: How the Microsoft Case Is Reframing the Rules of Competition.* Cambridge, Mass.: Perseus, 2000. Argues that the case against Microsoft is more bad politics than good law.

Jeffry Jensen

Cross-References

Champion v. Ames Upholds Federal Powers to Regulate Commerce (1903); AT&T Agrees to Be Broken Up as Part of an Antitrust Settlement (1982); Dow Jones Adds Microsoft and Intel (1999).

Chronological List of Events

Alphabetical List of Events

Category Index

Principal Personages

Subject Index